American Roma

American Roma

A Modern Investigation of Lived Experiences and Media Portrayals

Melanie R. Covert

LEXINGTON BOOKS
Lanham • Boulder • New York • London

Published by Lexington Books
An imprint of The Rowman & Littlefield Publishing Group, Inc.
4501 Forbes Boulevard, Suite 200, Lanham, Maryland 20706
www.rowman.com

Unit A, Whitacre Mews, 26-34 Stannary Street, London SE11 4AB

British Library Cataloguing in Publication Information Available

Library of Congress Cataloging-in-Publication Data

Names: Covert, Melanie R., author.
Title: American Roma : a modern investigation of lived experiences and media portrayals / Melanie R. Covert.
Description: Lanham, MD : Lexington Books, [2018] | Includes bibliographical references and index
Identifiers: LCCN 2018010950 (print) | LCCN 2018009929 (ebook) | ISBN 9781498558402 (Electronic) | ISBN 9781498558396 (cloth : alk. paper)
Subjects: LCSH: Romanies—United States—Social conditions. | Romanies in mass media. | Romanies in motion pictures. | Romanies—United States—Ethnic identity.
Classification: LCC DX201 (print) | LCC DX201 .C68 2018 (ebook) | DDC 305.8914/97073—dc23
LC record available at https://lccn.loc.gov/2018010950

Printed in the United States of America

To Shaun, whose love and support I could never deserve.

To the men and women who shared their stories with me even at great cost to themselves

and

to Daniel Niederjohn, for everything.

Contents

Preface   ix

Acknowledgments   xiii

Introduction: The Roma: Who They Are   xv

1 Roma Media Representations: Fantasy and Fiction   1

2 Discrimination and Prejudice in the Daily Lives of the Roma   33

3 Roma Lives and Attitudes: A Look into the Past and the Present   69

4 The Price of Roma Prejudice: Structural and Personal Marginalization   109

5 Roma and Education   135

6 Roma Identity and Traditional Lifestyles: Protective Barriers in a Hostile World   165

7 Roma Activism and Final Thoughts   201

References   213

Index   225

About the Author   231

Preface

On a Monday morning December 1985 I was born and the world, in my opinion, hardly took notice. My mom says it was because people had to go to work—I was born in the morning after all. Whatever the reason, hardly anyone came to see me. Conversely, on the day my older brother was born, in true Roma fashion, the entire extended family, it seems, came to see him causing the nurses to note they had never seen so many people coming for one baby. But there I was, failing to make an impression on the world with my appearance. My father died before I was born so, on the day of my birth, I was given my mother's maiden name, the name of her father. And this, symbolically, marked me as property of her people and past.

We are Romanichal, English Roma (sometimes called gypsies). I don't remember asking questions about my father or his people until I was older but even then I suppose it didn't occur to me that his existence meant that half of me was born from somewhere else. I grew up looking exactly like my mother and, having never seen a picture of my father, assumed all my genes came from her. It is a strange thing, learning to be whole as half a person. But we were Roma and that's what I knew.

We lived in many places in the very early years of my life, campgrounds or trailer parks surrounded by family, and visited with our Roma family often. We stayed with older cousins, those we referred to as "Aunts" out of respect, in pull-along trailers that once served as both a home and business for those relatives who told fortunes. Around the time I came to acknowledge my own existence, maybe around 4 or 5, we lived in an apartment community surrounded by many of these older "Aunts" and a slew of other cousins and family who would visit in the summer from Alabama, Texas and elsewhere. My two elderly "Aunts" lived across the street from one another, "Aunts" who would offer to make you a pork chop when you walked in the door and paid me a dollar to push back their cuticles. "Aunts" who, some said, once made their money telling fortunes but who I had only seen telling them for family.

My family spoke in a mixture of English and the language of the Romani-chal. A mixture we also spoke at home. Words that were part of our language every day. No one ever told me not to say those words when I started school, but somehow I knew. Over time I stopped using them altogether.

I didn't know then that the time I spent with these relatives in my neighborhood was a unique moment. They were the generation who had lived their lives on the road, engaged in what many consider to be traditional Roma occupations, sometimes run from towns, sometimes isolated from the world of those who were not Roma. I didn't know when we visited my great aunts what it meant that they had been educated, working women of their generation, or that they too had grown up in the house of a fortune teller. They too had sometimes moved from town to town. I knew these things but they were the story of my family. I didn't know the lives of those who weren't Roma. I didn't understand we were different. I knew we had words for people who weren't us but who we were in comparison to who weren't was lost on me. We just were.

And that was how I first came to know the world around me.

From that time, for reasons that belong in her own story, my mother decided to separate from her people. Finding refuge in her faith, she hoped to pass on the ideals of this faith to us rather than then customs and norms of her people that she had left largely behind. Despite our separation, as I grew older, I was raised with many of the same expectations. Ideas about modesty, appropriateness, gender roles, what is clean and unclean. I wasn't allowed to go to the houses of many other people and certainly could not spend the night. I didn't tell people I was Roma.

A story for another time is what happened in those early years and the ones following in my life. Despite the separation from our people, the life we lived and the many challenges we faced was, in part at least, a direct result of the world my mother had been raised in.

As life progressed, I entered a PhD program; I had every intention of carrying on the research relating to mental health and race I began in my master's program. At the same time one of my younger brothers was discovering more about our Roma roots. Having been raised largely after the separation, he had learned little in the way of what it meant to be Roma, our family history or anything beyond the negative views he often heard from my mother. He sent me a book, *We Are the Roma*. In it, in so many ways, I found again the story of me. It pushed me to see what else I could learn about the American Roma, my people, and sadly, I found many dead ends.

I decided then that I held a very privileged place, A Roma in academia, an American Roma, a Roma woman with an opportunity to speak, if not on behalf of Roma, about the Roma in America. I had an opportunity to connect the world of academia, and American Roma, with the struggle of Roma worldwide. And that is how this work came to be. I would not presume to speak entirely on behalf of Roma; they are far too diverse to be summed up in a few chapters or narratives. I hope instead to provide a glimpse into the lives of some of the Roma in America, to bring to light their struggles, to underscore their existence as a people and to connect them with the greater Roma community worldwide.

Acknowledgments

No work is achieved without the support of one's personal and professional community. I would like to thank Rosalind Chou, James Ainsworth, and Tomeka Davis for their advice and guidance. I would like to acknowledge the many men and women who not only lent their stories to this work but many of whom also lent their scholarly expertise, personal connections and insights to the completion of this work but who cannot be named here for the sake of anonymity. I would like to thank my graduate student Leslie Small for her help in editing. I would also like to acknowledge the support of friends and family who spent a lot of time asking about and supporting a study that they did not know much about but that they were excited and invested in as a way of supporting me.

Introduction

The Roma: Who They Are

In a proposal to city hall, Rome's social policy councilor advised other city officials that Roma (referred to often as gypsies) residing within their city should be hired to sort the city's garbage, citing their "skills in rummaging through waste" (RT News, 2015). The social policy advisor viewed this occupation as an opportunity for Roma to come outside of their camps and earn a living given that, "A lot of these people rummage through rubbish and find materials, they have become skillful." While many of her political counterparts viewed her proposition as an absurdity, her attitude toward these marginalized people, known as the Roma, is shared worldwide.

In France alone, Euroactiv reports over 13,000 Roma were evicted from their homes in 2014, leaving many without homes and even more with an interruption in their attempts to assimilate (2015). Euroactiv also reported that the Czech Republic was cited by the European Commission as violating European Union antidiscrimination laws after multiple infractions were found including the practice of requiring Roma children to sit in the back of schoolrooms and that children placed in schools for the mentally disabled were disproportionately Roma, making up over 30 percent of the school's population. The plight of Roma worldwide is often dire. Faced with intense discrimination individually and politically, academics and activists alike have sought to better understand and support the Roma cause.

The plight of the present-day Roma in Europe continues to be a desperate one. The experience of Roma in Europe has been compared to being Black in the American South during the era of Jim Crow (Lane, Spencer & Jones, 2014). European Roma face significant persecution, lack state protection and are often found in destitute living conditions (Ceneda, 2002; Oprea, 2004).

European Roma lack social power (Petrova, 2004), face resistance from mainstream institutions (Levinson, 2007) and are vilified in the media (Lane, Spencer & Jones).

Though Roma worldwide are a recognized and marginalized minority, they are given little recognition within the United States. Despite the seeming lack of overt oppression among American Roma, they may still struggle with many of the challenges to assimilation or integration faced by Roma globally. Few Roma in the United States have a visible place in Roma discourse. Researchers have not yet asked enough questions of American Roma to determine if many of the cultural barriers that Roma encounter worldwide are relevant to their lives in America. This lack of available information on Roma in the United States leaves many questions about how American Roma fit into the worldwide community and discourse.

Though Roma today have become increasingly "famous" due to the success of *My Big Fat American Gyspy Wedding* (Popplewell, 2012) and similar shows, few in America know who the Roma are. It is the hope of many Roma activists and scholars that the stereotypes produced by such shows can be countered as Roma continue to speak on their own behalf. Providing countering images to those being touted outside the community is one method of resistance. By providing alternate images throughout this text, I hope to add to the narrative of existence. A narrative about Roma created by Roma. Before I delve into their lives specifically, I want to introduce them as a people group to those unacquainted with the reality of their existence in America. The Roma are more than stereotypes or a "free spirited" way of living. They are a minority, widely persecuted worldwide and largely invisible in the United States.

WHO ARE THE ROMA?

Historical accounts of Roma in the United States remain widely untold. Despite gaining attention for their marginalized position worldwide, American Roma are a little studied group. Little scholarship exists that focuses on the lives of American Roma specifically. Among those who write about the Roma are Hancock, a linguist, historian and leading scholar of the Roma. His texts and references address American Roma and discuss in-depth Roma origins but they are most often focused on the European Roma community. Gropper's (1975) work, *Gypsies in the City*, discussed cultural patterns among Roma residing in New York. Though not Roma herself, she was able to provide a scholarly perspective on the lives of Roma, a foundational and groundbreaking work that provided one of the first scholarly accounts of American Roma. In similar fashion, Miller's *Church of Cheese*, (2009) and Sutherland's *Gypsies: The Hidden Americans* (1975) bring a scholarly account of the lives of Roma. Though not Roma, they have been given access and invited to witness the "backstage" of Roma lives, though some criticism toward their work as outsiders exists. Marafioti (2012), like Hancock, writes as an insider and is able to give an account of being Roma from both an American and European perspective. These texts are among the few in existence which can be highlighted for their focus on American Roma and provide meaningful and historical insight.

In Hancock's book, *Danger! Educated Gypsy* (2010) a detailed history of Roma people is provided. Hancock provides a scholarly review of the historical origins of the Roma, utilizing his background in linguistics and the work of other Roma scholars to discuss origins and potential migration patterns for Roma as far back as the sixth century. While specific dates and locations are debated among scholars, Hancock's review identifies the major themes of Roma history that have become widely accepted.

The Roma were believed to originate in India from which they eventually migrated due to a myriad of societal and geographical factors, among them invasion and persecution. As their migration toward and dispersement throughout Europe progressed, countries began to acknowledge their presence with anti-Ziganist laws and, at times, sought to control this nomadic people with enslavement. Many Roma became enslaved throughout Europe. In some places, this enslavement continued until the late 1800s. Hancock notes, in sixteenth-century England Roma were required to be branded and enslaved for at least two years (2002). In much the same manner as the Jewish people, Roma have faced persecution from each host country they have encountered. Authors such as Gropper (1975) and Fonesca (1995) have provided their own evidence in support of these major themes. Gropper provides her own review of Roma linguists and scholarly conclusions concerning Roma origins and history. While the specifics discussed by these scholars are not always in agreement, the major themes identified here commonly emerge.

The Roma have been historically viewed by their hosts as uneducated, dark-skinned mystics with a proclivity for crime, even more rejected for their desire not to assimilate into whatever host country they encountered. In those places where enslavement was avoided, the Roma were controlled with oppressive legislation and public persecution (Hancock, 2002). Clark (2004) points out that today, what is often labeled as Roma can be summed up into five common, erroneous beliefs. This summation is based on hundreds of years of historical inaccuracies and interpretation of Roma behavior by outsiders. These beliefs about Roma include: (1) Blackness, (2) False sense of Roma "Nobility" (i.e., king of the Gyspy), (3) Involvement with the occult, (4) Proclivity toward crime (historically this included the theft of White offspring), and (5) Overt sexuality of men and women. Historically, mainstream society would use their erroneous observations of the Roma to justify social and interpersonal discrimination which interfered with the Roma preferred way of life and led to hundreds of years of anti-Ziganist discrimination. This discrimination still exists today as evidenced by countless Roma narratives in which racism, unequal treatment in schools, housing and jobs are encountered and many Roma are pushed to the margins of society (Euroactiv, 2015: RT News, 2015).

In the United States today, it is estimated that over 3 million Roma are in existence (Minahan, 2013). Hancock (2002) and Gropper (1975) discuss Roma origins and identify that many scholars believe the ancestors of the American Roma were either transported to America from countries that wished to dispose of them, a result of their prejudiced beliefs, or came willingly to escape a persecuted life. Christopher Columbus brought many Roma unwillingly to the new world for the purpose of labor (Minahan, 2013). While many Roma were forced into the new world, by the 1800s, they were electing to come due to wars in Europe and the absolution of slave laws overseas. Roma immigration to the United States was banned in the late 1800s only to later be rescinded, with a rise in Roma immigration taking place during the time of the great world wars (Minahan, 2013).

While America may have held some promise of a new life for Roma, worldwide their plight did not improve. Anti-Ziganist campaigns continued and Roma became the target for racism, ostracism and bullying. During World War II, in addition to his "Final Solution" to the problem of the Jews, Hitler developed also a "Final Solution" to the problem of the Roma. By 1937 Roma, along with Jews and Africans, no longer had civil rights in Nazi Germany. The Roma were considered a societal disease to be disposed of in order to ensure the purity of the German race. Nazi records underestimate Roma deaths to be around 2 million individuals killed throughout World War II (Hancock, 2002; Fonesca, 1995). Since that time, scholarship and advocacy in European countries have brought about some improvement for Roma people. However, Roma continue to face harsh prejudice and discrimination publicly and privately (Hancock 2002; Saul & Tebbutt, 2004). In America, Roma have paved their own way as a minority often overlooked, with some maintaining ties to their ancestral homes and histories while others find themselves left out of the worldwide discourse on the Roma experience.

As previously stated, the intention of this book is not to reestablish or propose new information to the origins of Roma, specifically those in Europe, but to add to the current body of knowledge related to Roma lives in America. While little is known about the American Roma, what is known has been largely defined by non-Roma scholars who are often believed to be influenced by societal prejudices and commonly held stereotypes, scholars who may only be able to relate the story of the Roma as untrusted/trusted outsiders (Sutherland, 1975; Belton, 2005). Many scholars refer to the American Roma as living with a "duality of existence," much like that of

Dubois' "Double consciousness" in which, to exist within society, one must play dual roles. One must live in two minds in order to avoid previously encountered discrimination (Dubois, 1968). In his travels across Europe, W. E. B. Dubois was at times mistaken for a Roma. Experiencing this prejudice directed at the Roma (and Jewish) populations opened his eyes to the reality of minority life in Europe. He also stated that the prejudice he experienced in Europe as a mistaken Roma resembled that of his experience in America as a Black man. Dubois understood the emotional work required to exist as an unwanted minority in such a society. For some in America, living outside of the visibility of such a society or at least playing a part in that society has been the easiest course of action, leaving outsiders to doubt their existence (Belton, 2005; Hancock, 2002).

The Roma are people who very much exist, sometimes lacking adequate representation. They may choose to separate themselves from mainstream society and leave their stories untold or may be forced to do so. Because mainstream society has been a historical source of discrimination, viewed as immoral and likely to influence away from traditional cultural values (Derrington, 2005; Sutherland, 1975), interaction with the mainstream more than is necessary for work and some education may be discouraged. Disclosure of Roma identity to outsiders is unnecessary and unlikely for many Roma (Derrington & Kendall, 2004; Belton, 2005; Sutherland, 1975). Other Roma may simply be busy with the business of living their daily lives: raising families, establishing careers, pursuing individual goals. They may or may not acknowledge the history of their identity and may feel themselves removed from the experiences of Roma worldwide depending on their own encounters with prejudice. They may themselves be unaware of the state of Roma worldwide and may belittle the importance of their narrative in the greater conversation.

The many challenges and considerations faced by Roma in America were important to navigate as I moved forward in my research. Each, I found, was a factor motivating me toward uncovering narratives that needed to be spoken, to compiling a history that needed to continue to be told and to expose the presence of a minority in America that has most often gone unnoticed by the majority.

METHODOLOGY

I knew at the onset of this study that it was going to be challenging to find many Roma willing to engage in an open interview about their lives and views. The reasons already identified for this resistance will be discussed in depth throughout the coming chapters. Much distrust exists toward academics due to their treatment of Roma. As an insider, I knew that my position would afford me greater access to the community, a privilege I did not take lightly. To gain access to individuals, I started with two veins of referrals, some coming from within academia and some found within my own family. Due to the small nature of the Roma population and marriage practices, some of those interviewed possessed some relation to me, sometimes unknown to me until we met through the interview. Most interviews began by discussing who our people are, their surnames, their locations and familial lines. Some are cousins, some distant cousins; others have no relation at all because they come from other Roma groups and geographical locations. I engaged in the tried-and-true snowball technique to garner other referrals eventually managing to engage with Roma across the country and some who reside internationally.

Those who agreed to participate engaged in a semi-structured interview lasting anywhere from 1 to 3 hours in person in their homes, over Skype or telephone. They were asked a range of questions about their ethnicity, their education, experiences with prejudice and discrimination, current and past practices and connection with their Roma heritage. Their stories have been woven within the coming chapters to show both the similarities and the range of experiences among American Roma and to show their connection with the global Roma experience.

In order to develop the connection between Roma and those worldwide, I use European Roma as a comparison group for those in America throughout this text. This decision was based on a number of factors. European Roma are more widely studied than Roma in the United States, giving a wealth of information regarding the Roma experience. Both European and American Roma experience a reluctance to reveal their identities and a feeling of "otherness." Both are currently seeing a decrease in "traditional" lifestyles. Most Roma in the United States have some European origins. Both experience an intersection of sexism and poverty along with issues of race. Scholars from both locations often feel Roma women are left out of feminist discourse. Both have experienced being exposed to the mainstream through biased other media portrayals (Ceneda, 2002; Lane, Spencer & Jones, 2014; Levinson, 2007; Petrova, 2004). The incorporation of the lives of European Roma throughout this text brings a broader, richer perspective of Roma lives and will, hopefully, further highlight the parallels between American and European Roma.

As previously stated, this is in no way meant to be an exhaustive representation of Roma nor a complete picture of their lives in America. It is not meant to establish their origins or migration patterns as there are far better academic texts in which one can find those discourses. It is not meant to be the final word on how Roma define themselves. This text gives a general picture of the Roma experience in America and a current look into Roma lives. It will, I hope, allow for the Roma who were interviewed to speak on their own behalf. While a Roma, and a proud one, I am also an academic, and in recognizing this intersection and its potential implications, the reader may find I take a backseat in the discourse to come. In writing this book, in my own way, I speak as a Roma, but more importantly, I make room for other Roma to speak on their own behalf.

For those unacquainted with the Roma, or only acquainted through the stereotype of the gyspy, I begin by introducing the Roma in a general way before delving into their lived experiences both historically and in the present day. For the readers' reference, I include here a table of those interviewed including their ages, occupations and geographical locations. All names have been changed and attempts to mask identity, as much as possible, have been taken. Those identified as engaging in "traditional" Roma occupations have self-identified their occupations as "being on the road" or "traveling" and indicate that their occupations, or those of their husbands, is reflective of those occupations historically engaged in by Roma which have seen a sharp decline in the present day.

Roma have been known to engage in many occupations, as various as any found within American society. What is known as stereotypically Roma is often work that was traditionally held by Roma, work that allowed some to ply trades that did not require formal education, work that allowed or required travel and that could be taught to younger generations skillfully. These occupations may be held by men or women. This may have included metalworking, woodworking, automobile trading, horse trading, auto-mechanics, paving, construction, carnival work, fortune telling, crafts and door-to-door sales to name a few. Often these occupations allowed Roma to work for themselves and in partnership with other Roma. Those considered to be more "traditional" Roma are often defined by these or similar careers and find themselves traveling often due to the demands of working professions based on both weather and market saturation.

A LOOK AHEAD

In the coming chapters, I hope to shed further light on the life of the American Roma. I will discuss their lives through the eyes of available literature and narratives but also through the 23 narratives I have collected. These narratives come from Roma all across America, some living lives that may be considered "traditional" for Roma while others work white collar occupations. They include men and women whose ages range from early twenties to early eighties. Their names have been changed to ensure their anonymity. They represent the spectrum of Roma experiences and, if nothing else, exemplify that Roma cannot be defined as homogenously as popular media has portrayed them to be.

Name	Age	Occupation	Geographic Location
Gertie	50's	House Manager	Southeast United States
Ruby	40's	Teacher	Southeast United States
Peaches	80's	Retired/Former Bookeeper	Southeast United States
Fener	40's	Retired Nurse	Southeast United Sates
Phoebe	40's	Teacher	Northeast United States
Rachel	20's	College Student	Northwest United States
Allie	40's	Marketing	Midwest United States
Vaidy	40's	Professor	Northeast United States
Gayle	30's	Higher Education	Northwest United States
Gracie	60's	Author	Southwest United States
Marilla	60's	Office Admin	Northeast United States
Louisa	40's	On the road-Traditional Roma occupation part-time/ Sales	Midwest United Sates
Josephine	30's	Travels in traditional Roma occupations	Southeast United States
Fey	60's	Museum Curator	Northwest United States
Anne	40's	Former Nurse	Southeast United States
Gilbert	40's	Non-Profit	International
Donald	50's	Pastor	Midwest United States
Teddy	30's	Government/Non-Profit	Southeast United States
Al	70's	Traditional Roma occupations	Southwestern United States
Henry	40's	Consultant	Northeast United States
Eddie	50's	Contractor	Southwest United States
Benny	30's	Distiller	Midwest United States

While introducing the lives of the American Roma and relating their narratives, I will also discuss challenges to successful acculturation encountered by many Roma. I will do this through the lens of Milton Gordon's theory of Assimilation (1964), Berry's Fourfold model of acculturation (1997) and Margaret Gibson's proposed "Accommodation without Assimilation (1988)." This will give both a language and structure to my inquisition into the lives of American Roma.

LEXICON

Throughout this book I will use language that may be, will most likely be, unfamiliar to the reader. Unless noting a specified group, Roma will be the term most often used throughout this text. For the purposes of this text and for ease of read, many groups will be understood within this label. I do not assume homogeneity of these groups by placing them under a singular label nor will assume to fully define each individual group. I will, at times, discuss a particular sect of the Roma throughout the text and will seek to identify each group by their preferred name. I will here briefly introduce the myriad of people groups I will be discussing under the umbrella of Roma. While not all of these groups have the same origins or current cultural practices they may be connected through language (Petrova, 2004), may share similar points of suffering or economic struggles (Petrova) and they may be grouped together by government agencies differently than how they may define themselves.

Roma is a broad term encompassing a large group of people, many who speak the Roma language and, as previously discussed, may trace their origins to India (Hancock, 2002). Many within this group may be historically categorized as gypsy but prefer to be identified as Roma due to the pejorative nature of the gypsy label and the baggage that comes along with this identification (Petrova, 2004). Those within this group may self-identify as Roma as a means of identification for activism and political reasoning (The Traveller Movement, 2015). They may not associate with "gypsies" who do not share their language or national heritage and therefore may prefer not to be associated under that label (Petrova, 2004). They may include Eastern European Roma, many of whom came to the United States after 1880, often found in larger ethnic enclaves throughout the United States (Salo, 2002) and the Romanichal, who have immigrated to America earlier in the 1800s and whose presence can be traced in England as early as the 1500s (Salo).

Despite the preference of many to be called Roma, gypsy is often used historically and in literature to define Roma. Some may also choose not to be called Roma and may prefer or feel pride in the term gypsy (Petrova, 2004). Recent groups have begun to appropriate this term to define their lifestyle without ethnic connections (Matros, 2004). The connections, specifically social and economic connections of gypsies and Roma are acknowledged in places like the United Kingdom by placing them under the label of GRT. GRTs are often grouped together based on cultural experiences or social positions though they have separate languages (Traveller Movement, 2015).

Their economic and social disadvantage ties them together and their social attitudes resemble one another (Equality and Human Rights, 2016).

GRT includes not only gypsies and Roma but also travelers. Travelers may or may not identify themselves as gypsies but they are not ethnically Roma and most lack ethnic connections to India (Petrova, 2004; Matros, 2004). Travelers may be Irish, English or Scottish. Many Irish travelers immigrated to the Southern United States while many Scottish travelers may be found in Canada (Salo, 2002). Many travelers lead a nomadic lifestyle though many are also settled and have a separate identity, heritage and culture from those who identify themselves as Roma. Irish travelers can trace their ancestry to twelfth-century Ireland (The Traveller Movement, 2015). Census data in many European countries combines travelers with gypsies, again connecting them socially and economically, if not ethnically (Salo).

The last group that will be discussed briefly in this text are the Sinti. Said to be German gypsies, they are sometimes assumed under the title of Roma but at others times they are identified as distinctly their own group (Petrova, 2004). Only one individual interviewed for this study falls within this category and they self-identified within the context of Roma/Gypsy. Because of this and because of their similar social position they will also be assumed under the heading of Roma for the purposes of discussion throughout the remainder of the book.

I include Sinti within this group based on the self-identification of Sinti found within the literature and among those interviewed as well as the precedent within academic literature; however, it should be noted that some Sinti would not necessarily consider themselves Roma and that some scholars have noted the existence of large cultural divides between the two (Gropper, 1975).

I often use the term Roma or Romani as an all-encompassing title but they are in no way entirely homogenous. Hancock (2010) points out that among the various groups of Roma, immigrants, Romanichal, Islamic Roma, and so on, a lack of contact often exists. If and when I change terms throughout the text, I am doing so out of respect for how the individuals themselves wished to be identified. Gypsy is used based on the self-identification of the individual or the way they are noted in a specific text. In a coming chapter, I discuss in-depth the feelings that Roma possess about this term. Another term I will use frequently is "gadje," "gadjo" or "gorja," these terms have identical meanings. They may mean anyone who is not Roma and will most often mean White, non-Roma individuals. These terms will be essential to the reader as they navigate the narratives to come.

SOME IMPORTANT THOUGHTS ON WHAT'S TO COME

Before delving into the narratives and historical data that make up the bulk of this work, I felt it was important to remind the reader of how American Roma are perceived through the eyes of mainstream society, specifically within media sources. Some may read this book and find themselves asking, "Who *are* the Roma? I have never heard of this group in my life." I believe the reader will find they have heard of the Roma in many forms from many outlets historically and in the present day. Undoubtedly these stereotypical portrayals will be all too familiar and will, I hope, bring a narrative which will so strongly contrast with what is presented throughout the remainder of the book, it will be impossible to deny why these representations are so problematic. The Roma's unique position of being largely invisible in the United States as a people group with the majority of their notoriety coming from mainstream media is, I propose, a dangerous one. These portrayals have the potential to have significant negative social and individual affects. As we take a look at the lives of the American Roma, beyond the narrative of popular it will be more than obvious why.

Chapter two will unfold discrimination as a part of the Roma experience. Chapter three will explore Roma history in the United States, assimilation theory and Roma attitudes and traditions. Chapter four will continue to examine structural and personal prejudice encountered by Roma and the determinantal effects these occurrences have on Roma socially and economically. Chapter five explores Roma experiences in education, attitudes toward and barriers to education. Chapter six identifies the strategies Roma possess for effectively coping with prejudice. It also explores the factors that impact Roma identity development. The final chapter concludes with a discussion of Roma activism and ideas for future research.

Chapter One

Roma Media Representations

Fantasy and Fiction

In 1921, the *Topeka State Journal* reported that a camp of gypsies had settled outside the city and were granted a permit to tell fortunes. While in residence, money from two local businesses was reported missing. The owners identified that the missing cash was a result of these "gypsies." The gypsy camps were searched and the oldest member of the camp was detained while the other camp members were questioned. Community members were told there would be no release until they paid the missing funds back to the store owners though no evidence of their crime, including the existence of the money, had been found within their camp. Once they provided a confession and pooled the money to pay back the shop owners, their elderly relative was released and they, according to the article, "Accepted an invitation to depart." The article also stated: "The undesirables were then urged to depart by License Collector Mattingly and Topeka is forced to exist without the diviners of the future. . . . Today, Topeka has no gypsy inhabitants." The article clearly identified that gypsies had been relegated to the role of outsiders. The sarcastic tone of the article left the reader with little doubt of the value placed on the lives discussed within and any Roma reading the article may be left with little doubt that they were socially unwanted and outcast.

Research on minority portrayals in entertainment media overwhelmingly identifies that negative portrayals of minorities influence the attitudes they encounter from society (Esses, Medianu & Lawson, 2013; Fryberg et al., 2008; Leavitt et al., 2015; Mastro & Greenberg, 2000; Schemer, 2012; Schlueter & Davidov, 2013). Of all ways to disseminate mainstream attitudes about minority groups, mainstream media is the most common, and perhaps, the most damaging (Mastro & Greenberg, 2000). Portrayals of minorities influence the attitudes of the majority group, encouraging stereotypical thinking and may, at times, increase prejudice (Bissell & Parrott, 2013). Recently, several Roma and non-Roma researchers have begun to challenge and dissect Roma representations in popular media, giving voice to the bias that exists in many mediums (Deaton, 2013; Velez, 2012; Silverman, 2014; Schneeweis and Foss, 2016). Critics of popular media identify the positioning of Roma as "other" in popular media. They are often without positive representations of their own and their cultural production has been relegated by outsiders to the areas of music. Even within that realm they may be perceived as "takers" or "cultural sponges" leaving them open to appropriation and lack of credit for their own cultural productions (Silverman, 2014).

The impact of these portrayals will be discussed at length in later chapters, however, it is important to discuss first how Roma have been portrayed historically and in present-day media. Dating far back into American histories, Roma have been plagued with stereotypical or biased portrayals in a variety of mediums, ranging from newsprint to blockbuster movies, portrayals that would create a fictional image of Roma in the minds of mainstream America. As previously stated, this list is not meant to be exhaustive but should illuminate the major themes of Roma portrayals in historical and present-day media.

ROMA PORTRAYALS IN MEDIA

American Portrayals

The *Topeka State Journal* was not the only newspaper in America's history reporting crimes pinned on Roma. The Library of Congress holds an archive of American newspapers from 1836–1922. An initial search of articles relating to gypsy/Roma activity produced over 100,000 references many retelling narratives of Roma stealing children or money. Some articles simply made an announcement, stating "Gypsies visit city" (*Little Falls Herald*, 1920) describing their clothing and actions while others chronicle for several pages their "depraved" life of stealing children and robbing others from town to town (*The Day Book*, 1913).

For a time, early in American history, the presence of Roma (most often referred to as gypsy by newspapers), inside or outside towns, in rural locations and even at fairs and marketplaces was not an unusual sight. Their presence was known and felt and their existence was well recognized by what was largely the main source of media at that time, the newspaper. For reasons that will be discussed throughout this book, as time went on, Roma slowly faded from public eye in America. Roma would reappear sporadically, though they often made only small appearances in movies or television shows where they were portrayed stereotypically, as caricatures, not as an unrecognized and persecuted minority (Dobreva, 2009).

Due to the somewhat invisible nature of Roma in America, it was much more difficult to find general sentiments regarding their portrayals in mainstream media. Specific examples, as will later be explored, were much more abundant. In 2014, Juliann Beaudoin utilized qualitative research to highlight the plight of the Canadian Roma immigrant. Her research coincides with the experiences of Roma worldwide. Beaudoin shows that media portrayals of Roma, even in North America, help to cement the erroneous beliefs of outsiders regarding Roma. These beliefs can and have led to a resistance toward Roma immigrants and Roma efforts to assimilate.

Beaudoin (2014) provides several examples of media contributions to the general distaste for Roma in Canadian society. Beaudoin reports on a television segment by a conservative TV personality. The segment aired publicly in Canada and highlights racist attitudes toward Roma that have permeated Canadian society:

> Gypsies aren't a race, they aren't a religion, they aren't a linguistic group. They're the medieval prototype of the Occupy Wall Street movement. A shiftless group of hobos that doesn't believe in property rights for themselves—they're nomads—or for others. They rob people blind. (Levitz, 2012 as cited in Beaudoin, 159)

The program highlights some of the most deep-seated emotions held by Canadian natives. The quote exemplifies the problematic language of this program, language that removes Roma personhood and ethnic identity simultaneously. The program also exemplifies the resistance to not only Roma assimilation but to the acknowledgment of Roma as a legitimate minority. While there was a general negative reaction to the airing of this program and others like it among Roma in Canada and their allies, little can be done to fight against these messages by those within the Roma community who are unacquainted with the workings of popular press. Mike, one of Beaudoin's (2014) informants describes the limitations this way: "refugees with language barriers, they don't know how the media works. You know, I've had people ask me, "How much do I have to pay to get my story in the paper?" And I just find that sad (Mike, 174). Because of their social stratification, some Roma may lack the education or social resources to adequately combat negative media portrayals. Roma immigrants, such as those in Canada, have the added barrier of language preventing them from responding to discriminatory messages in a socially positive way. Because of the situation among Canadian Roma immigrants, advocates have begun to use media to fight against Roma prejudice and to counter the negative representation of Canadian Roma worldwide.

I discussed the impact of negative representations on Roma lives with Rachel, the youngest of the Roma I interviewed. Rachel, a woman in her twenties from the Northeast, described the general impact of negative media attention in her own life:

> It's awful, I've had [someone] who used to be my friend, she's posting statuses about oh Gypsies are so crazy and I'm like you know that we are not actually like that right and she's like what do you mean "we"? And I messaged her privately and I'm like yeah surprise, "Hi." She started spewing out the most racist garbage I have ever heard my entire life, and she unfriended me and I was like "really?" That was probably just because of [the media], that's all she knew.

Rachel identified that a person she considered a "friend" developed beliefs about Roma from popular media sources who portray Roma in a negative light. These beliefs lead not only to racist and abusive language but also to a willingness to end their friendship because of these deep-seated beliefs. These beliefs were strong enough to override the years of interaction and positive impressions that Rachel had made and led this "friend" to engage in marginalizing Rachel as a result of her identity.

Rachel also identified that the state of negative Roma portrayal and recognition in the media is, if anything, casual racism at best. Without a true recognition of Roma existence and identity, the impact of these portrayals is often unrecognized:

> Recently the first lady used the term "gypped" and she had been told before that some Roma find that offensive and she like doesn't want to apologize for it apparently. People are starting to recognize we are a group but the First Lady of the United States won't acknowledge that she said a hurtful word toward us. She doesn't want to say we are a real ethnic group or whatever. We had all these shows, would it be acceptable if they were about any other race. Would it be ok if there was show that was like my big fat Jewish wedding and it demonizes Jews like it demonizes the Roma, I don't think it would be allowed. I think it's almost like we're the last acceptable group to globally ridicule without any consequences.

The term "gypped" has historically been used as a racial slur against Roma, particularly in newsprint (Bruce, 1984). Rachel makes a significant point about Roma that is found throughout much of the literature on Roma lives; racism toward Roma is the last acceptable form of racism. This racism is often perpetrated through the media leaving many with, at the very least, questions regarding Roma lives and existence and, at the very worst, racist ideologies that were created centuries ago.

Portrayals in Europe

In Europe, the sentiment that racism against Gypsies, Roma and Travelers (GRT) is the last acceptable form of racism pervades (King, 2015). Though guidelines on how to portray GRT for journalists and others in the mainstream media were created, they are loosely adhered to. And, just as in North America, Roma possess little power to counter these negative images. Though they are often reported on in Europe, Roma are rarely consulted regarding their opinions or perspectives on significant issues about GRT lives (Plaut, 2012). GRTs in Europe may be viewed as "passive objects in a chess game of great powers . . . rather than active subjects" (Plaut). A qualitative study of Roma children in the United Kingdom highlights the fact that much of the bullying and discrimination experienced by Roma at school is a direct result of media attention. Roma within traditional communities may fail to recognize or understand this because they are not aware of how they have been portrayed, largely due to their unique lifestyles (Ureche & Franks, 2007).

Roma or GRT portrayals in Europe mirror those in America, showing stereotypical caricatures of Roma that are commonly recognized by the general public (Tremlett, 2013). When not portrayed in a racist or marginalizing way, actors and models appropriate the GRT lifestyle as a way to showcase a romanticized, carefree life (Tremlett). Roma are portrayed in a way that suggests homogeneity and GRT or Roma themselves lack control over their own representations (Tremlett), something that will be discussed in a coming chapter. Tremlett identifies how any of these approaches to Roma representations are problematic, "Whether 'noble savage' or 'bogeyman' whether celebrations or denigrations, these representations of Gypsies base their viewpoint on the same pivot Gypsies as different from the majority society" (1078). As Tremlett points out, whatever the vantage point of Roma representation, they all serve one purpose, to "other" Roma from the mainstream, creating an additional barrier for Roma relations with the gadje.

The average European's idea of Roma is limited by what they see in the mainstream media. A qualitative interview conducted with Roma children and community members in the United Kingdom confirms that true knowledge of Roma lives and their plight is lacking among "outsiders": "most of us only know anything about them from what we read in the press or see on the television and that is prejudiced and biased" (Lane, Spencer & Jones, 2014, 15). A Roma woman interviewed by Lane, Spencer and Jones (2014) concurs with this "outsider" opinion, stating "it's the paper and TV and professionals that make the settled community not like us" (19). What is known about Roma to those outside the community is most often funneled through the mainstream media. Those inside and outside the community are able to acknowledge the bias that comes along with these representations.

Much of the negative media attention that influences the attitude of the average European is a direct result of government involvement. This involvement poses a significant difference between European and American portrayals. Policy makers identify Roma as "beggars" (Ceneda, 2002). Government officials release statements or engage in broadcasts which serve to incite fear or prejudice toward Roma or do little to restrict those who engage in these behaviors. It is not uncommon for government officials to make negative comments about Roma (Lane, Spencer & Jones, 2014) even going so far as to say "the only good gypsy is a dead gypsy" (Ceneda).

Similar to the experiences reported by Rachel but on a much greater scale, Roma in Europe are affected not just on a societal level by negative media portrayals but also on a personal level. Erjavec, (2001) discusses how media representations of Roma are used to normalize discrimination against Roma and situate it as "rational." She describes a media story in which a Roma family was physically prevented from moving into a village because local villagers had experienced negative interactions with Roma in the past and, rather than being called out for their racist actions, they were portrayed as rational actors who were protecting themselves. Local media assisted the cause of the locals and failed to report that the house was legally owned by the Roma family. Reporters emphasized instead how one Roma family could lead to an onslaught of others. The Roma family was unable to live in the home they had purchased, leaving them without housing (Erjavec).

The situation just described is one of countless examples of discrimination experienced by Roma that is the direct result of media portrayals or intervention. Before identifying further the resulting discrimination experienced by Roma, it is important to understand more fully in what forms these portrayals come both in the United States and Europe, and how these are discussed within and outside the Roma community.

ROMA PORTRAYALS IN NEWSPAPERS: A SUITABLE TARGET

Historical Vilification of Roma

As already identified, newspapers have had significant impact on Roma lives. Newspapers are often the points of origination for much fear and distrust toward Roma. The various stereotypes surrounding Roma remain largely unchanged in newspapers and long-held prejudices are used many times over by journalists covering Roma issues (Okely, 2014). Newspapers portray Roma as criminals, dangerous individuals and "immigrants" who should be feared for the dangers that could accompany them (Okely). Okely identifies: "The Gypsies, with centuries of demonization, have become the ideal scapegoat for new uncertainties."

Roma are used as an easy way for journalists to draw readership due to the ease with which one can sensationalize Roma or easily prey on mainstream fears surrounding Roma (Oleaque, 2014):

> Their bad reputation in the eyes of society and the media seems to have been intensified, leading to an association of gypsies with wretchedness. . . . They have become a suitable target for any type of negative comment about them, always for the sake of sensationalism . . . Most of the time the gypsy matter is only dealt with to further ascribe it to a stigmatized description, since this is the most newsworthy and recognizable aspect (2).

As Oleaque describes, the Roma life is newsworthy because it has been sensationalized. Journalists who are able to capitalize on negative societal views of Roma do so for the sake of readership and popularity. Because it works, it continues, intensifying mainstream society's negative associations with Roma lives.

Schneeweis (2017) identified that the majority of news reports in the United States tend to focus on European Roma. She suggests that much of the discourse on Roma fails to connect with the current experience of Roma and often portrays them as homogenous. Those news outlets that take a sympathetic tone toward the plight of Roma may do so with a condescending tone.

As previously discussed, the Library of Congress' newspaper archives from the 1800s and early 1900s are a wealth of the American mainstream interaction with Roma. A sampling of the articles available from newspapers across the nation can give one significant insight into the ways that newspapers were used to create a narrative surrounding the "mysterious" Roma in the United States. Many of the articles discuss common themes such as gypsy kings and queens, witchcraft, kidnappings, unkempt children, artistic temperaments and romanticized lifestyles. Some identify that the advent of publicly available motor cars and the trend of taking motoring trips had made "gypsies" living in the countryside more visible (Cameron County Press, 1911).

In 1897 the *Atlanta Constitution* published an article talking about "gypsies" in a way that both mirrored the stereotypes of gypsies from the time of publication and challenged some of these stereotypes. The article discussed both their origins and their existence. It discussed the occupations of gypsies that included the traditional occupations familiar to the public at the time but also identified that many gypsies were also clergymen and rich men and women. They were identified as good men and fathers. The author states, "In so far as I know him, the American Gypsy is one of nature's gentleman, courteous, considerate and loyal sacrificing friend to his friend." Despite these positive affirmations uncharacteristic for news publications of the time, the author also identified that Roma were born with a desire to travel in their blood and that even among the settled individuals, those with careers who had seemingly largely assimilated in the mainstream, "The vagrant tendencies of the race can never be crushed out" (*Atlanta Constitution*, 1897).

In 1913, reporters from *The Sun* who had previously interacted with Roma in America and found them to be attractive with colorful clothes, decided to seek out Roma in Europe. To their great disappointment, the Roma they interacted with failed to meet their romanticized views and instead describe them as, "decidedly unproductive of romance, beauty or poetry. The English gypsies at home are not particularly attractive . . ." in describing their interaction in this way, they further perpetrate the romanticized view of Roma life and objectify European Roma as objects for entertainment rather than a severely marginalized and impoverished group.

Also in 1913, the *Day Book* of Chicago, Illinois, reports on a story in which a 9-year-old girl suddenly goes missing. The father reports he has observed a group of gypsies passing through the town recently and accuses them of stealing the girl. A search for the gypsies ensues, crossing over four states with newspapers from up to 500 miles away carrying the story of the child stolen by passing gypsies. The reporter himself appears somewhat sympathetic to the plight of the gypsies in this story. He identifies that many gypsy camps were searched and upset and that several gypsy families were accused of stealing their own children. The child in question had not been found at the time of publication.

In the article, the reporter acknowledges (in a rare representation of the Roma perspective on the story) that contrary to beliefs about their aggressive and criminal tendencies, the Roma were "the meekest people of the road" and:

> They protested to us always that they did not steal children. They told us that they were always suspected that everywhere they went they saw the haunted, scared eyes of mothers. [They said] but why should we want more children, the families of all gypsies are large.

Though rare in its ability to give Roma voice, this article further substantiates the popular idea that Roma steal children. It also further highlights the lack of rights held by Roma who were arrested and searched for crimes they were accused of despite a lack of evidence or even an eye witness. Another article published a few years later, in 1916, by the *St. Tammy Farmer* follows very much the same narrative. A boy went missing at the same time a "band of gypsies" arrived in a Pennsylvania town. Their camp was searched as well as their children and no evidence of criminal activity was found.

Among the more confusing and simultaneously racist articles I discovered within the archives was an article written by the *St. Mary Banner* in 1915. The article was reprinted many times over across the country. The article begins positively enough discussing the difficult plight of the "gypsies," their lack of housing, income and the stigma they encounter from the justice department. The reporter then begins to delve into what is believed to be the true nature of the gypsies including their involvement in the white slave trade: "There is evidence that the gypsies have sold their wives and daughters into captivity indicating that the morals of the gypsies are degenerating." He highlights their involvement in threatening local farmers who would not accept trade deals. This included accusations of poisoning cows and burning houses, "American communities . . . are looking upon the horse-trading fortune telling thieving gypsies with more suspicion than usual at this time." The article claims that gypsies had never been sent to jail for their crimes. These accusations provide confirming evidence to those who may have already held negative stereotypes about Roma and offer a prejudiced view of Roma to those unacquainted with their lives. To both groups, the article depicts Roma as dangerous outsiders, a threat to decent society.

The author goes on to identify that gypsies have been persecuted, enslaved and held down, which makes the remainder of the article all the more shocking. According to the author:

> In their religion, which is a religion of hate they have no word for God, soul or heaven . . . They have their own King whom they elect yearly . . . in Spain. The king is supposed to be inducted into office by the sacrifice of two White babies.

The article then identifies that the gypsies have now realized it is too risky to sacrifice White babies so, instead, they steal the babies who are then adopted by the king. Despite their residence in America, they have "never gone through the crucible which makes Americans out of foreigners." They are still very much in need of being domesticated. The author believes that it would "take many years to drive the thieving traits out of the American Gypsies . . ." One hardly needs to delve into this article before seeing the racist ideologies surrounding the Roma purported by the author (*St. Mary Banner*, 1915). By disseminating this "history" of the Roma in papers across the country, and mixing racism with a hollow form of compassion, commonly held beliefs about Roma could be further cemented. Those without information on this group would be ill-informed.

The theme of compassion mixed with overt racism pervaded the many articles gathered from these archives. A newspaper from 1892 (the *Daily Pacific*) discusses the history of gypsy oppression and counters the ideas that gypsies steal and work as little as possible. Despite these enlightened thoughts the author also identifies, "The general impression regarding the race is wrong—most of them are industrious in their own way—they do not like civilization." This quote is exemplary of even modern-day newsprints that consistently "other" Roma. Further, the author brought to mind his subjects by describing them in this way, "all have seen our wandering nomads traveling along our highways or bivouacking in their filthy tents and still more filthy camps." This quote serves to further confirm that gypsies are "dirty," among the most common of gypsy stereotypes and among the most common of reasons to reject interacting with them or accepting them into one's town or neighborhood.

Newspapers of this time also highlight the interaction of Roma and law enforcement, a theme that will be explored throughout this book. In this instance, as in other articles, Roma are portrayed as being constantly entangled with the law. In 1916, the *Ashland Tidings*, of Ashland, Oregon, reported on a robbery in this manner: "True to their inborn instincts, the horde of gypsies which passed through Ashland last Sunday failed to get out of the country without committing a serious depredation." The author goes on to describe how the "gypsies" held up a man for $20.50. The sheriff then "arrested three of the dark-skinned holdup men." Following their arrest the article indicates that, "the police and the mayor invited the gypsies to shorten their stay to no time at all" kicking the remaining Roma out of the town.

The article from the *Ashland Tidings* (1916) also points out that Roma are often entangled in legal issues in other major cities and in fact, they seem to enjoy the benefits rendered from these entanglements:

> It is said that in San Francisco during the winter the jails are filled with gypsies, who seemed to enjoy the confinement and the regular meals. Finally, a special ordinance was passed ejecting them from the city.

The author believes that Roma, so debase in their desires and morality, choose to engage in illegal activities in order to garner free room and board. This depiction of Roma life serves to bring further confirmation to the "criminal Roma" stereotype.

These news articles provide a significant look into the historical role that newspapers played in disseminating information about the Roma in America. As time went on, Roma became increasingly invisible as their mistrust toward outsiders grew and the fear of revealing their identity was passed from generation to generation. While print media has waned in popularity, other forms of media have arisen to take its place. Within these new forms can be found many of the same stereotypes and prejudices that historically plagued newspapers.

Modern American Press

As time progressed, many Romani fell somewhat out of the public eye; however, an inquiry into modern America newspapers will inevitably produce representation of Roma not unlike those already discussed. In 1970 the

Chicago Tribune published an article touting, "Fiction Cloaks Gypsy Lives." The article focused on the suspicion and fear that gypsies often inspire in those around them. Though the author acknowledged that gypsies often lived settled lives, paid their taxes and were otherwise normal contributing members of society, they continued to practice fortune telling, kept their children out of school, had frequent run-ins with the law, were inherently wanderers and were generally different individuals who would never be able to assimilate successfully (Yabush, 1970).

An article in 1987 from the same newspaper compared the lives of two different Roma families. Titled "Gypsies: the last outsiders," the article compares a blue eyed, blond haired gypsy family living the all-American dream, a settled home for their kids, a stable income, a middle-class existence made possible by education. This scene contrasted by the dark gypsy who lives a rough and nomadic existence, surrounded by the involvement of other migratory gypsies with a proclivity toward crime. The article goes on to discuss the tumultuous relationship of gypsies with public schools who can't seem to find gypsy kids, even among the settled individuals and with local police. The settled life is seen as an anomaly among gypsies, however, the subject of the article contradicts this idea. His story will be further discussed in coming chapters. The life of the itinerant gypsy is presented in contrast with the life of one who is acceptable to mainstream society (Yuenger, 1987).

Among the modern newsprint articles I was able to locate, one example confirmed that little has changed in the mind of the public as well as local law enforcement regarding the presence of Roma. A bulletin posted in Tampa Bay, Florida, in January 2016 warned residents to be on the lookout for gypsy scammers in their community (Lonon, 2016). They were accused of scamming local residents with shoddy paving jobs or outright theft of jewelry or money during the day. They specifically identified the group as gypsies and gave this warning: "Should a homeowner confront a gypsy, they will give excuses to explain their presence on the property." While it may very well be true that gypsies are committing these crimes, one thing is certain, gypsies continue to be presented in a homogenized way in newspapers. The rare modern mention of this group in newsprint highlights involvement with the law, craftiness, criminality, and lying. Unlike many other minority groups, there are no alternate representations to counter these images.

Deaton (2013) examined crime articles in Florida from 2011 to 2012. She largely followed the Marks family who were accused of defrauding their clients through fortune telling. She identified that many articles referenced his ethnicity though some did not. They are continually conceptualized as the more pejorative term gyspy rather than Roma. Federal agents are shown as displaying bias toward the family in court by highlighting the ethnicity of the family unnecessarily and portraying them in a stereoptical manner. Major themes highlighted by Deaton included the untrustworthy nature of Roma, the Roma threat to the dominant culture and its members, the exoticized nature of Roma, their predatory nature and living outside the norm. Deaton's research underscores the bias approach that both law enforcement and news media have taken to the portrayal of Romani who, like those in Europe, best serve the newspaper market when they are sensationalized.

ROMA IN EUROPEAN NEWSPAPERS
AND "THE WORST REPRESENTATIONS"

The representation in European newspapers is similar to the historical representations in America though they persist as widely today as in the past (Okely, 2014). Reporters write influenced by previously held judgments and lack accurate information about Roma or Gypsy, Roma and Travellers (GRT's). Okely reports "The Gypsies, with centuries of demonization, have become the ideal scapegoat for new uncertainties." Her words characterize the relationship between the Roma and newsprint throughout Europe. The Roma are more often than not vilified. Reports of Roma are situated in language that is prejudiced, promoting racism and discrimination (Lane, Spencer & Jones, 2014). Tereskinas (2002) discusses the lengths at which newspapers go to represent Roma in a negative light when compared with other minority groups:

> Roma people merit the worst representations as the least socially integrated, criminal and exotic group. The press frequently refers to the Roma minority as criminal, deviant, socially insecure, inscrutable, and manipulative. In the police reports published in the newspaper, *Lietuvos rytas*, the ethnicity of Roma is always emphasized. (8)

Roma are more likely to be depicted in a negative light than other minority groups. Their ethnicity is emphasized due to the immediate negative associations journalists know will be elicited from readers.

Plaut (2012) identifies: "Roma have consistently been portrayed as passive objects in a chess game of great power . . . rather than active subjects." Newspapers often discuss the Roma "problem" but rarely consult them directly (Morris, 2000). "Many Travellers will not see or cannot read the things that are written about them. Not only are they taunted, denigrated and laughed at, it is done behind their back" (Morris, 213). Though sometimes unaware of what is being reported on specifically, traditional European Roma are more than aware that the media portrays them in a negative light. A qualitative study by Lane, Spencer and Jones (2014) uncovers Roma sentiments toward their representations and the way they are treated by journalists:

Newspapers follow you to camps [their homes] and take photos of your property . . . The media are rubbish, they just make a fool of Travelers and make up stories in their own head (20)

While Morris identifies that Roma may not always have access to how they are being depicted, Lane, Spencer and Jones highlight the fact that Roma routinely encounter journalists in their daily lives and have an inherent understanding of journalists' attitudes toward Roma.

In places such as Bulgaria, it is reported that 90 percent of hate speech in print media is directed at Roma (Danova, 1998 as cited in Erjavec). In Italy, print media comes in a variety of forms directed at the Roma community. These forms include media hysteria about Roma presence. They include government-issued emergency decrees allowing for the eviction of any minority deemed a "threat" which unfairly target Roma. Newspapers compare Roma to "animals." Molotov bombs and violence against Roma are reported on as citizens and government officials ask for manpower to be used to remove Roma from Italy (Sigona, 2008). In her 2000 article on Gypsy Travelers and the media, Morris cites this notice posted in a local newspaper regarding Roma:

KEEP THIS SCUM OUT (And it IS time to hound 'em, Chief Constable). They call themselves tinkers, itinerants new age travellers. We call them parasites. The scum of the earth who live off the backs of others. They contribute nothing but trouble . . . They set up filthy, disease-ridden camps on roadsides and in parks and offend every decent citizen. (214)

This notice is a shocking example of the overt prejudice Roma encounter throughout Europe and is representative of countless examples of the way that Roma are targeted through newsprint.

In the United Kingdom, a code exists that states a person's race should be mentioned only when it is strictly relevant to what is being reported (Morris, 2000). Despite this rule, the ethnicity of GRT in Europe is rarely overlooked and is often overemphasized. Local newspapers make life challenging for those traveling by spreading false statements about them before they arrive in a town, resulting in a pre-existing resistance to their presence (Morris). They are most often represented in newspapers as a group that is inherently bad (Morris 2000; Plaut, 2012). There can be little doubt that the dissemination of information which is outright opposed to Roma is often channeled through newspapers, however, indirect and even fictional portrayals in mediums such as movies have the potential to disseminate these same messages.

ROMA IN THE MOVIES "A ROMANTICIZED VIEW"

The Hunchback of Notre Dame

While newspapers most often seek to villainize Roma, their portrayal in movies is largely a romanticized depiction of their existence. Though portrayed in many films throughout American history, among the most notable portrayals are those that have occurred more recently. *The Hunchback of Notre Dame* is a Disney film that focuses on the relationship between a Roma woman and a disabled Roma man. Criticism for the film's portrayal of Roma can be found among various Roma activists and bloggers. Among these, on Tumblr, the author of "Roma in Art, Literature, and Music" (Tasbeeh, 2015) identifies just what is so problematic with this romanticized portrayal of Roma. The author of this article points out that the source material for this movie, originally by Victor Hugo, is incredibly racist, far beyond what Disney would be willing to portray. She also states that Quasimodo's character, though Roma, has been "white washed," that the other Roma in the film are merely "racial caricatures" and that "racial slurs" are used throughout the film.

Among the larger news sites and academic scholars little can be found in the way of protest and any protest found gives way to religious objectors, feminists and others concerned with disabled persons (Whittington-Walsh, 2002). Like it or not, the movie is among the most recognized portrayals of Roma. Among those interviewed for this book, many agreed when they identify as Roma, "Oh, you mean like Hunch Back of Notre Dame?" is a common response from those otherwise unacquainted with Roma.

Thinner

In Stephen King's Novel *Thinner*, (King, 1984) made into a movie in 1996 by Paramount pictures, gypsies are portrayed in all of their most stereotyped glory. The story follows a successful lawyer with a weight problem who hits and kills an elderly gypsy woman in a case of distracted driving. He is acquitted from any guilt and upon his exit from the courtroom is cursed, along with the judge and police officer on the case, by the woman's father. The main character quickly begins to waste away to the point of near death as he seeks to end the curse by confronting the man who cursed him (Holland, 1996).

The film is rife with stereotypes from the beginning of the film. The gypsies arrive in town in a caravan of old cars piled high with their belongings. The women are objectified in the opening scenes. They are characterized wearing revealing clothing and portrayed as having a seductive air. Main characters of the movie discuss offering a young gyspy woman money to get on her knees or to show herself. Later the woman lifts up her skirt but then flicks off the man in protest to his objectification. She is shown as lacking modesty, masculine and violent throughout the remainder of the film.

The pejorative term "gyp" is used frequently throughout the film, a term that many Romani view as a racial slur. The main character discussed catching diseases and lice from the gypsies invoking an age-old stereotype that gypsies are dirty or do not care about their personal hygiene. The gyspy characters are portrayed as magical, vindictive, making trouble, seen dancing around fires, violent and working as carnival workers. Further, the gypsies in this movie are given Italian accents and it is implied they are engaged in abusing their animals, restricting their food either for protection or for dog fighting.

The only positive portrayal of the gypsies in this film includes their value of family and a singular line spoken by the man who "cursed" the main character. When asking the main character why he killed his daughter, the man explains that he didn't see her in the road. The gypsy father responds "You never see us." This one statement embodies the experience of many Roma in America and certainly in American film. Roma remain invisible in America to many and in film their true nature is often hidden by derogatory and archaic portrayals such as those found in *Thinner*. The gypsies are never given a redeeming moment in the film; they are only forced to lift the curse when both animals and humans within the camp are killed.

Sherlock: Game of Shadows

Among other recent depictions of Roma life, *Sherlock: Game of Shadows* was released in 2011, starring Robert Downey Jr. and Jude Law (Silver et. al, 2011). In the film, the pair travel across Europe with a "band of gypsies" to stop Professor Moriarity's evil schemes. Sadly, the portrayal of Roma in this film falls very much into the romanticized notion of Roma. The first scene that introduces a Roma character shows a Roma woman clearly sexually objectified in her portrayal, telling fortunes and engaging in dishonest schemes.

The sexualization of Roma, particularly Roma women, is a known and harmful stereotype (Hancock, 2008; 2010) that *Sherlock* eagerly plays into. Throughout the movie Roma are portrayed as adventurers, good at fighting and engaged in underground criminal dealings. Critical reception of this movie was even scarcer than with *The Hunchback of Notre Dame* (Hahn, Trousdale &Wise, 1996) though their portrayals are essentially along the same themes. Critical reviews that were located indicate a feeling that the portrayal of this Roma woman is positive and have this to say regarding her portrayal:

It was encouraging to see a woman involved who didn't have to be either man's love interest, who could hold her own in a fight without toting a machine gun or breaking out tae kwon do, and wasn't being flaunted on screen in an overtly sexual manner. (Asher-Perrin, 2011)

The author of the article felt that the independence of the woman portrayed, her ability to fight for herself and her lack of romantic entanglement qualified the role as an empowered one.

The author goes on to say that she believes the women portrayed by the director of *Sherlock* are portrayed with a "surprising amount of respect." Despite this, this particular author fails to acknowledge once that this woman is being portrayed as a Roma and, though she discussed most of the film's themes and characters at length, fails to ever mention the aid Sherlock received from the Roma and how they play into the outcome of the film (Asher-Perrin, 2011). Though center stage in this film, they are invisible in their stereotypical portrayals and the Roma woman is, as so many Roma are, allowed to be either a woman or Roma but not both.

It should be noted that both *The Hunchback of Notre Dame* and *Sherlock: Game of Shadows,* though they are American films, portray Roma in Europe in a romanticized light, making them, if anything, a subject of lore or fantasy. These portrayals are often a factor in the resistance of American Roma to acknowledge their ethnicity and existence. Gertie, a Roma woman in her fifties, acknowledges the role that movie portrayals have played as an intermediary between Roma and the outside world; "Yeah, I mean very few people know anything about the personal lives of gypsies. I think they have a romanticized view from the movie or the media." Gertie's views align with the general consensus that media portrayals are the main source of information about Roma for those outside of their community.

Borat

Borat, a 2006 feature film starring Sascha Barron Cohen, featured Roma villagers as imaginary citizens of an imaginary village. Meant to exemplify the backward nature of these villagers in a humorous manner, the filmmaker failed to adequately portray the depth of poverty or social isolation faced by these villagers in real life. As Carpenter (2007) points out, the villagers were paid to be in the film unaware of the context. They were given no agency in the situation. "Because of the way they are presented in the film, viewers may have interpreted their situation as humorously backward, instead of as people in need of economic opportunities" (Carpenter, 2007). Some European countries sought to ban the film because of the treatment and portrayal of the Roma (Meyers, 2006).

This list is hardly exhaustive; many other movie portrayals in America exist, most following along the same lines of stereotypical portrayal. One can look further into these portrayals by examining the works of Schneewies (2017) and Schneeweis and Foss (2016).

The Challenge to Modern Portrayals in America

In recent movies, controversy has surrounded the portrayal of Marvel's character, The Scarlet Witch, or Wanda Maximoff, in the *Avengers* franchise (Whedon & Feige, 2015) among other notable characters. While revelation of her Roma origins may or may not lend itself to the "mystical" trope associated with the Roma, the fact remains that writers of Marvel comics created a powerful super hero with Roma origins that remain unacknowledged. Her backstory in the comics highlights the persecution and prejudice faced by her parents, who are both Roma and Jewish, and survivors of the Holocaust. Despite her special powers, her backstory has the potential to highlight the history of the Roma people in a realistic way and bring their story into the notice of mainstream America and others worldwide. When casting the movie, this character was cast as a blonde-haired blue-eyed woman, a possible but not common look for the majority of Roma. Her origins were largely ignored and her ethnicity has gone unnoticed (Abed-Santos, 2013).

Some fans have argued that an outright acknowledgment and understanding of these origins is not essential and all but irrelevant in the *Avengers* portrayal. Some Roma activists would argue that this character and her brother have the ability to help Roma worldwide view themselves as survivors. Acknowledging their ancestry and the history surrounding it could bring the plight of the Roma into the life of a powerful protagonist, rather than a victim. The "white washing" of these characters has taken a rare opportunity for a positive portrayal of the Roma and a chance to educate the public on their tragic history away, for the time being (Fernandez, 2016). An opportunity has been lost for Hollywood to become further informed regarding Roma portrayals and to bring a new type of diversity to their casting. This is unfortunate for a country that is far behind Europe in their on-screen portrayal of Roma people. Gilbert, forty-seven, identifies the opportunity that exists for Hollywood:

> You have Roma characters that could be brought forth and used as super heroes. That would be fantastic. You need a, you have a Black superhero and an Asian Superhero you need a Roma one too, you need positive portrayals in Roma media. But will Hollywood be smart enough to have their writers reveal that part of the character? I don't know, they need to find someone to help them do that.

Gilbert feels that this could be an opportunity for both Roma and Hollywood but questions if writers will make the right decision. Recent events involving at least one writer from Marvel at New York Comic Con cast doubt on this possibility.

At New York Comic Con 2016, Marvel held a Panel on LGBT and diversity issues. Vincent Rodriguez, founder of ROMApop addressed many of these issues by raising questions about Roma characters to the panel. Peter David, a marvel writer on the panel, responded by relating a story about his experiences in Roma with "gypsies" who, according to his narrative, had purposely and horribly mangled a child in order to beg. He identified how this horrific scene had stayed with him and then effectively shut down Rodriquez. Yelling at the top of his voice "We are done. . . . No. . . . I DON'T WANT TO HEAR IT!" David reduced the Roma in one vignette to criminally viscous beggars, without even familial sentiment denying their right to a voice and furthering despicable stereotypes about Roma (Rodriguez, 2016).

In response, Rodriguez relates in an official statement put out by Romapop (2016) that he and other Roma allies filed a grievance with NYCC based on David's statement. Following the end of the event they were issued a private notice that David's statements were not condoned and that they would be following up in-house about the incident. No public statement from Marvel was made. Peter David released a statement that was deemed inadequate by Roma activists and supporters.

Rodriguez and other Roma took to Twitter to call on Marvel and David to follow through on their commitment to diversity and to make amends publicly to the Roma community. Rodriguez and others sought to provide countering information to David to no avail. David is only one of many who lack adequate information about the Roma, both in America and especially Europe where, as previously discussed, the lives of Roma are tragic in many respects. David's exceptionalism lies in the very public platform he holds in the media, one which allows him to disseminate his vitriol toward the Roma in a way that could have significant ramifications worldwide. As long as writers such as David hold these attitudes, it is unlikely that Roma movie representations in America will deviate from their standard tropes. Movie representations will reflect the held beliefs of their writers.

One response to this whitewashing of Roma characters has been to bring visibility to Roma characters' origins long before the movies are produced, in hopes of becoming an advocate for accurate portrayal. A recent article from Nerds of Color (2017) a group of contributors made of persons of color with an interest in pop culture representations in comics, movies and TV, discussed a portrayal now in the works from DC Comics. In the article, the contributor highlights the soon-to-be produced *Nightwing* wing film. *Nightwing* is the name given to Dick Grayson, formerly Robin of Batman and Robin. Nerds of Color discuss the revelation of Grayson's Roma identity in the D.C. canon and hope to shed light on this identity, question the possibility of negative Roma representation as it is currently written in the canon and express hope for a more positive representation in the future. Nerds of Color provide many suggestions for reclaiming positive Roma representation in the upcoming film. This type of proactive advocacy is a response to the many negative representations of Roma in Hollywood, representations that continue as writers are unwilling to explore their bias, educate themselves or simply acknowledge the true existence of Roma in America.

Modern Movie Portrayals in Europe

In Europe, Roma portrayals and their criticisms are more readily available than in the United States. In Eastern Europe, for example, Imre (2003) identifies that Roma are often exoticized and their lifestyles are idealized on screen. Roma are commonly "othered" by these films and perpetuate the narrative that Roma who become successful financially or otherwise are an exception to the Roma community. He sees this as a serious affront to the Roma community, stating "representation can constitute an act of violence." He also acknowledges that this type of representation has led Roma to be skeptical of filmmakers even from within their own communities. Imre criticizes filmmakers for failing to acknowledge their position of privilege being outside of the Roma community and how this may impact or bias the way they represent Roma on the screen.

In no way is this list exhaustive in its discussion of films that portray the Roma. The list of Roma portrayals and appearances in movies is quite long; however, these examples give a glimpse into the ways in which mainstream America and Europe continue to be exposed to Roma as a people. While documentaries and other forms of film arise to counter these images, they have yet to make a significant mark on the lives of many in the mainstream. Beyond the impact that these films and others have made, television has moved to the forefront of controversy in its role as the primary mode of representation for Roma, certainly in America but, to some extent, in Europe as well.

ROMA ON TELEVISION

Though screen portrayals of Roma have not been adequate in accurate portrayal, what is known about their impact is limited. The medium of Roma portrayal known for the most significant impact on the lives of the Roma is television. Roma portrayals on television have risen in popularity in recent years in both Europe and the United States. These portrayals, like other mediums, fail to adequately convey the many challenges Roma face in their everyday life and, instead, promote either a romanticized view of the Roma or an image meant to incite fear or distrust. One need only to observe statements made by those outside of the Roma community to understand the impact that these portrayals have on deeply held prejudices.

A recent viral video (LiveLink, 2016) of Irish Traveler women produced a flood of racist commentary, many commentators indicating that the public behavior of these women only confirmed what they previously believed about GRTs. One individual, from America, had this to say regarding "gypsies" from Ireland and their portrayal in the video: "For anyone who has had dealings with Irish gypos in any way, shape, or form you will know that they are literally the scum of the earth" (American, Comments Post). Not only does this commentator use a derogatory term (gypo) but they also categorize an entire marginalized group as the very lowest of the low, based on what they have observed through the medium of television.

The commentator's sentiments were mirrored by another commentator in Europe who felt the way television was portraying the gypsy community was entirely reflective of the many deficits in their culture:

> Gypsy women are by far the most ignorant people compared to almost anyone. Not just illiterate and unable to read the time, but (as revealed on TV last year), they often don't even understand days of the week. The men in their despicable criminal communities actually prevent them from having any education. Any. (European, Comments Post)

Unacquainted with any real information regarding the Roma way of life, many viewers from mainstream society reach their own conclusions regarding the lives of the Roma and many, such as these commentators, have chosen to share this with others, spreading further the prejudice and misinformation that originates from television portrayals. These attitudes most often turn to actions which can have serious ramifications for Roma as will be discussed in the coming chapters.

Historical Portrayals in the United States

In the United States, Roma appeared historically on television in romanticized and stereotypical roles just as they had in movies. We will discuss here at some length an example of representation that was typical of the portrayal of Roma throughout the history of U.S. television. In 1966, an episode of the *Andy Griffith Show* aired titled "The Gypsies" (Maclane & Rafkin, 1966). This episode depicts the arrival of a family of gypsies on the outskirts of town. The gypsies begin selling goods and telling fortunes throughout the town, prompting the sheriff to ask them to move on. The gypsies place a "curse" on the town due to their lack of hospitality, causing fear in the townspeople. The gypsies decide to remove the curse and they are eventually found out to be nothing but conmen. The sheriff asks them to leave Mayberry and not return.

I chose this episode of *The Andy Griffith Show* (Maclane & Rafkin, 1966) because the episode successfully represents every major stereotype associated with the Roma, "good" and bad. At the beginning of the episode, Sheriff Andy Taylor and his girlfriend see smoke coming from a field on the outskirts of town. They stop to investigate. The scene changes to four gypsies— two men and two women—cooking over a campfire while the men play cards and guitar. They sit in front of a brightly painted caravan and are all clad in bright-colored clothing and gold. The younger woman of the group suddenly exclaims, "Policeman is coming." She picks up a tambourine and the man his guitar. They all begin to dance and sing and laugh as they wait for the sheriff to arrive. This one scene manages to capture the gypsy life in its romanticized glory, colorful clothing, music and dancing, a carefree lifestyle. It also hints at a darker side to gypsy life, putting on a show for law enforcement, having something to hide.

As Sheriff Taylor arrives at their camp, one of the men greet him by saying "Welcome to the gay, carefree camp of the Gypsies!" The men become overly flattering of the sheriff and his girlfriend and the young woman begin to act suggestively toward the sheriff. They introduce their mother as the "Queen of the Gypsies." The sheriff warns the "gypsies" about having a fire lit due to the dry season. As he leaves he wonders if they plan to stay or if they are just passing through. "What difference does it make?" his girlfriend asks. "We've had gypsies here before," he says with a knowing look and decides to head back to their camp.

The gypsies see the sheriff returning and immediately fall back into their singing and dancing as he approaches. He questions how long they plan to stay outside of Mayberry and explains his questioning: "The reason I ask is last year we had some gypsies pass through here and they went around and started cheating people, they had a lot of different angles."

The gypsies respond in the negative: those must have been "bad" gypsies but we are "gay and carefree" and would never sell "worthless" junk. This scene begins what is the theme for the remainder of the episode, the darker side to the gypsy life, lying and hustling others. Sheriff Taylor's response to them is unfortunately a fairly accurate depiction of historical interactions with law enforcement. Sheriff Taylor views gypsies in a homogenized and prejudicial manner and insinuates that a long-term stay would be unwelcome.

The scenes following show the gypsies going from door to door selling fake gold earrings, telling stories and flattering their customers to make a sell. They tell fortunes for money, which Sheriff Taylor believes is dangerous and dishonest. He visits their camp again and finds the elderly mother is drinking heavily. The gypsies once again begin to sing and dance. Sheriff Taylor tells them it's time to "move on." In retaliation they come to the town square and put on a ritual dance in which they place a "curse" on the town. They state that rain will not fall in Mayberry until the gypsies are allowed to return. Both this scene and a scene toward the end of the episode where they "lift" the curse play into the mystical nature of the gypsies, able to curse or bless someone at will. As the gypsies leave town for good, having been "found out" as hustlers by the entire town, Opie asks his father, Sheriff Taylor, "Can gypsies do any magic at all?" "Yes, yes they can," he answers "They can take out a pair of worthless earrings, show them to your Aunt B and make 12 and ½ dollars disappear like nothing." His statements leave the viewer with the underlying message that despite all their showmanship and fancy words, the gypsies are nothing more than common thieves and hustlers (Maclane & Rafkin, 1966).

MODERN PORTRAYALS ON AMERICAN TELEVISION

The only stereotype the episode of *The Andy Griffith Show* did not hit on was that of stealing children. This portrayal was representative of many other shows of the time, each allowing the portrayal of a people little was known about to take on a life of its own and portrayed to the viewer that these were accurate representations of gypsy lives. In modern times, Roma lives have made small appearances in stereotypical portrayals on shows such as *Star Trek: The Next Generation* (Roddenbery & Snodgrass, 1989) and in outlandish and culturally unaware portrayals on shows such a *Bones* (Hanson, Reichs & Charles, 2014).

Schneeweis and Foss (2016) examined 84 fictional and 17 reality television portrayals ranging from 1954 to 2014. Through their review 5 major themes of depiction emerged. These themes included the ethnic other, gypsy tradition, swindling, magical and irresistible fortune teller and the misunderstood. Schneeweis and Foss point out that even in those depictions sympathetic to Roma, characterization as an "other" remain:

> The role of Gypsies as outsiders and peripheral characters persists, accompanied in contemporary depictions by the more politically correct construction of "the misunderstood" Gypsy, albeit still limited and presented as an outsider (1151).

These portrayals continue to relegate gypsies to the role of an outsider, fail to acknowledge their positive social contributions and preserve the aura of mystery surrounding Roma lives. (Schneeweis & Foss, 2017).

Among the more popular modern television shows that portray Roma in the United States, is *The Riches* (Lipkin, 2007). The show aired from 2007–2008 for two seasons and starred Minni Driver and Eddie Izzard as a pair of Irish Travelers who get into a car accident, killing a wealthy family. The family takes on the identity of the wealthy individuals and proceed to "con" the town's residents into believing they belong as the "Riches." The show came out to positive critical reviews and a wide viewership. While seen as entertaining, much of the show falls into the stereotype that the life of the Roma is most often tied up in poverty and criminality. Once again, through this portrayal, negative ideas about travelers, or Roma, become legitimate as they are played out in prime time television. Despite the fact that Roma are largely without a voice on how their representations are portrayed, viewers believe these portrayals to be "realistic" (Kabachnick, 2009).

The writers of many shows that portray Roma imply that criminality is an "ingrained" characteristic of their DNA. To some, this is seen as "an attempt to forgive Irish Travellers, since their need for grifting is beyond their control." It is almost has if they have no choice in the matter, it is in their blood, and thus, one cannot hold them accountable for their actions (Kabachnik, 2009). Kabachnik identifies what is problematic with the way identity is constructed for Roma within the show *The Riches*, "Irish Traveler culture is constructed as an insular, criminal group that is diametrically opposed to and exploitive of, everyone else." Kabachnick, following an extensive dissection of this show, was left with one conclusion, "If there is one thing we can learn from *The Riches*, it is that we still have a long way to go before Irish Travellers begin to be represented as any other ethnic group would expect to be."

Hemlock Grove

Set in Hemlock Grove, Pennsylvania, the show chronicles strange occurrences in the town investigated by the son of the town's wealthiest family and his new friend, a boy of Romani origins who is suspected of carrying out the horrible crimes that have recently befallen the town. Not only is Peter a Romani, he is also secretly a werewolf. Peter's portrayal as a Romani is at best problematic and the portrayal of other Roma characters in the show hardly fare better.

When interviewed about his preparation for the role, Landon Liboiron who plays Peter in the series, describes reading many books on the culture. Liboiron views his portrayal of Peter as positive, identifying that there have been few positive portrayals of gypsies on TV. Despite this, many of Peter's descriptions and explanation of gypsies and gypsy culture play into stereotypes that are the source of criticism surrounding gypsy portrayals. Liboiron discusses hoping on the road to camp on the spur of the moment "like a gypsy would." He also talks about gypsy preference for "bedazzling" themselves with gold and describes what makes the gypsy "magic." While seemingly well intended, Liboiron's interview highlights a lack of understanding surrounding gypsy portrayals or the elements which make up gypsy identity, ethnicity and culture.

Fangs for the Fantasy, a blog devoted to both the world of urban fantasy and social justice provide a scouring critique of the treatment of Roma characters in *Hemlock Grove*. Their observations include "anti Roma prejudice" noting the use of "trash and scum" as adjectives describing gypsies. Their feelings toward the portrayal of Roma were concisely stated in this sentence: "I don't think an episode went by without some anti-ziganism of some kind." Main Roma characters are identified as being representative of negative stereotypes including thievery and the possession of magical powers (or the claim of possession). Additionally, they are "othered" by those they regularly interact with and fail to adequately portray their culture in a positive light (Fangs for the Fantasy, 2013). Despite critiques like those coming from Fangs for the Fantasy and others interested in highlighting disparities in media portrayals, *Hemlock Grove* was an overwhelming success for Netflix in its first season and continued for three seasons.

Buffy the Vampire Slayer

Beaudoin (2014) explores with a critical eye Roma representation in *Buffy the Vampire Slayer*. Giving a brief history of the Roma who cursed Angel the vampire with a soul, she identifies that Roma portrayals did at times fall very much into stereotypical tropes. In contrast to this, she also finds that a main Roma character within the show, Jenny Calender, was able to defy stereo-types and proved to be a "dynamic and multifaceted Romani character who . . . contributed to a positive Romani portrayal." She also believes that stereotypes of Roma were at times challenged in the show, real issues affect-ing Roma were discussed and specific Roma clans were identified as Roma justice was portrayed. Despite this, there were many negative aspects to the portrayal of Roma including sexualization, othering, dehumanization and language including association of Roma with the word "dirty." Beaudoin asserts that Buffy presents a complex picture that is at once stereotypical and challenging of stereotypes, one that deserves to be further examined in Ro-mani ethnic discussions.

Criminal Minds

A more current portrayal of "traditional" Romani lifestyles occurs in Season 4 of *Criminal Minds*. The episode "Bloodline" centers around a Romani family who, through enacting an ancient ritual, becomes the center of a multiple murder investigation. The episode opening sets the stage for what's to come as a mystical, almost dreamlike score plays. A family from Alabama begins to speak with their almost ten-year-old son about becoming a "man" soon. The story progresses as the family breaks into a home in the dead of night, murders a man and woman and steals a little girl from her bed.

From there, the investigation begins and the stereotypes surrounding Romani unfold, one after another. The viewer learns that the family is of Romani origin from the investigators as they seek to profile the killers. Identified as Eastern European Roma, gypsies, they are said to be highly superstitious and obsessed with ritual. While the investigative team throws the Roma a bone stating, "Someone has perverted the Roma culture" and indicating Roma are "not usually prone to violence" we are given to understand that Romani are typically nomadic who often bring with them a wave of petty theft.

As the investigation continues we see the family characterized as brutal, cold, kidnappers (one of the oldest and most bizarre of the Roma stereotypes). Though described as tight-knit when it comes to their own family they are shown to be without feeling toward others. They live in a mobile home, identified by the camp manager as dirty, superstitious; later they are said to be stealers of children, grooming their offspring to kill, and poisoners of the mind. They are portrayed as hunters, magical, experts at petty theft from a young age, doing what is needed to survive and putting the purity of the family first. Garcia, a character feeding the team information, immediately brings to mind the romanticized image of Roma held by most Americans citing Cher's "Gypsies, tramps and thieves." Through her information she identifies 100s of years of petty theft, kidnapping and ritualistic murder.

King of Romania, a blog dedicated to "all things Romania," pulls apart the many ironies and misconceptions that take place in this episode, first pointing out that the Romani family is said to be stealing children to acquire new blood for the family while also being labeled as so insular they do not allow adult Romani to marry those outside the culture as adults. King of Romania also points out the contradictory use of Romani language and English throughout the episode. In summary, King of Romani states "Its racist piece of garbage plotline . . ."

Though harsh, one might be inclined to agree with King of Romania's conclusion. While representing one voice among many supporters and detractors of the show, he is one of many bloggers who took issue with this episode. For this episode specifically, King of Romani hits on the concern of this episode from the perspective of the general public, beyond the critical eye of the academic or even social justice advocate. And that is what makes this portrayal particularly troubling. The inconsistencies, the moments of outright stereotypical portrayal seem to be obviously inappropriate, yet they go unchecked throughout the show with the minor exceptions of Romani culture being seen as "perverted" and identified as not usually violent.

My Big Fat Gypsy Wedding

Few of the portrayals discussed have been able to effectively convey that the Roma are a legitimate minority or immigrant group living in modern America. This changed when TLC adapted a widely popular British television show, *My Big Fat Gypsy Wedding* (Popplewell, 2012) and brought it to

America to give a "real" look into the outlandish world of the "Gypsies." *My Big Fat American Gypsy Wedding* documented the marriage customs of Roma in the United States. For many Americans, this was the first real-life exposure to Roma and it was wrought with stereotypes and poor representations of their true lives. The show premiered on TLC in 2002 and, as of 2017, continues to air. It has been wildly popular with mainstream audiences and has received significant criticism from the Roma community. Those in support of the show have dubbed it "horrifying, bizarre and compulsively watchable (Bosch, 2012)." Bosch describes the Roma on the show as exhibiting the "deeply conflicting dual traditions of extreme conservatism in slutty clothing." The show, which originated in the United Kingdom, was equally as popular as the American version, if not more so, and because Roma are quite visible in European society, served to do further harm to a minority group already surviving on the fringes of society (Plunkett, 2012).

My Big Fat American Gypsy Wedding has left society with questions about the true origin and nature of Roma and their ethnicity. Girlsaskguys.com (n.d.) is a website on which men and women can anonymously ask each other about any topic and are given answers by as many individuals as are willing to contribute. Within these anonymous though public conversations one can get a significant glimpse into the attitudes of the general American public toward Roma. One can also plainly see how their attitudes have been influenced by popular media.

The following is a conversation that took place about Roma identity:

> Girl : How are the self-described gypsies/travelers of America actually gypsies? My understanding of gypsies were the tan/olive skinned eastern Europeans so how are those guys gypsies when they can blend in with the cast members of MTV's Buckwild?
>
> *Girl:* Being a gypsy isn't about skin color, it's their ethnic background . . . Essentially they're "white" but from different cultures. Those gypsies on TLC are trailer park trash though. Supposedly they're 10xworse in the UK, which is probably why they're disliked . . . not condoning or supporting racism/discrimination toward them btw.

This conversation highlights some of the unfortunate consequences of the portrayal of Roma on *My Big Fat American Gypsy Wedding* (Poppelwell, 2012). The images and stereotypes conveyed through the show have left those having this conversation confused regarding who the Roma actually are and have helped to cement the negative attitudes already held by others. Despite Girl #2's claim that she is not supporting or condoning racism toward Roma, she indicates that Roma are both "trailer trash" and "10X worse in the UK." Girl #2 obviously believes that a separation between racist attitudes and actions is quite large, how else would she fail to see that it is the dissemination of these attitudes that qualifies as racism and leads to discrimination (girlsaskguys.com, n.d.).

Similar conversations about the impact of this particular television portrayal could be found elsewhere on the site. One poster indicated that she felt the show actually failed to live up to the negative stereotypes she has heard regarding Roma, however, another poster was immediately available to provide answers, erroneous at best, regarding her questions about Roma. These questions would have already been answered had the show adequately explained and portrayed the life of the American Roma (girlsaskguys.com, n.d.):

> *Girl*: I watch *My Big Fat American Gypsy Wedding* and they don't seem so terrible, but then again they're in America and I'm American. They say they don't steal or commit crimes as stereotyped. But, I've always seen people in the UK talk badly about gypsies and how they steal and when they leave one area (cause they're travelers), they leave the area dirty and a mess and they're known for taking pets.
> *Guy*: On one hand, they are widely considered an underclass in most countries they are in, so they are naturally treated and thought of badly by others by default . . . they DO frequently engage in criminal behavior, scams/swindles, violence, intimidation, and often live a very "ghetto" lifestyle and make big messes that others have to clean up.

While there is no way to determine where the guy in this conversation developed his information, one can certainly see that the misinformation provided by *My Big Fat American Gypsy Wedding* (Herman, 2012) has created an opportunity for misinformation to multiply and become further seated in the attitudes of those who bother to watch.

Another example of confusion produced by this show and the ignorance with which individuals readily speak up regarding the existence of Roma in America can be found in the following online conversation (girlsaskguys.com, n.d.):

> *Girl*: So I was watching a TV show on TLC about gypsies and I don't know what they are. I find it crazy that they let their daughter's dress the way they do and basically make them marry before they are 18 to become stay at home wives. So please help me understand how that can be acceptable. Thanks guys.
> *Guy*: I'm from 'Murica. We don't have gypsy problems.
> *Girl2*: What about that big fat American gypsy weddings program and the spin off series gypsy sisters?
> *Guy*: Never seen either of those. Or heard of for that fact.
> *Girl2*: Well, saying that there are no gypsies in America is pretty ignorant
> *Guy*: I didn't say we didn't have them. We have everybody. I'm just saying it's not a problem.
> *Girl3*: When I ask people they usually tell me they're thieves and not people to trust. I wouldn't know because I've never met one. I hear about them now because of the T/V show "American Gypsy" and the Disney Character Esme-

ralda . . . Disney makes everything look cute but gypsies are pretty much Satanists.

This conversation is rife with ignorance regarding the Roma life and existence and there can be little doubt where much of this comes from. Television shows such as *My Big Fat American Gypsy Wedding* among others have created a narrative surrounding a little known group. Conversely, the guy in this conversation identifies that there is no gypsy "problem" in America and acknowledges he has never viewed these television programs and yet now, one can only worry that he will investigate these singular points of reference for the mainstream and further delve into a world of misinformation. One could argue that a show such as *My Big Fat America Gypsy Wedding* (Herman, 2012) creates an opportunity for education from reliable sources as much as it does opportunities for misinformation. While Roma activists have sought to bring countering images, as will be discussed later in the chapter, Roma rarely own the shaping of their identity in the mainstream, as will be discussed in a chapter to come.

It can be difficult for Roma to face the reality that their identity, something held so tightly to in Roma history, has been publicly exposed on national television, and not in a way that would improve the relationship between Roma and mainstream society. Gracie, a woman in her sixties from the Southeast United States, discussed at length how television portrayals, and specifically *My Big Fat American Gypsy Wedding* (Herman, 2012), has forced many Roma to reveal themselves, something they never intended to do:

> I tended to not talk about being Roma to outsiders so I never intended to do that but I think there are a group of us now who believe that if we don't do that then things will be bad. So I mean if you let TLC interpret who you are then that's who you are to the public.

The extent that *My Big Fat American Gypsy Wedding* (Herman, 2012) has negatively portrayed Roma has forced American Roma, like Gracie, to take a stance in defense of their identity out of fear. These Roma fear that what has been a historical truth for Roma in America, and in the present day for European Roma, could again become the reality for American Roma.

My Big Fat American Gypsy Wedding is problematic for a number of reasons. Comanescu (2015) identifies that the show typically focuses on outdated practices of the Roma. The show consistently "others" Roma by portraying them as a secretive and entirely isolated community. Comanescu identifies:

> The large social issue of discrimination that perhaps lies at the root of the tensions between Romani and the majority population becomes solely an issue

of Roma cultural identity. Discrimination is legitimized by providing evidence that the Roma simply cannot be integrated.

The audience is presented with reality scripting and is encouraged to understand these actions as inherent to the Roma community:

> Because Roma tend to be defined in terms of behavior, rather than other characteristics, almost inevitably any antisocial behavior will be pinned down to some innate characteristic of their culture.

Comanescu does acknowledge that the American version of this show at least provides some historical context. He points out, in a reference to Roma scholar Ian Hancock, that because America is a land of immigrants who possess varying physical features, the Roma of these shows do not differ physically from American Whites. This lack of physical variation supports the mainstream idea that rather than being an ethnicity, being gypsy is a set of actions. This idea aides viewers of shows such as *My Big Fat American Gypsy Wedding* in accepting that the actions portrayed on the show are markers of what it means to be a "gypsy."

American Gypsies

Despite the obvious connection of shows like *My Big Fat Gypsy Wedding* (Herman, 2012; Poppelwell, 2012) with harmful outcomes, they continue to air and have resulted in the development of spin-offs such as *Gypsy Sisters* (Thomas & Tarantino, 2012) and shows produced in an eagerness to capitalize on the popularity of the mainstream's interest in Roma lives such as *American Gypsies* (Kriss & Lipera, 2012). *American Gypsies* is an equally problematic television show that has been protested by members of the Roma community, anticipating the harm it is likely to cause (Nicoara, 2012). The show, produced by National Geographic, has been criticized for portraying Roma life in an exotic light, confirming stereotypes and othering of Roma (Nicoara).

In 2014, a petition was created through causes.com to bring an end to *American Gypsies.* Among the claims against the show was the claim that *American Gypsies* "misrepresents Romani for financial gain at the expense of Roma culture, livelihood and social status" (Jasaroska, 2014). The petition went on to say that those willing to sign would agree to take part in "any potential class action lawsuit and/or any other legal action which may serve the purpose of holding these offending parties responsible . . ."

While many signed the petition, the creators of the petition were unable to reach their target goal. The show, though no longer in production, continues to be aired causing Roma to feel they must speak out in defense of themselves and their communities:

> I'm An American Gypsy and I am sick of the way my culture is portrayed on television . . .(Reddit User, 2014)

> The "American Gypsy" TV show burning Millions of Romany souls. (Petition Signer, Anonymous)

> I am an American integrated Roma, and these shows make me very disappointed to call myself American. I'm sick of having to fear persecution for being who I am. People are ignorant, and they take what they read and see on television for granted. Enough is enough. Never again. (Man, Signed Petition, Anonymous)

> National Geographic is demonizing Romani through negative, inaccurate and irresponsible portrayals in mass media, this is causing a great harm for the Gypsies, therefore these shows, must be stopped immediately! (Petition Signer, Anonymous)

Each individual who commented on the petition shared commonalties in what they hoped to express. Themes of frustration, acknowledgment of negative outcomes resulting from these portrayals and a desire to see them at an end were common among the commentators. While protests against the misappropriation of Roma identity are loud, they continue to occur with regularity. In 2017, Netflix debuted an original series titled *Gypsy* (Rubin et al., 2017). Roma activists and supporters took to Twitter to protest the appropriation of this term, often used as a racial slur, with no acknowledgment from Netflix.

Among many narratives about Roma television portrayals, only one person interviewed seemed to take a somewhat positive stance on the issue. While Henry, in his forties, agrees that Roma portrayals were "mostly terrible" and that he wishes "there were no reality television shows about Roma because it's the form of a program that makes everyone look like an asshole," he believes, in a sense, this may also be a form of equality:

> Sure the portrayals of Roma on reality television is mostly terrible but that's equality because the portrayal of most groups on reality television is exclusively terrible. Any show where a 30 second pitch includes the ethnicity, the show portrays that ethnicity as idiotic so were getting equal treatment. In Arranged all the other couples look worse than the Roma couple and they look like the most down to earth with strong family values . . . It's the first time I have even seen a Roma on a reality television show and not been embarrassed . . . As far as the future it looks pretty bright.

Henry takes a positivistic view of Roma's place in television with the impression that perhaps the future will include both equality and positive portrayal for the Roma.

Because Roma representations exist in a limited capacity in U.S. media, each new representation carries with it the burden of representation for Roma in America. Representations continue to be stereotypical at best and as King of Romani so eloquently states "racist pieces of garbage" at worst. While this may be said to be true of many minority representations, one would be hard pressed to find few if *ANY* alternate representations of Roma that disconfirm the negative stereotypes typical of Roma portrayals. Contact theory makes clear that even contact within media representations may create a solidified impression of an individual not belonging to one's social group (Schiappa, Gregg & Hewes, 2005) and even ONE particularly powerful representation may solidify these negative impressions. This knowledge is troubling when one considers the ongoing stereotypical portrayal of Roma in the media that is without countering or disconfirming evidence. Episodes such as "Blood-line" pull what many would consider to be "traditional" Roma from obscurity only to sacrifice them on the altar of sensationalism and to leverage the historical images that they have sought to escape into bait for ratings. Isolated episodes, movies and entire series such as those that have been discussed combine to create a narrative of Roma identity that continues largely unchallenged to the mainstream mind leaving Roma to remain a thing of legend, a collection of television tropes or a unknown threat existing on the outskirts of America for hundreds of years giving little account for their behavior.

Movies and television shows such as those discussed paint the Romani in a mystical and other-worldly light, bringing some to doubt their existence in the modern day and minimizing their role as a legitimate people group who identify themselves by their ethnic and cultural connections rather than their fabled reputations. Beaudoin (2014) and Schneeweis and Foss (2016) have noted other portrayals such as *Buffy the Vampire Slayer* further contribute to the lore of the Romani and all fail to give voice to their historical and present narrative.

CONCLUSION

When examined with a critical eye, common themes emerge in media portrayals both in the United States and in Europe: themes of "otherness," alienation, being immigrants in their own home, and secrecy. Roma in both Europe and the United States are portrayed, even in current times, as dirty, conniving, mystical, otherworldly, exoticized and romanticized, violent, dangerous and something to be feared. Roma have spoken against negative media portrayals as they are able, seeking to counter these negative images and identify the potential for negative consequences. At the conclusion of the book we will identify more specifically and broadly the amazing contributions of Roma activists, fighting daily against these types of portrayals.

The impact of these portrayals on Roma's day-to-day lives and their ability to successfully choose their own strategy for acculturation or, at minimum, successful coexistence in the world of the gadje is important to understanding the lived experiences of Roma. Before diving into a discussion of the daily lives of Roma and how they choose their interactions with the outside world it is vital to understand the challenges Roma face and what has influenced many of their attitudes and life decisions. A departure from the mystical or care-free life painted by mainstream media, and often on the receiving end of prejudice, the lives of the Roma have, for as long as they have existed in America, been plagued by marginalization. To an even greater extent, European Roma have been significantly marginalized. It is their experiences worldwide that prompted me to investigate the challenges that other American Roma face. Myself being an "N" of only one, I wanted to gather the narratives of other American Roma, I wanted to discover how much of the persecution experienced by European Roma was shared historically and in the modern day. What I found was significantly shocking. After compiling my research, I felt it was important to lay out these experiences before delving into the daily lives of Roma. In order to have an understanding of Roma life in America, one must first understand what, in many respects, has led Roma to remain hidden for so long.

Chapter Two

Discrimination and Prejudice in the Daily Lives of the Roma

In 1929 a police officer in Atlanta was taken into custody charged with what the newspapers deemed a "slaying" of a Roma man, Nicholas Adams, who had stopped to change his tire. The man was asked to move on because he was making a disturbance and, according to the officer, he lunged at the officer unprovoked with a tire iron. The police officer shot Adams at close range in the stomach several times killing him in front of his four small children (*The Atlanta Constitution*, 1929).

PREJUDICE IN THE DAILY LIVES OF ROMA

In America's history and even into the present day, actions motivated by prejudice are not uncommon in the life of the Roma. Whether encountered in the halls of a university or in daily lives on the road, Roma have found that prejudice and discrimination may be a part of their everyday existence. While Roma in America do not often face discrimination to the level of severity found across Europe, they may find common ground in their own narratives of marginalization and a history of being "othered" by the very country they belong to.

In 2017, the European Roma Rights Centre highlighted in its blog (Heller) the ongoing issues for Roma seeking to obtain clean water and basic hygiene services. Investigators found that in areas such as Portugal conditions were, "comparable to the worst of situations I have seen thus far." Roma are unable to access what those in the general population are more than able to acquire. The report cited that many countries are failing to adhere to rights recognized by the UN which mandate that those most marginalized be assisted an accessing these necessities. Conditions for Roma across Europe have been found lacking, with Roma communities unable to access clean water or sanitation services. Amnesty International points out that in places such as Slovenia, Roma can barely acquire the water required to drink and bathe regularly (2016). Allies and activists have identified that this lack of access to clean water comes as a direct result of prejudice toward Roma and ongoing structural discrimination.

Discrimination in the lives of Roma worldwide is a well-documented occurrence (Hancock, 2002). From verbal and physical attacks to social stratification and ostracism, Roma have historically encountered discrimination wherever they have sought to establish themselves (Hancock). In 2013, *Time Magazine* reported on the rise of anti-Roma sentiments as economic times worsened. Many Roma experienced restricted access to necessities like water in Hungary while in other parts of the world Roma have been unable to find jobs and homes in the face of discriminative legislation and cultural bias (Harris, 2013).

In 2013, National Public Radio reported on a Roma family in Ireland whose blond, blue-eyed children were removed from their home. Authorities believed the children may have been abducted (an age-old stereotype held about Roma) because the children did not resemble their parents (Peralta, 2013). The children were returned to their parents after a DNA test confirmed their identity but their story remains a powerful reminder of the strength of prejudice held against Roma worldwide. As I previously identified, it was my wish to understand how American Roma fit into this larger narrative of prejudice and discrimination. The underlying stereotypes and prejudice that often motivate stratifying behaviors toward Roma around the world are the very same that have impacted Roma lives in America for centuries.

Because of their sometimes invisible lives in the United States, the plight of discrimination faced by the American Roma often goes unnoticed. Of the 23 interviews I completed, 18 reported experiences of covert or overt discrimination. Many have accepted this as a way of life for Roma. A lifetime of discrimination has led many Roma to retreat further into a life of separation in which they seek to remain invisible in hopes that through invisibility they may avoid discriminative practices; others simply remain silent about their identity, preferring a life of being anonymously Roma. Others herald the creation of reality shows like *Gypsy Sisters* and *My Big Fat Gypsy Wedding* (Popplewell, 2012; Thomas & Tarantino, 2012) as an end to the invisible life of the Roma. They have chosen to fight back through activism, education and openness. While intellectual strides have been made to address the experience of the Roma within the United States, their stories remain largely untold and justice is often exchanged for the separate and quiet existence that many desire.

The discrimination and prejudice faced by Roma in this section has been divided in several ways. First, I explore historical discriminations which were described by many of the older individuals that I interviewed. These individuals shed light on the lives of Roma fifty to sixty years ago in the United States. I then explore current instances of discrimination encountered by respondents. Following this, I explore the development of mistrust as a result of discrimination and the resultant "hiding" of the Roma identity. I then discuss Roma interactions with law enforcement, a subject which will be explored further in other chapters. Finally, I talk about gender specific discrimination experienced by the community of Roma women. By providing such a range of representations I hoped to come to an understanding of the role that discrimination and prejudice play in the lives of the Roma. This will perhaps help the reader see beyond the stereotypes of the modern media. Further, the establishment of this understanding will be important as we move into the next chapter and seek to understand the acculturative practices of Roma and their everyday lives in the United States.

HISTORICAL DISCRIMINATION

Forced Assimilation

For the first seven years of her life, Fey, currently in her sixties, grew up in what she describes as a traditional Sinti community in the Northeast United States in the 1950s. She recalls a loving and nurturing community surrounded by strong, empowered women and a loving, extended family. At the age of seven, Fey, her brother and cousins, along with the other children in the community, were taken from their homes and entered into a forced assimilation program. The children were first placed in orphanages and fostered out to white families. Fey recalls her grandmother seeking to be reunited with her brother time and time again, seeking to understand why this was done to the community. Fey's grandmother was charged with kidnapping following her last attempt at being reunited and died shortly after. Fey emotionally recounted this, stating:

> My brother and I had a very hard time because the community sort of broke up after the kids were taken away. No matter what they did, they couldn't get us back and my grandmother had died after that kidnapping charge and this was a woman who saved her kids from the Holocaust and then to come to this country and have her grandkids taken from her. I will never forgive this country for that . . .

Fey's grandmother had come to America hoping for freedom from the oppression and prejudice she had encountered during World War II. Instead, she found a society, similar to many in Europe that was unwilling to accept the preference for separation from gadje life within their community. The city officials' answer to this group of individuals who would not assimilate by choice was forcible assimilation but, as Gordon's foundational assimilation has shown (1964), true assimilation cannot fully exist unless there is an end to discrimination. For Fey and her relatives, this discrimination would only end by hiding who they truly were.

Fey was placed with many different families throughout the program; she was punished for speaking the language of her people and discouraged from recalling the customs of her community. Fey found herself forced to exist within the world of the gadje, stripped of her true identity. Fey described the last step in attempting to erase the identity of her past, "My name was changed, I was a White girl." By forcing Fey and her fellow Roma to outwardly conform to gadje norms, even to the smallest detail, such as her name, an important message was conveyed. A life of separation from the world of the gadje was unacceptable. Hancock's (2010) account of life for Roma in Britain and United Kingdom corroborate with Fey's experience as he recounts similar experiences within his own family. At odds with the expectations of mainstream society, Fey and Hancock's family found that one must choose to assimilate or be marginalized, there would be no middle ground. While this was the message conveyed to Fey and her family members, other respondents found that their attempts at assimilation were met with complete resistance, they were unwanted and found themselves pushed to the margins.

The Impact of the Civil Rights Movement

Gracie's family were among those who found themselves pushed to the margins, whether they hoped to assimilate or not, unless they were willing and able to hide their identity. She was raised in a mill town in the Southeast in the 1950s. Her father was full Roma while her mother was partial Roma a fact that was concealed by her mother until later in life. Gracie found discrimination within her own family as her mother raised her to believe that something was amiss with her Roma relatives on her father's side. While Gracie recalls "passing" as a typical White girl due to the light color of her skin, she recalls:

> Some of us could pass, some of us couldn't. I can pass for the most part and one of my brothers couldn't. . . . I remember kids throwing rocks at us saying your mother must have been with the Indian mail man.

Fey grew up with many questions regarding her background and race, "Sometimes my father would whisper in my ear, you know we're not White and if he would try to talk about it, my mother would shush him." Though

Gracie's mother tried to silence the realties her father was seeking to convey, Gracie could not remain ignorant to the disparity in treatment that her family, especially those siblings who were not able to pass, experienced. As Gracie got older, the truth of her father's words remained with her.

At the age of fourteen, Gracie joined the Civil Rights movement along with her brother as a response to the language and behavior they observed in the White Citizens Counsel:

> My brother met a member of SNCC and they invited us to a meeting and things kind of went from there and it started to make sense to me about my background by talking to these Black kids about race and what it is and what it isn't and it was a way to talk about things because my family wouldn't talk about it at all so I spent a lot of time in the civil rights movement . . . a lot of it was trying to figure out this whole thing of being mixed race and how people talked about it and how people felt about it.

Where Gracie had found herself unable to be fully part of the White world she was seeking to pass in, she found a place among the members of SNCC who could understand her experiences and help her make sense of why she found herself constantly unable to be fully a part of that world, why full assimilation seemed unreachable, why her family had been pushed to the margins. Gracie and her brother are not alone in identifying the cause of American civil rights movement as one that closely resembled their own fight for equality. In his book, *Gypsy Movements*, (2014) Jud Nirenberg describes the development of civil rights action among Roma in Eastern Europe. By borrowing purpose, structure and language from the American civil rights movement, they would not only be able to structure a movement relevant to their own cause but would create a movement with language easily identifiable to American allies.

Gracie's involvement in the civil rights movement opened a door for her father to recount a painful experience to her years later when she was on a visit home from college. Gracie recalled, growing up, though her parents worked at the local mill, they never lived in the mill housing though it was cheaper and closer to her parents' work. She stated she never understood her parents' choices until that day:

> I went somewhere with my father, I don't know where and we pulled into our yard and instead of getting out he just set there for a minute and he looked at me and said, "You know, I am glad you did what you did, I think Dr. King was right." He told me this story, he told me when he and my mother were a very young married couple. . . . they lived in a mill village. . . . I never understood why we didn't live in them, my father was adamant he wouldn't live in a mill village, he wanted to live on the outskirts of town . . .

Gracie had observed a desire for separation though she misunderstood its intent. This life of separation often made her feel like the girl from the "wrong side of the tracks." She carried with her many questions regarding the separate life she experienced with her family. Many of Gracie's questions were answered on this day:

> I was always curious about it so on this day when I was in college he told me that when they lived [in a mill town] his family came to visit. They lived in a town nearby and when they left, the man who was the supervisor of housing for the mill came to him. . . . He came to see my father and he said to him "I don't ever want you to have those niggers here again." My father said, well, they are not Black, they are Indian and the guy said "I don't care who they are, they are dark and you can't ever have them here again." So my parents moved out and from that time on my parents refused to live in a mill village.

Gracie believed that her father told her this story as an example of his experiences as a Roma. He wanted her to understand why he had made the choices he had made for his family. Gracie realized that it was this type of discrimination that had led both her father and mother to try to pass as a different group that was more socially accepted in the town from that time on. The act of "passing," for Roma in America, is not an unusual act as will be discussed later in the chapter. As a result of discrimination, Gracie grew up on the outskirts of her town in housing which was more expensive and not comparable in quality or size to that of the mill housing, away from where her friends resided. Gracie grew up knowing that, in some way, she was different but was encouraged to hide that difference in order to find acceptance in her town, an experience shared by many Roma of her time. Assimilation was not aspired to because assimilation was never truly a possibility. For families like Gracie's "passing" was as much as could be hoped for. This would influence many families, families such as Peaches,' to look on the world of the gadje with a leery eye.

Fascination or Discrimination:
Varying Perspectives on Gadje Acceptance

Peaches was the oldest respondent in the study—at the time of the interview she was in her early eighties. She described her life growing up in the 1940s in the Deep South as typical of Romanichal, a particular group within the Roma. Her mother was a fortune teller. Her mother and father would "put up" in a town, setting up their mobile home (for some Roma at that time it may have meant a tent or cheap housing) and a sign that advertised their occupation. Her father advertised the business by carrying cards around to the townspeople, careful to avoid areas that were known to report activity by Roma to the police regardless of whether they were disturbing the public or not. In her recollection, her classmates and neighbors were accepting of her family, in fact, she described their approach to her life as "fascination":

> Mama told them when she registered us in school. They knew we [told fortunes] and they knew we were gypsy. . . . The wanted to know everything there was to know about it and I wasn't about to tell them. It was none of their business.

Peaches described the fascination of her classmates and the many lasting friendships that her parents possessed with non-Roma in the town, which was unusual for some Roma families at the time, as proof that they faced no discrimination.

Fascination, celebration or appropriation can exist alongside prejudice, often does, marking a line between the idealized and the reality of Roma existence. Two articles published in the *Atlanta Constitution* underscore this dichotomy. The one identifies that a group of girls from a local church would be holding a fund-raiser called "a gypsy encampment" in which an encampment would be simulated on the lawn of someone's home with food and music (*Atlanta Constitution*, 1887). The fund-raiser, meant to provide novelty enjoyment for the churchgoers while raising money for charity, is a prime example of appropriation and of the idealized. The second article from the same paper states that citizens were complaining about a gypsy encampment outside of the city, requesting that they be asked to move on (*Atlanta Constitution*, 1920), highlighting the reality. While separated by years, the articles represent the danger of appropriation in which the idealized life of a minority group is used for amusement, financial gain or inspiration while the reality of their existence is simultaneously ignored or outright opposed. Despite her belief in her classmates' and parents' friend's fascination with her culture and her adamant denial that any discrimination existed, Peaches still identified that not all was revealed to those who were outside of her family.

Though Peaches did not, according to her narrative, move as often as other Romanichal, she and her family did relocate every few years for work or as a way to avoid harassment from local law enforcement. Though fascination existed, Peaches very clearly identified that discrimination also persisted, "I think most Romanichal knew they were discriminated against but it was just the way it was." Peaches had experienced positive interaction with gadje friends and classmates, believing them to look on her culture in a positive light and yet, she also knew that discrimination and mistreatment from the gadje was simply a part of her existence. The actions of her father, careful to avoid making trouble when entering a new town, exemplified existence outside the world of the gadje. It would be difficult for any family to assimilate within a culture they were consistently being run out of. Separation rather than isolation was the rule for Peaches' family but assimilation, without question, would be an impossibility.

"Run Out of Town" — The Reality of Roma Life

Peaches' experiences growing up were unlike many Roma who were unable to establish any connection with the towns they temporarily settled in and were more frequently "run out of town" for a myriad of reasons. Gertie, in her early fifties, recalled her mother's experiences: "It affected my mother very much. . . . If someone in the town complained about you, you got run off by the police so it was very hard on mom, she wanted to live a normal life. It was very embarrassing for her." Many traditional Roma have historically made their living in occupations that allow them to travel and settle in many places. Unfortunately, as Peaches and Gertie's mother experienced, this often drew them to the attention of the local authorities who would target Roma as troublemakers or cheats. Ruby, another respondent in her forties, also identified that her parents were run out of town growing up which led to a life of secrecy about her own identity.

Vaidy, a woman in her forties from the Northeast, also recounted that her parents experienced being run out of town. She recalled it this way:

> I know that my mother's family was run out of town several times and I know that my mother and my aunt and my uncle and a lot of my cousins were not allowed to go to school because of being Roma, they were kicked out of school.

Eddie, fifty-one from the Southwest, related hearing of similar experiences among his older relatives:

> back in times when they used to come out, and they used to set up tents in a town. The [gadje] would come out and throw rocks at the tent and the cars and the police didn't do nothing about it . . . My mom told me one story about how they [the gadje] were sitting there throwing rocks at the tents and stuff. My mom was born [in the 30s] so this might have been the early 50s or something. So my one Aunt that was out there, the neighbors across the street are just sitting there watching. They were sitting there at their house watching it, they were watching rock after rock after rock. So my aunt picks up a rock and throws it through a window across the street. Immediately the police come out and put an end to that, they wasn't going to have no rock throwing.

Eddie recounts a common experience, settling outside of a town only to be harassed by local individuals. Eddie identifies his mother and aunt having rocks thrown at them by local individuals only to watch as people sit on their porch and take in the harassment like a show. Eddie's family expected no assistance from the police, it was only when Eddie's family became fed up and turned the tables that the police showed up to intervene. As Eddie states, this is just one of many narratives that led to the feeling one must keep Roma identity "under wraps, so then you are a double agent . . . there's a lot of stigma involved . . . so you really aren't gonna level much with a lot of your peers who aren't Romanichal." As Al, in his seventies stated, "You are just asking for trouble and once that word comes out and you say gypsy, people associate that with some kind of crime, it's automatic."

"We Lived It"—Prejudice as a Normal Part of the Roma Experience

Fener, in her mid-forties, identified how her older relatives spoke about the discrimination they encountered:

> We were, you know, they used to say "dirty gypsies" you know, "stealers" and my grandparents and my mom and dad say they thought that gypsies were going to steal children.

The encounters Fener described were in line with literature (Clark, 2004) that erroneously identifies these stereotypes as commonalities of the Roma. At the beginning of this chapter, I discussed a current news article in which a Roma family in Europe was accused of stealing children (Peralta, 2013). The prejudice encountered by Fener's family persists worldwide today and that is why these types of stories have become a part of the shared knowledge of the Roma. Though it is part of the shared knowledge, it is not something that is always spoken in words.

When asked if her family ever sat her down to discuss their experiences of discrimination, Fener responded by giving a keen insight into the under-stood nature of discrimination as part of the Roma experience:

> We lived it. That was my life so we just knew, I don't know how, I just knew. That's the way it was you didn't have to sit down and be told . . . I lived in the middle of it. I could hear the older ones talking when I was younger. It's not like we were being hid from it, we just knew. We just knew how it was.

That was the life of many from the older generation, no words were spoken, no lessons passed on, it was their experience, their daily life, they knew they were treated differently. Fener was not the only respondent to identify this type of discriminatory treatment. I found Marilla described the treatment she encountered to be an even more explicit example.

"The Minute They Found Out"
—The Impact of Discrimination on Identity

Marilla, a women from the Northeast in her early sixties, experienced this differential treatment firsthand. She moved often with her family growing up. Initially, they would find acceptance in their new home, until her familial origins were discovered:

> Once people did find out, when I was growing up they didn't want any part of us . . . It confused me as a child I could not intellectually process why I was being shunned I didn't realize it was because we were Gypsy.

Like many Roma who identify facing prejudice and discrimination, Marilla knew she was treated differently but couldn't quite put her finger on the how or why until she was older and could intellectually process the complexities of social prejudice. Although she identified that many younger generations have it easy, especially those who can "pass" as White, Marilla continued to encounter the same discrimination she encountered as a child into her adult life. When asked if anyone ever found out about her background and treated her differently because of it, Marilla quickly responded that this was indeed the case, "Yes, the moment they did [found out] everything changed. An employer found out and took every opportunity to speak poorly to me. They put me down in a hole you know."

Like Fener, Marilla found herself living a marginalized existence. Even when Roma have attempted, historically, to assimilate into the world around them, they were often met with prejudice and suspicion brought about by age-old stereotypes. This has only served to push the two worlds further away and has led many Roma, historically, to view complete separation as their only option. Though lifestyles of Roma changed as the years progressed, these deeply held views on separation remained.

Like Roma worldwide, prejudice and discrimination have been a part of the Roma experience historically. Though I was able to collect many narratives of historical discrimination in the United States, I have no doubt that many stories remain untold. Henry conceptualized the attitudes of older Roma in this way:

> They may say they know discrimination is wrong but they still seem ashamed to sort of admit that they have been subjected to it. And they seem to take pride in not being bothered by it and thinking it's no big deal. . . . I think the attitude about complaining about it is its being a crybaby, we survived it and it didn't get to us and there's no real harm and we are too tough to care. "Oh I barely remember that happening, yes, yes it happened on occasion but who cares."

Unlike older generations of Roma, Henry identified, individuals of his generation view prejudice and discrimination in an alternate way, "Our attitude is that we have a right to be angry and to talk about it and somehow not just a right but somehow politically its socially noble for us to make a big deal about it because we shouldn't let it go, and let people get away with it." Henry's words rung true and prompted me to want to discover if discrimination were as much a part of the younger Roma's experience as the older and if they were in fact responding to it in an alternate way.

CURRENT DISCRIMINATION

Most respondents identified that with the passing of years, Roma have forsaken the "traditional" lifestyle of traveling, though some still hold to it and have transitioned to a more outwardly assimilated lifestyle. This will be discussed more in-depth in a coming chapter. Despite this outward assimilation, many still prefer separation between themselves and gadje. Their lives may be identified as accommodation without assimilation, doing what is necessary to get by (Gibson, 1988).

Though these changes in lifestyle have occurred, prejudice and discriminative practices toward Roma remain very much prevalent. In its simplest form, this looks like stereotypes that Roma may encounter almost on a daily basis. These include stereotypes about Roma being cheats, thieves, stealing children and placing curses on people. These arose in almost every interview conducted. In a more severe form, this may include physical violence or being targeted by the police. The first respondent representing the lives of Roma today reported a mixture of each of these forms of discrimination in her narrative.

"He Couldn't Deny It"—Facing the Reality of Discrimination in the Present Day

Rachel represents a new generation of college-educated Roma women. Rachel is a women in her twenties who resides in the Northwest United States. Staying connected with her Roma roots and community is an important part of her life. Her story was wrought with experience after experience of discrimination and outright racism. Rachel resides in an area of the United States where outsiders are familiar enough with Roma practices and physical features to easily recognize them within their community. Prejudice against Roma is tightly held as Rachel experienced many times growing up. Rachel identified how the knowledge of this prejudice began to dawn on her as she got older:

> When we were young, my dad would try to hide things from me because he
> didn't want me to be upset . . . you know all sorts of assaults that happened to
> family members including my dad. . . . At first he would ty to say you know oh
> this and that but finally he couldn't deny it anymore you know, I was old
> enough to understand what was happening, it's pretty bad here actually.

Rachel's father had hoped to protect her from the reality of prejudice in her
life as young Roma, but over time, the frequency and intensity of these
occurrences made ignorance impossible. Rachel grew into an understanding
of just how bad discrimination for her people was in the United States.

As she grew older, Rachel had her own experiences in which she encountered prejudiced attitudes and discrimination. During an internship with a
mayoral campaign, Rachel was confronted with strongly held prejudiced
attitudes that nearly led to violence:

> We were going door to door to try and talk to people. I went in to this Jewish
> neighborhood and you know a lot of them come from Europe so they have
> more exposure to us. I was harassed and almost assaulted and they were
> calling me you know slurs in Yiddish but I knew what they meant and it was
> very scary. And I quit. I was like I can't do this.

For Rachel, overt prejudice is a reality. She has encountered prejudice from a
variety of sources. Because she resides in an area of the country where Roma
are identifiable, the opportunities for facing overt prejudice are many. She
has found this to be true in many jobs she has held, jobs in which she came
face-to-face with deeply held stereotypes about Roma.

These stereotypes prevent individuals from viewing Roma as the marginalized group they are and fail to pay respect to the difficult experiences
many have lived. Rachel agreed that the stereotypes held by mainstream
society affects what is expected of Roma which can eventually lead to discriminative practices. Rachel acknowledges that some things have marginal-
ly improved for Roma in the United States such as the removal of laws
banning Roma from owning land or property but even some of these measures are very recent. In 1998, New Jersey removed the last law from their
books that allowed them to regulate gypsy property ownership, residence and
travel. For some Roma, the absence of these laws on official record has not
prevented law enforcement or others from continuing to engage in discriminative practices.

In Rachel's experience, racism and discrimination are a reality for Roma
in the United States. She acknowledges that while not everyone knows about
Roma in the United States, a lot do. She says, "You have to be careful."
When asked if the gypsy stereotype negatively affected societal expectations
for Roma, she agreed they did. The dream of Milton Gordon's assimilation
(1964) where both the minority and the majority come to an accepting of one

another, in the current state of society, is an unreachable one because prejudice remains. For many respondents in the study, assimilation has only been possible by giving up something and for most, this has meant giving up, or hiding their ethnic identity. For those unwilling to make that choice, a life of separation, according to Berry's model of acculturation, is preferred.

"It's Just Really Bad"—Invisible Discrimination in the Life of Traveling Roma

The preference for separation was evident in Louisa's family. After listening to her story, there can be little wonder why. Louisa, in her forties, is one of the few women interviewed who still hold too many of the traditional ways of life. Her husband works a "traditional" job for Roma men and they are often on the road for work. Perhaps because of this, Louisa has some of the most vivid accounts of discrimination and prejudice in the present day:

> I'll argue over a dollar because of how we are treated. We [she and her grandmother] went into a store, Ross and they went over the intercom, security on all aisles, security on all aisles like, yeah there's that.
>
> Whenever you call to make a reservation [at an rv camp] and then you come and they see who you are "Oh that spot is full you have to leave, you can't stay there."

Like other respondents, Louisa encountered small instances of being singled out within the world of the gadje. In her life, being treated unfairly due to stereotypes held about her community has become an almost daily occurrence.

Louisa recalled events that happened to her grandparents and recognizes these events continue to occur in her community, "Granny's father got arrested and they beat him. He died from internal injuries ten days after they let him out of jail." Louisa identified that harassment by the police is not a thing of the past:

> When you are pulled up in a campground, don't be surprised if you are surrounded, the police will block off all the entrances. They will block every entrance to the place in the middle of the night and run checks on everybody's license in the place . . .

In many of the towns where Louisa and her family travel for work, their community is known and sometimes watched by local authorities. Age-old stereotypes influence the reception they receive from town to town. As Louisa identified, they are often met with immediate distrust from law enforcement officials who take every opportunity to make it impossible for them to make a living:

> The first time he [her husband] was arrested because we were ignorant. . . . we had no idea . . . they made up a charge. . . . When they took him to the jail and they were booking him the police said "What are these guys here for what did they do? They haven't done anything" and they said "Oh, they're just these gypsy fly by nights you know the ones that's always coming in town" . . . They keep their trucks and auction them off, They see them driving down the road and pull them over and give them so many tickets they can't drive, it's just really bad.

This treatment from local authorities makes her fearful for what the future holds for her family and her son:

> I don't want him working outdoors because nowadays it's not if you go to jail it's when you go to jail and it's not for what you are doing but it's for who you are. . . . I can't send my son to go to work to make a living to go to jail. I don't have the money to get him out.

Louisa is fearful that her son will encounter the same discriminatory treatment her husband and other male relatives have encountered if she allows him to follow a traditional career path. Because of the potential for danger and negative encounters with the law, she has encouraged her son to go to college and find an alternate way.

For the sake of survival, Louisa's family views separation as their only option in a world that is constantly seeking to drive them out. Louisa's family faces marginalization on a constant basis. She discussed being called a "fly by night" though she and her family lived in houses within the town. For Louisa, it seemed that even when she and her family attempted to be a part of the gadje's world in any small way, they were only met with resistance, continuing to solidify the intergenerational mistrust that exists toward the gadje.

"Go back to India"—Childhood Encounters with Prejudice

On one hand, Gilbert, in his forties and currently residing overseas, states that he rarely if ever encountered prejudice in his professional or school life until he moved to Europe. On the other, he acknowledges that there were moments from his life and his mother's that stick out as singular moments of prejudice, enough to make an impression on him. He recalled an occurrence from his childhood:

> Once in the summer when I got really dark, one of the neighbors who we got into an argument with because we were playing basketball in the backyard or something told me to go back to India.

Gilbert acknowledged this caused confusion in his younger self, enough to bring it to his mother's attention. Up to that time, she had not disclosed his

Roma heritage. She chose that moment to disclose their heritage, a heritage she herself had kept hidden with hopes that her family would successfully assimilate and not experience what she, an immigrant to the United States from Slovakia, had experienced in her birth country as a Roma.

No but Yes—The Changing Narrative of Discrimination

Like Gilbert, Teddy, thirty-nine from Southeast United States, stated that he did not recall many occurrences of prejudice in the United States, unlike, as Gilbert also pointed out, Roma living in Europe. Despite this statement, he too was able to identify at least one example of ongoing prejudice toward Roma in the United States. He also highlighted interactions with the general public in which stereotypes impact their engagement with social institutions. "You have people that discriminate against you on the issues of funeral home situations or halls for weddings." Teddy highlighted Roma interaction with law enforcement in which they can be, at times, unfairly targeted. This is a theme that will run in some facet throughout this book:

> [There was] a situation in Georgia actually, a guy actually passed away in jail in Augusta, Georgia, last year. They could never pin down the judge on discrimination but it was referenced in court the kind of background he [the defendant] had. Just the amount of sentencing that was put on him. I would say you maybe could not make a case to persecute the judge on the issue of discrimination but it was clear that there was an issue there and it was because he was a Rumni man. It was an awful situation. He ended up not getting the treatment and health care he needed in jail and he ended up passing away in jail, it's been a mess.

Teddy references a case, if true, in which prejudice of law enforcement and the judicial system led to the unnecessarily harsh treatment and ultimate death of an individual. Throughout many of the narratives I collected the unnecessary disclosure of Roma identity in environments where prejudice could lead to detrimental outcomes was common. Despite Teddy's revelation of these types of prejudice being in existence, Teddy went on to say "So I think things have improved in the US, we're more of an integrated society here anyway and there is less a chance of someone discerning Roma people." He, like Gilbert, left me unsure if the reality of prejudice as part of the modern Roma experience matched that of Roma in America's history. My interview with Henry afforded some profound words with which I could perhaps conceptualize the current state of Roma lives in America.

Discrimination that Depends

Henry is in his early forties. He resides in the Northeast United States. He is a professional individual who is married to a non-Roma woman. Henry would, by no account, be categorized as a Roma with a "traditional" life or occupation yet he holds tightly to his Roma roots, language and participates heavily in Roma activism. Henry recalled various moments where he encountered prejudice about his Roma roots. He stated "My mother would say nasty things about Roma to my face." His mother, herself not Roma, would assert her families' superiority over his father's Roma roots. "They definitely felt they were a better sort of people. And they didn't hide it very well and sometimes my mother said it openly to me, don't forget that we are better than them." Henry agreed that this left him with a few identity complexes growing up.

Henry acknowledged he lived a fairly normal, assimilated life growing up and felt little in the way of discrimination, toward his Roma identity at least. When asked about his families' experience with discrimination, he acknowledges that though they had experienced prejudice, getting them to discuss it was difficult: "they didn't share those stories of their own initiative, I would have to push for them. But they did have stories about being turned away from places, not being able to stay in a hotel for example, things like that."

For Henry, the attitudes of mainstream America toward Roma are largely unimportant. Henry conceptualized Roma lives and how they are impacted by these attitudes in this way:

> I don't think stereotypes are a barrier to me or that they will be a barrier to my son or to anyone that wants to go to college and eventually have a White collar job but what I shouldn't forget and what the reader shouldn't forget that there are lots of Roma Americans that are not aiming for a White collar life. If you are aiming to be a used car dealer or if you want to be an independent skilled laborer contractor who goes into people's homes and fixes appliances then I think that being out as a Gypsy would definitely come against you in your business practice. I have talked to Roma and Romanichal Americans . . . they say that on a handful of occasions the client became aware that they were gypsies and that was the end of the business relationship. Because gypsies would mean cheat and people don't think of that as a stereotype they think of that as the definition of the word, you people are cheats. That's what it means that's what you are telling me right, to say that people don't face discrimination or it doesn't impact what they do, and I think it depends on what they are aspiring to do.

Unlike the older generations of Roma who largely lived the traditional lifestyles Henry is describing, the Roma of today occupy professions and residences of wide variation. Henry conceptualizes that the lives of some Roma in terms of their encounter with Roma prejudice may vary based on where they find themselves situated within society. As a result, he cannot confidently say that discrimination or prejudice is not part of the modern experience. Many narratives I collected do support the idea that it is part of the modern experience of Roma. In many cases, it may be much more covert and, whether in traditional or professional settings, the fear of what could and what has been continues to lead many Roma to hide their true identity and mistrust the outside world.

MISTRUST

Given both current and historical experiences of prejudice and discrimination, it is not surprising that Roma Americans, like other Roma worldwide have developed a culture of mistrust toward the outside world. Throughout each interview that was conducted, mistrust was evident.

When asked if they remember anyone in their family speaking about race and racial issues, interviewees responded with a range of recollections that showed a common theme of mistrust. Some were instilled with a belief that "Gorjas" or "gadje" were dirty and that they should remain separate. Others were told not to trust gadje, that there were many differences between Roma and gadje and though they might associate, there remained an understood line between the two. Even in some of the more liberally minded families, the line remained:

> It was up to us who we married, We dated, a lot of Romanichal weren't allowed to date, we dated Gorjas and brought them home, we didn't hide it, they knew we were dating it was ok with them but at the same time they both knew when we got married we were going to marry a Romanichal.—Peaches, eighties

Even in Peaches's family, where the dating of the gadje was allowed, a firm line remained, one that Peaches understood and respected. Certain lines would not be crossed, and though these boundaries were often unspoken, Peaches understood the social retribution that would occur by crossing them.

From an early age, Fener's family also instilled this sense of being separate as a form of protection, "We were always kind of told to keep to ourselves because I think the way outsiders viewed our family so long and treated us. . . . it was instilled in us to be leery of them."

Despite this lesson, Fener took a unique perceptive on the idea of "mistrust":

> Mistrust is not the right word sweetheart, it's not the word, it's cautious, you're cautious of people. It was, we were told this, my father's generation were treated so badly because of who they were. That's why our parents didn't want that happening to us you know they saw how bad it could be but I never really mistrust people it's just really leery of them.

Despite a more positive outlook on those who are not Roma instilled by her parents, Rachel, in her mid-twenties, found the rest of her family to be much less trusting of the outside world. Rachel recalled a lesson that her aunt passed on:

> They [her family] are very aware of the discrepancy in how we are treated in this country. You know my Aunt. . . . She always says you know don't trust anyone who isn't Roma who isn't us. Don't put too much trust in gadje. . . . Don't trust anyone from the outside because you know they will hurt you.

While Rachel's parents sought to counter this by encouraging her to treat everyone equally the rest of her family encouraged her to remain separate and mistrustful of non-Roma by not forming friendships with them and not eating in their home.

Most of the interviews conducted echoed a sentiment of remaining separate from non-Roma and maintaining an air of mistrust. The refusal to eat food from those outside the community is just one form, a very important form that this mistrust took. Even those interviewees who reported having friendships outside of their community often identified that crossing the boundary of entering a non-Roma home or eating their food was not allowed. In most families, at least growing up, friendships with non-Roma outside of school were not encouraged and very often discouraged through words and actions. Gertie recalled her great aunt hanging up on friends who were not Roma when they would call her home.

As the thread of mistrust was noted in interview after interview, something else began to emerge. Undoubtedly the mistrust of non-Roma persisted for, as has already been discussed, good reason. As a result of this, many Roma took to hiding their identity in various ways. As a means of survival in a world surrounded by prejudice Roma would lie about their ethnicity. A culture of secrecy was cultivated. This culture persists today and was encountered as time after time potential interviewees declined to participate citing that the things we would be discussing in the interview, the life of the American Roma, were not things that should be openly talked about and certainly never put on paper. Hiding, for the Roma, was a traditional way of life and many, in one way or another, carry this with them even today. Henry discussed why the idea of being so identifiable as Roma became such a liability to the older generations:

> I guess they believe that being identifiable meant that you were going to face discrimination and I guess that everything previous generations went through in Europe and even some discrimination that my grandparents may have experienced New York led them to think their whole lives it was important to pass whenever they could. My father wanted to and still wants to pass whenever possible.

While Henry stated that most people his age were most likely not taught that hiding their ethnicity was a way to deal with potential discrimination, the narratives I collected paint a very different picture. Many were taught to hide, be vague or outright lie about their identity to "outsiders" even those among the youngest of my respondents. Both hiding and passing were common themes that emerged throughout most of the narratives I collected.

The deceptions perpetrated by those interviewed who sought to hide their identity were not always similar; some said they were Irish, others Native American. The underlying motivation however, was always the same. No one could know who you are. Never tell what you are. Hide who you are. These were messages passed from generation to generation motivated by mistrust, birthed from lifetimes of discrimination.

TODAY

For many of the interviewees the point at which they finally decided to identify who they are is a pivotal point in their lives. The mistrust that led to years of hiding had to be overcome with the knowledge that what was once feared could still very much be a reality. While others who were interviewed identified passing as German, White, and Native American some would simply lie about knowing what a Roma was or avoid the question of race at all costs. For some, the façade continues as a form of protection or simply because the strength of the cultural norms instilled within them remains.

For others, there was no need to hide. Anne recalls that by the time she was fifteen her dad had passed away. There was no longer a voice encouraging them to hide so she and her brother would tell anyone who they were because they were already noticeably different. Few people in the United States. can confidently identify Roma but, as previously discussed, the rise of reality television featuring Roma has increased the negative ideas many hold. Fey despairs that these shows have reversed progress that has been made among Roma to proudly identify their heritage. As was evidenced in the lives of many who were interviewed, the hiding of identity carries on today as a protective factor for many in the Roma community. Encountering discrimination continues to be a part of the Roma experience as evidenced by the stories in this study. This finding however, is not surprising given the lives of Roma worldwide.

General Experience of Discrimination—"No Life for the Gypsies"

The experience of Roma in Europe is an established narrative; there can be little doubt that they experience significant discrimination and social stratification. Though on a lesser scale, the same could be said for Roma in North America. In Canada, Roma are viewed as immigrants and outsiders (Beaudoin, 2014). Many have come to Canada to escape the racism of their home countries. Sadly, these immigrants, though not facing outright hostility or violence, face a lack of trust. This lack of trust is fueled by newspaper reports which doubt their claims of oppression from their home countries and increase the belief that they have come to Canada in hopes of filing bogus claims for help from the government. Canadians not of Roma origin have a difficult time understanding how many Roma, who appear White to their eyes, could be recognized and persecuted in the manner they claim. This confusion creates significant distrust toward Roma which is exacerbated by the way they are portrayed in print media (Beaudoin).

Several Roma within Beaudoin's study identify the difficulties they face in their home countries:

> And in the Czech Republic, in all of Europe, it's horrible, there's no life for Gypsies. It's almost like Hitler. Yeah, like Hitler. Nobody knows—nobody can imagine how life is there. And not just for our family, but all Roma people, they are afraid to live there (Elana, new Roma refugee to Canada)

> Like on Facebook, there is one page where there are all Gypsy people, and they put information, like what's going on . . . there was [a picture of] the dead body of a Gypsy, without eyes, without organs and everything, and they said, like this one, we will do to every Gypsy who we find until they disappear from this country (Elena)

Their experiences, fueled by the media in their home country, make it all the more difficult to experience resistance to their presence and their desire to become a part of Canadian society.

As previously discussed, in the United States, Roma have historically been portrayed as con-artists and thieves who make their living conning individuals through their trades including fortune telling. An article in *The Harvard Crimson* (Lacalle, 2009) identifies the lasting effects that these portrayals have had on U.S. laws that remain in some states today:

> Even in the U.S., the law seems to be biased against Gypsies. A Gypsy in Maryland recently enlisted the American Civil Liberties Union to fight a law that outlaws fortune telling. The practice is banned because many consider it fraudulent based on the belief that predicting the future is impossible. The Gypsy involved in the case, however, stated, it's not like you choose it. You're born with it.

Many Roma consider fortune telling not only a trade but a gift they are born with. Laws created to prevent them from plying their trade and using this gift not only prevented them from making a living but also allowed them to be turned away from towns. The law prevented them from establishing permanent residences in the United States.

As previously discussed, historical portrayals of Roma in the United States—most notably in newspapers—created a culture of mistrust and vilification toward the Roma. The result was an unwelcome atmosphere leaving many Roma to face a life of poverty, discrimination and prejudice. Ruby, a woman in her forties from the Southeast United States, describes the life of her father, a man currently in his late seventies, growing up in this America:

> My dad, later in life, told me about going on the road with my grandfather and how he would make clay pots and try to sell them door to door, just anything and everything he could like to get chickens or flour for food. They were really poor, there was a lot of poverty, they had leaky roofs and shacks with no floors. There was a lot of poverty he experienced that he didn't talk about a lot or share a whole lot about.

Vaidy, a Roma woman in her forties from the Northeast United States, has encountered this culture of resistance and vilification firsthand. While teaching an undergraduate class this exchange took place:

> They said you call a people who take their children out begging and their children suffer in the hot sun and there should be a law against that and you know sometimes they take White children so they could have more attractive begging things. So I slapped my hand on the desk and I was in the middle of a lecture and I said I am sorry that is a racist stereotype. We do not steal children and that is not appropriate for an academic classroom.

Vaidy saw firsthand the impact that attitudes commonly passed through media outlets has on the way those in the mainstream feel and act toward Roma. This is especially true for those who are unlikely to have ever encountered Roma personally. Rachel identifies that experiences such as Vaidy's are not uncommon in the life of the American Roma:

> The main issue is no one actually cares, if you make a joke about poor White people, White people are going to get pissed off, that happens a lot but the only people it's acceptable [to mock] are Roma but no one really cares but it's like we kind of get lost.

Rachel acknowledges that experiences of both overt and covert prejudice are a normal part of the Roma experience and they continue in large part because few care about their occurrence outside of the Roma community. To Rachel, the real life of the Roma is invisible to anyone but themselves.

Unfiltered Prejudice

With few countering images to those the media routinely portray, Roma are subject to age-old stereotypes. Often unrecognizable to outsiders, Roma in the United States face unfiltered prejudice and discrimination akin to Vaidy's experiences. Rachel identifies that this often makes things more difficult for Roma in the United States because they can never be sure who to trust with the revelation of their identity, unlike Europe where Roma are much more recognizable:

> A lot of people don't know about us in the US but a lot of people do so you have to be careful, in Europe everybody knows so it's a little bit easier I think but here, people have a lot of opinions about it. . . . I'm not very dark but I do have olive skin and I do have a very Roma nose you know . . . and I think I look you know, very Roma. I've been abroad and you know people recognize me for what I am without having to talk to me. I think that contributes a lot. I don't think most Americans know what kind of features we have.

The inability of Americans to distinguish a Roma based solely on looks is both a blessing and a curse. For some, it means they are able to slip in and out of the mainstream as they choose, or are able to successfully assimilate without facing resistance from those who are unaware of their identity but who potentially hold racist attitudes toward Roma. On the other side, this leaves Roma to combat the belief that being Roma or gypsy is more a way of life than an ethnicity and to combat negative attitudes associated with this invisible people. Media outlets have disseminated and cemented these beliefs, leading to racist, interpersonal interactions such as those described by Vaidy and Rachel and much more, as will be discussed further in the chapter.

It is impossible to discuss the lives of Roma in the United States without addressing the state of Roma worldwide. There can be little doubt that the lives of Roma around the world are far worse than those in America and yet it is, at least partially, the experience of persecution based on their common identities that ties the communities together.

Prejudice in Europe—"They Are Being Exploited"

While underlying prejudiced attitudes toward Roma may be identical in America and Europe, in Europe, the situation for Roma is dire. Asylum Aid reports in 2002 (Ceneda) that there has been a significant increase in racial violence toward the Roma in Eastern and Central Europe, these locations have a significant bias toward, and campaign against, Roma in newsprint media. Roma in these areas are being forced to abandon their homes and immigrate elsewhere and they are being denied asylum. Anti-Roma campaigns released by governments as well as newspapers and radio follow them regardless of the countries they find themselves in (Ceneda, 2002). In Romania, Roma experience mob violence and violent harassment by the countries' police.

Green (2016) reports that there are allegations of Traveler families being put on secret blacklists at holiday camps where they seek to take their families on vacation. When they attempted to investigate why they were being turned away from camps when they had prior reservations, they were threatened with arrests. The Travellers believe they have been placed on a blacklist due to their ethnicity, recognizable by their last names. In March of 2016 *The Local* reported that Roma families in Linz, Austria, had experienced the third arson attack on Roma camps that year. The homes of fifteen people who were living in tents were burned to the ground. Local newspapers identify the victims as "beggars," fail to identify the racial motivations behind the attacks and minimize the incident by stating that no one was physically in danger.

Not only do these stories occur as a result of a culture of vilification surrounding Roma, but the lack of accountability by those who commit these actions. The journalists who report on these stories but refuse to hold anyone accountable continue to perpetrate an environment where the victimization of Roma will also be portrayed as warranted or misunderstood. The lack of accountability in the media lends itself to a continuation of these types of occurrences because few speak on the Roma's behalf.

INTERPERSONAL PREJUDICE

Interpersonal Prejudice in America

Roma in the United States fear or face prejudice and discrimination on an interpersonal level from the gadje. Even those who exist as fully assimilated members of the mainstream may carry around a fear of facing this type of racism. Many carry memories of times that relatives or they themselves have experienced this prejudice firsthand, a prejudice that separates them and makes them feel "othered" in their own country. A Roma woman in New Jersey, posting on a Facebook forum about the issues surrounding Gypsy stereotypes, had this to say about her experience with interpersonal prejudice:

> I feel like the "gypsy trope" makes them think Roma aren't real, like they're just in stories or something . . . Even though those stories were often racist tales people told their kids to make them stay away from us. It pisses me off a lot. It's like we're invisible in America.

This woman recognizes the harm of the "gypsy trope." This trope, paraded throughout American media as the main theme of Roma representation, has led the majority to not only deny the existence of Roma, and thus their ethnicity, but has also led others to remain careless of how they speak of Roma. These individuals encourage their children to remain separate from

Roma if they encounter them. Interacting with those who do not acknowledge the Roma's existence leaves many to feel invisible.

Because many people do not acknowledge Roma existence or buy into the difficulties they face even in the United States, Roma encounter a large amount of interpersonal prejudice online. This prejudice may originate in social media spaces or online forums meant to give the general public a space to exchange ideas and discuss their opinions openly. These types of online forums become meeting spaces where individuals, who again are unlikely to encounter Roma personally, freely share their strongly held prejudices widely influenced by popular media.

As previously discussed, girlsaskguys.com (n.d.) is a public forum in which questions can be asked and answered anonymously by anyone worldwide about any topic. The following are opinions about Roma posted by American men and women meant to educate others. The first was submitted by a man from the United States:

> And they are very insular and actively resist assimilating into the cultures around them, which prevents the situation from improving very much. It's pretty much standard ghetto behavior with a few additional quirks of their own thrown in. They don't want "help" and have no interest in changing.

One can see what is problematic with these attitudes from this quote alone. The poster villainizes the Roma and accuses them of engaging in "ghetto" lifestyle, making the poverty that many experience inherent. He also blames them for their current situation by making resistance to assimilation about their stubbornness and lack of desire to change rather than highlighting the years of racism and prejudice that have made them fearful of how they will be treated by the mainstream. In addition, he fails to recognize that many Roma in the United States have managed to assimilate successfully into mainstream society while holding onto their Roma roots. In his narrative, Roma are inherently ghetto and blamed entirely for their experience while society is left unaccountable (girlsaskguys.com, n.d.).

Another American man, postulating on cultural differences in America highlights this "fact" about Roma: "Gypsies in some countries openly steal and their children are trained to steal. They consider it acceptable." A woman from the United States gave her own narrative of Roma worldwide:

> It's a culture of broken people that are basically doomed to wander the country-side of European countries. There are not that many "morals" . . . That is why they dress in scandalous clothing to attract men . . . even the younger ones expose and degrade themselves. I remember seeing a picture of a family of "modern gypsies" and the grandmother, the mother and the daughters all had eyes that were dead. The "modern"; Gypsies are not respected and are subjected to discrimination daily. The Men are "Gods" and the women are servants.

The opinions of both individuals, speaking with an air of fact but void of vindictiveness, genuinely perceive Roma as they have been portrayed: to be void of basic societal norms and morals. They view them as living under archaic rules and, even in seeing the plight of discrimination and poor treatment, say so with the air of blaming the victim. Society, again, has remained unnamed as having any responsibility in their plight (girlsaskguys.com, n.d.).

Even those individuals who express an "admiration" for Roma are often actually expressing a desire to appropriate their culture and reduce Roma to a set of behaviors rather than an ethnicity, thus denying their existence, leaving them to feel invisible. Another quote from girlrsaskguys (n.d.) exemplifies this type of admiration:

> Girl: I wanna be one
> Guy: You really don't.
> Girl: Lol why? It's more that I wanna have a nomad life before I settle.
> Guy: That's fine, but you don't want to be a typical gypsy Traveller. "Excuse me, a bunch of kids from this campsite just set fire to those cars over there and robbed the local shop!" The response, "sorry about that, boys will be boys."

While the girl expressed a desire to take on the gypsy "lifestyle" of traveling, she lacked any knowledge of the many challenges Roma living this lifestyle face. The responder felt the need to gloss over their experiences of marginalization and to criminalize Roma and their way of life as one without morals, heedless to the rules of "civilized" society.

I titled this section "Interpersonal Racism in America" because this type of racism, though directed at the group is experienced person to person. Whether that person has made a Roma reading these comments feel invisible or marginalized or whether it has led to the mistreatment of Roma they encounter individually. Roma are most likely affected by these attitudes, as already stated multiple times, because there is no thought given to filter these racist beliefs. Not only are these opinions spoken openly online but also in person. Failure to acknowledge the ethnicity and existence of Roma or, as already stated, a perpetration of the "gypsy trope" by the media leave individuals with the belief that Roma are nothing more than an act. Those speaking on behalf of the majority fail to acknowledge that Roma exist as a marginalized group and, at the very least, are a people who exist and have feelings.

The following are just a few more people that Roma may have the opportunity to encounter in their everyday lives (girlsaskguys.com, n.d.):

> Girl: It seems like the only people who look down on gypsies are Europeans. Literally no one here in the U.S. cares or thinks less of them.
> Guy: That's because we don't have gypsies. If we did then plenty of Americans would hate them.

Girl2: Those that I see on streets need some fashion advice and a shower. A normal understandable vocabulary wouldn't hurt either, and normal people behavior.

Guy2: If you saw them regularly you would understand. They are generally extremely violent they beat their kids on public transport and yell at each other all the time and most stealing and murder and theft has a Roma perpetrator . . . People always say "well of course they are like that, they live in poverty and people are wary of them but that doesn't justify the violence, the yelling, spitting . . . you don't see a non-Roma person doing that.

The anonymity of the online world provides these girls and guys the ability to express their true opinions of Roma in an unfiltered way. Though these opinions are expressed online, given the content of their posts, it is evident that these attitudes are carried with them into their everyday lives, lending themselves at the very least to covert forms of interpersonal prejudice.

Interpersonal Prejudice Europe

As in America, prejudice toward the Roma is in existence however, because Roma are more known and more visible in Europe, this prejudice takes on more severe forms than in the United States. The following are some examples of Roma experiences of prejudice and discrimination that have taken place in Europe and were posted publicly on Facebook (2016) as a way to expose this discrimination when other mediums, such as local newspapers, failed to acknowledge its occurrence:

JUST WANTED PEOPLE TO KNOW THAT A PUB IN MY VILLAGE THAT MY FAMILY BEEN GOING TO FOR OVER 50 YRS BARRED ALL TRAVLLER EVEN WOMEN AND CHILDREN ALL BECOUSE THE LANDLORD CAN ANY TIPS IM TAKING IT FURTHER THANKS ALL. (Traveller Woman, UK)

Customer notice, please be aware that we have travelers in the park and ride. Police have been notified. Please be vigilant and report any suspicious behaviors to reception. (Facebook post highlighting posted notice in UK neighborhood that listed all Roma companies that lived on the street.)

Well I'm in my late sixties and for as long as I can remember it's always been the same and I can't see it changing to be honest even when my kids went to school they put the gypsy children in a different room from the gorger kids and playtime they wouldn't let them out to mix with other children and that was in the seventies that's the reason I took my children out of school and they never had any more schooling I wonder what would happen if they done that to the refugees ay. (Facebook Post, UK Man, 2016)

Through these posts, one is able to see that Roma in Europe are banned from frequenting commercial establishments, segregated in public schools and among peers and are targeted as criminals, all as a result of simply being recognizably Roma.

Individuals in Europe are vocal regarding their attitudes toward Roma even when expressing racist or discriminatory thoughts. On a survey from girlsaskguys.com, 21 percent of girls and 32 percent of boys said "gypsies are scum." Others had this to say about Roma, even those they have encountered (girlsaskguys.com, n.d.):

> Guy: Well, the gipsy culture is a little different, they are encouraged to trick people and steal. Most of them complain about not being able to get jobs or help when they take any chance to screw people over. Now I know this sounds racist but this is the truth about the majority, I've met gypsies that were really good friends. PS: They are usually very charismatic and they like to use that.
> Girl: Their lifestyle is not the same as the mainstream, and the government finds them harder to control. They do sometimes participate in activities that are looked down upon such as tricking people out of their money, panhandling, and pick pocketing. They generally do not like for people who are not gypsies to know anything about them. People hate them because they don't understand them, have had some bad experiences with them, and therefore, fear them.

Similar to the opinions expressed by Americans, the feelings toward Roma center on their criminality, their lack of morals and their resistance to assimilation. Again, what they fail to discuss are the challenges they face as a marginalized people and the reasons behind Roma resistance to assimilation. The respondent in the quote above even relied on a form of the cliché "some of my best friends are" in order, it would seem, to qualify the validity of his statements and to excuse what he himself identifies as sounding racist. The boldness with which these opinions are shared as factual, the level to which Roma are presented as homogenized individuals and the buy-in to racist ideologies create an environment in which hostility and social stratification are permitted.

A study conducted by Ureche and Franks in 2007 catalogues the experiences of GRT young people from England, Britain and Ireland. There are 201 participants ages 7–30 who share their experiences of interpersonal violence. The goal of the study is to emphasize the importance of positive contact between GRT and non-GRTs to reduce the amount of derogatory words that are used toward Roma. Research shows that contact, including contact through the media (known as para-social contact) can significantly impact the increase or decrease of prejudice between individuals (Schiappa, Gregg & Hewes, 2005). The researchers were able to collect chilling narratives of interactions between GRTs and those outside their communities.

Researchers identify that "Roma, gypsies and travelers . . . experienced prejudice, bigotry and institutional racism as part of their daily lives" (Schiappa, Gregg & Hewes, 2005). Many reported the experience of being denied service due to their ethnicity, "We don't like everyone knowing though. It's bad then (because) they put up signs saying 'No Travellers" (English Traveller). Other individuals describe their experiences dealing with non-GRTs at school and their parents:

> Yes, I went [to school] until some girls poured water all over me because I was a 'dirty Traveler.' My Mam went up to school and asked them what they were going to do about it but they did nothing so Mam said I wasn't going again 'cos it was disrespectful to ignore her complaints. (English gypsy taken out of school because of bullying. 33)

> . . . they kind of drag their children away like we have Aids or something. (GRT parent, 42)

Schoolchildren experience prejudice at an interpersonal level when they are bullied, assaulted or rejected by their non-Roma peers (Schiappa, Gregg & Hewes, 2005).

These types of experiences described are representative of the interpersonal interactions that Roma experience on a regular basis. Ureche and Franks (2007) identify many of their respondents found this troubling not just because of the harm young people already experience but because of where it has the potential to lead. One researcher related the worries of the aunt of one study participant whose own mother died in a concentration camp:

> She said she is worried now because people are turning more and more against the Gypsies and particularly the Roma. . . . it is a small step, she says, from spitting at someone in the street or beating someone up to putting them in camps and killing them. (6)

Having experienced firsthand the progression that prejudice can take from an interpersonal level to societal discrimination the respondent seeks to conceptualize the current situation of Roma in Europe. The respondent expresses fears that the behavior she is currently witnessing toward the Roma is only steps away from revisiting past atrocities committed against Roma and other minority groups.

The change from individual to institutional racism is certainly a concern for many Roma in America as well as Europe. Government institutions such as the police force rely on public notices and newspaper profiles to perpetuate fear and suspicion of Roma, leaving individuals as well as towns to resist their presence. Without many advocates, Roma become easy targets for law enforcement, making their desire for invisibility harder to achieve. Reality television as well as a continual presence in newsprint highlighting criminal activity of the Roma, and nothing else, further contributes to their vilification and increases their likelihood of being targeted by the police.

POLICE AND THE ROMA

American Interactions with Police

Historically, interactions between Roma and police in the United States have not been favorable. As I discuss in the previous chapter, law enforcement has been largely suspicious of the presence of Roma and instrumental in contributing to the passing on of stereotypes surrounding Roma in posted statements and contributions to newspapers. Police officers have been cited as saying that gypsies are the "evilest, cleverest, best organized society of criminals in existence." One such officer felt his assignment to investigate gypsy crime in society to be the sleaziest assignment an officer could be given (Yuenger, 1987).

A 2001 article in *Police: Law Enforcement Magazine* features an article titled "Gypsies: King of Con" (Hall, 2001). The article, though noting they do wish to imply that not all people of the gypsy culture are involved in crime, begins with this description of gypsies in America:

> We have all heard or know about organized crime. But did you know there is an organized crime family specializing in fraud that has successfully operated throughout the world for almost 2,000 years? Their success nets them millions, tax-free, every year. Less than 5% of their victims complain and when they do, are often met with laughter, misreporting or ignorance by law enforcement.

This statement, despite the disclaimer at the beginning of the article, immediately homogenizes and criminalizes Roma in the United States. Additionally, while it may very well be true that some Roma engage in conning others or in criminal activity, the assertion that their cons net Roma millions of tax-free dollars gives one the impression that they are secretly living a life of luxury and not dealing with poverty as many, in reality, are.

Reality television shows such as *My Big Fat American Gypsy Wedding* (Herman, 2012) further contribute to this narrative, leaving many to believe that the lavish weddings enjoyed by Roma women with custom-made dresses are typical of their lives. These shows also portray sketchy business practices and interactions with the law, raising their visibility to other law enforcement and leading some to be distrustful of Roma who appear to be living in poverty, believing it is merely a part of their "con." Deaton's (2013) content analysis of Florida newspapers from 2011–2012 uncovered a narrative within that suggested many Roma are living extravagantly outside what the mainstream can afford through ill-gotten means. While wealth may be distributed among Roma as in any other group found within the United States, this type of narrative is dangerous as it gives the impression that Roma, like those discussed in Canada, are hiding their wealth and fail to account for the social stratification that many Romani face. This may be particularly true for those engaged in "traditional" Roma occupations for whom poverty or economic stratification may be a reality.

The article in *Police Magazine* goes on to report that each Roma group has its "criminal specialty" (Hall, 2001). Gypsies are listed as "experts at false identification" and are said to be largely without the ability to read or write. "Gypsies choose a lifestyle of thievery, one that is as natural to them as eating and sleeping." The article then discusses the various cons gypsies are engaged in and how to fight against them. There is in fact a "South Florida Gypsy Crimes Task Force" that has been developed to focus their efforts on gypsies committing crimes in their area. While this may seem a reasonable step in gypsy crime if it is indeed running rampant to the extent reported, by reframing this perhaps one can see where the issue lies.

It would be unlikely that a task force called the "South Florida Islamic Crimes Task Force" or the "South Florida Asian Crimes Task Force" would be something allowed to exist. Without question those things, in the form of racial profiling, do exist within police departments but are operated in a manner where profiling is meant to be done covertly. For Roma, racial profiling is not only done outright but is applauded and, as the article states, has gained national recognition. This recognition places Roma seeking to legitimately support their families, in a position of fear and has led to the evacuation of Roma from cities. It has also led to laws being passed that prevent their ability to conduct business, own property or simply reside in certain areas.

A national association exists that specifically trains policemen to target Roma and Travellers in the United States. The National Association of Bunco Investigators held a conference in 2015 on Elder Exploitation and Nomadic Organized Crime that offered two days of workshops identifying the criminal world of Roma and Travellers. The workshops offered include, "Introduction to the Criminal Gypsies and Travelers," "Fortune Telling Fraud," and "The Travelers: English, Irish and Scottish: Nomadic Bands of Home Repair Con-Artists" (NABI, 2015).

Hancock (2010) reviews literature associated with racial profiling of Roma within American police departments. Deaton (2013) found documented occurrences of discrimination and profiling toward Roma by federal agents in court. While undeniable in their targeting of "Gypsies" police are reluctant to admit this targeting necessarily affects the Roma. Police deny that those they are calling gypsy are in fact the Roma people and instead may be defined by lifestyles and criminal profiles. Thus, they lack accountability for their targeting of the Roma people and the Roma have little support for a case of civil rights infringement. Roma may view police distrustfully as they may fail to take into account Roma culture. Donald and Brooks (2009) identifies one such case where underage Roma women were searched without a warrant by police officers. According to custom of this particular sect of Roma, they were then considered "unclean" leaving them open to the derision of others within their community and impinging their ability to marry. They eventually sued and won a case with a city, victorious not only in fiscal means but in holding the city and police department accountable for their discriminatory actions.

Among the Roma women I interviewed, many identify negative interactions between police and Roma. Gertie, a Roma woman in her fifties from Southeast United States, describes the life of her family and its relationship to the police:

> Gertie: If someone in the town complained about you, you got run off by the police. Basically the same thing that they would be run out of towns.
> *Interviewer: That was because of who they were or because of the type of work they did?*
> Gertie: Because of who they were and it was because they told fortunes.
> *Interviewer: Do you think there were things that happened [with the police] to your family they didn't talk about because it was difficult for them?*
> Gertie: Uh, probably not because they didn't get caught very much back then.
> *Interviewer: So do you think, were they normally run out of town or do you think they were able to leave town before they got run out?*
> Gertie: They traveled a lot, they stayed like a step ahead of the police.

Gertie describes the experiences of her family that occurred in the early half of the twentieth century. It was during this time that newspaper articles warning residents of Roma presence were not uncommon. This notoriety caused residents to be on the lookout for Roma presence and led to targeting by police who let Roma know they were unwelcome in many towns. Ruby, a women in her forties from the Southeast, describes a similar scenario: "Yeah I mean that they were run out of town that the police, the muskers, would shake them down for money when they found out that they were running a business without a license." Ruby was able to recall narratives about Roma interactions with police related by her parents and grandparents.

The targeting of Roma seeking to support their families with nontraditional means and in nontraditional lifestyles is both a historical occurrence and a modern one. The work of organizations such as the Association of Bunco Investigators and the "South Florida Gypsy Crimes Task Force" is alive and well. Louisa, in her thirties, describes the interactions many of the men who work jobs traditional to Roma have had with police:

> They know the gypsies are ignorant so they know they will pay whatever it takes to get them out. They used to do that to them all the time. Then when we was in Minnesota they were arrested on theft by deception charge. The next

day they dropped the charges and released him but at the time my husband had 5,000 dollars on him that the police kept just because they felt like it . . . we never seen a dollar of that money back. That was like to pay for the men. That was supposed to cover all the material and pay all the men.

Louisa reports many experiences of being unfairly targeted by the police based on their identity only to later be released without consequence but not before it cost them jobs, time they could be working or traveling, or money. Louisa also commented on the situation for Roma and other minorities:

It's just a really racist town in Florida, one of the police officers . . . in that same town shot a Black guy [multiple] times and when they asked him why they shot him that many times, he said well I ran out of bullets, like if he'd had more he would have shot him more. It's for who you are not what you done, it's who you are.

Many Roma fear not only for their livelihood, but they are fearful their children will be profiled and sent to jail on trumped-up charges. Louisa was able to conceptualize these fears by situating them within narrative of Black interactions with law enforcement.

There can be little doubt that the Roma encounter significant prejudice from police in the United States. For those whose goal is living largely invisible lives, media portrayals serve to only bring them to the forefront in a criminalized and fear-inducing manner. The situation for Roma in Europe is all the more dire due to their heightened visibility. In addition, it is the common practice for local councils to pass laws making the Roma way of life largely illegal, effectively outlawing portions of their historical identity and making them targets for law enforcement.

Police Interactions in Europe

American experiences with police mirror those of their European counterparts in many ways. One could argue that in Europe, Roma criminals are created and punished simultaneously by the government. As I discuss in an upcoming chapter, traditional Roma lifestyles are becoming more and more "illegal," impacting Roma identity in a significant way. As already recounted, media in Europe, be it newspaper, news stations, radio broadcasts or posted notices serve the police by creating a culture of fear surrounding Roma which helps to justify their actions. The Roma in Europe hold an understandable mistrust toward police in many communities (Heaslip, 2015).

An article by *The Guardian* identifies that it is rare for women to call police for help, even when victimized because the community would look down on this as a betrayal, possibly leading to the individual being ostracized (Bindel, 2011). Even if the police were called, few believe that police would be of much help, as one woman interviewed in a study on the intersectional oppression of Roma women identifies, "I gave up calling the police . . . when we call them, they often say, 'Let it be, Gypsy business'" (Kushi, 2016). Mistrust of police by Roma has many historical underpinnings (Beaudoin, 2014). Even in situations where police reach out to Roma communities, a large amount of distrust remains. These feelings were conceptualized by a Roma woman who participated in a study on Roma identities (Beaudoin):

> Are we under surveillance? Are we feeding information to the police? Why do they want to partner with us? What role are we playing in giving them access to Roma Community members that they want? What role are we playing in gathering information? For deportations? (261)

Another Roma woman, participating in a study on vulnerability within the Gypsy/Traveling community also identifies with these fears:

> We also had a fear of the law, a very deep fear of any police officers or any people like that, because it has been inbred in us to fear the law and not to trust anyone from the local community. (Heaslip, 2015, 92)

The respondent from Heaslip's study has a narrative corresponding to respondents from America. Roma hold deep-seated fear and mistrust toward the law that has been passed down in their community.

A Roma woman in her twenties from the same study identifies that Roma mistrust is not unwarranted. Roma see that they are being targeted by law enforcement and surveilled for no apparent reason:

> Two sites I spoke about you've got cameras, you wouldn't get a camera outside the front of the house so why do Travelers. It's like you go home tonight and they put a camera outside your house. That cameras watching every move we make and it ain't nice. (Roma Woman, age twenty, as cited in Heaslip, 2015, 88)

Like American Roma, Roma in Europe believe they are being unfairly targeted, especially when they are routinely watched and forced from their homes (Lane, Spencer & Jones, 2014). One Irish Travelling youth reports to Ureche and Franks (2007) that being Traveler is itself enough to warrant the notice of the police, "If they know then they use it against you. The police they do it worse than anyone." Roma are targeted because of their ethnicity and made to feel as if they are somehow guilty, simply by existing. As one respondent states, "You're a 'T' so you must be up to something" (Irish Traveler, 41).

Targeting of Roma by police whether in America or Europe is further evidence of prejudice and discrimination as a part of the Roma lived experience. The reluctance of police officials to allow Roma to successfully establish themselves vocationally or physically and the continued fear-mongering disseminated through mainstream media will be discussed further in coming chapters. The last area for examination is gender specific. The lives of Roma women in the United States and worldwide carry additional challenges, attracting additional kinds of prejudice. While the interviews I conducted produced some evidence in collaboration with the lives of Roma women worldwide, I thought it also appropriate to give voice to Roma women in Europe who have and continue to face significant prejudice.

GENDERED VIOLENCE IN AMERICA AND EUROPE

As it exists in America, there is an intersection between gender, violence, race and ethnicity among European Roma women (Ceneda, 2002). European woman experience significantly more ethnically motivated violence as well as social exclusion. Portrayals of Roma women are most often used to represent the life of the Roma, most significantly through shows such as *My Big Fat Gypsy Wedding* (Herman, 2012; Poppelwell, 2012).

Among all types of violence perpetrated against Roma women worldwide, one has come to the forefront. Studies have conclusively proven that Roma women were forcibly sterilized in countries such as Hungary, Czech Republic and Slovakia (Albert, 2011), and likely, historically in the United Kingdom (Hancock, 2010). During the Holocaust, many Roma were killed, as many as 95 percent of Czech's Roma population alone was killed during that time, however, many Roma women were forcibly sterilized as a way to control the Roma population (Thomas, 2006). The practice became common in Eastern Europe in the 1970s, a time when women were often sterilized during cesarean sections without consent. Some women were coerced into the procedure through promises of money or threats of having their government benefits cut off or having their children taken away (Albert, 2011; OpenSociety, 2011). Some reports identify that this practice continued into the 90s (Kushi, 2016; Open Society) while others identify sterilizations as recent as 2002 (Albert). A report from the U.S. state department regarding their investigation into the Czech Republic reports sterilizations as recent as 2004 (Thomas, 2006).

There has been no confirmed end to these practices and little to no accountability has been expressed. Representatives from the Czech Republic minimize the sterilizations as "procedural shortcomings" while other countries fail to acknowledge the extent to which these procedures took place, sometimes in the tens or hundreds of thousands (Albert, 2011: Thomas, 2006). Recently, some accountability has taken place; however, efforts to bring restitution have failed (Van der Zee, 2016). Van der Zee collected the stories of women who had undergone these experiences. Elan, a Roma woman in her forties, shares her story in a play that highlights the experiences of Roma women who have undergone forced sterilization: "To be able to have children is so important for a woman. When they took that away from me, I felt worthless, I completely lost my self-esteem." Elan is able to put into words what was taken away from her and from other women who experienced these procedures, both personally and emotionally.

The portrayal of forced sterilization in the media is significant to not only the recognition of their experiences but the ways in which it is addressed or stopped. Despite efforts to bring notoriety to this occurrence, the language utilized about these procedures has the ability to minimize the violence of the action, to clinically justify it or to justify it based on popular social beliefs as many in the Eugenics movement were able to accomplish (Hirsch, 2012; Thomas, 2006). The way Roma have been historically treated by the media has contributed significantly to the care that society gives about the elimination of their future children and the continuation of their race.

In the United States, forced sterilization has historically been linked with the Black community as well as those in poverty or those deemed "defective" (Open Society, 2011). There is no concrete evidence at this time that Roma women in the United States. have experienced forced sterilization, though the United States cannot be said to be without guilt in the targeting of Roma families. I have already recounted the story of Fey, a woman in her sixties living in the Northwest. Fey told a story of her experience with forced assimilation as a child growing up in New York. The children of her community were taken, placed in orphanages and adopted out to White families where they were given new names and were prevented from speaking about their heritage. It is interesting to note, that many of the newspapers of that day highlight the lives of Roma only to identify their proclivity to steal children all the while the government was perpetrating that very crime against the Roma community. As previously stated, it is often the silence of the media on such matters that has the potential to harm as much as the stereotypical accounts.

Roma women face considerable stress as they exist at the intersections of race, gender and oftentimes, poverty, worldwide, a fact that will be considered in further depth in the coming chapters. The cultural violence Roma women experience, including the objectification of women who are very much a marginalized minority, has been exacerbated by the negative media portrayals they face in the modern world. These media portrayals serve to erase the challenges faced by Roma women, highlighting instead facets of their lives that are unrealistic at best, and damaging at their worst.

CONCLUSION

When one considers what prejudice toward Roma has led to worldwide, it becomes all the more evident why these occurrences must be acknowledged and changed. Roma have long chosen to remain separate from the world of the gadje, a practice that continues today. Though this may be the result of a people who simply prefer to keep to their own ways, their decision to remain separate has been solidified due to the historical and current prejudice that many Roma encounter.

John Berry (1997) proposed a fourfold model of acculturation, identifying that immigrants and minorities may choose to adopt one of four modes of acculturation or move through them in a linear model. Among the four modes, assimilation, integration, marginalization and isolation, Berry proposes that two of the four modes, assimilation and integration, were the most likely to produce positive mental health and social outcomes. Despite this projection, through choice or social stratification, many immigrants and minorities are unable to follow these "recommended" paths of acculturation due the complex barriers posed by mainstream society. They may lack the social capital to follow their chosen method of acculturation or lack the desire to do so because of ongoing experiences with discrimination (Williams & Berry, 1991). Berry and others show that the process of acculturation can last for multiple generations (1997) and thus the negative outcomes of engaging in the process of acculturation are experienced intergenerationally.

The experiences related in this chapter represent decades of prejudice and racism and allow for a better understanding of the lives of minority, multigenerational and recent immigrant Roma families. It was important to give a foundation not only of media representations of Roma from the previous chapter but also of their experiences with prejudice and discrimination both historically and today. This foundation should provide a lens through which the remainder of the book can be read. In the coming chapter, I will discuss the lived experiences of Roma, their choices related to assimilation and their attitudes about family work and education.

Chapter Three

Roma Lives and Attitudes

A Look into the Past and the Present

In 1866, President Andrew Johnson rejected Congress' attempts to pass the Civil Rights Act, vetoing it based on a number of grounds. Congress was able to overrule this veto and pass the act by a two-thirds majority. The night that the president sent his rejection to Congress, it was accompanied by a note. Though some were ready to adjourn for the night, others felt that it was imperative that the note be read aloud and placed on record. In doing so, a record of President Johnson's feelings toward the Roma, those he referred to as "the people called Gypsies" (Johnson, 1866), and likely those of many of his contemporaries was left behind. With good reason this act and Johnson's subsequent protest of its passing has been found most often in the discourse of Black, Indian and Chinese American rights and history in the United States. One hardly need read closely into Johnson's words however to understand that his protests were not merely directed at these groups but also at gypsies.

President Johnson states that among his hesitations for passing the bill and ultimately rejecting it is the understanding that the bill would give these groups, including gypsies, a birthright to citizenship in the United States. From the time of its passing, anyone born within the United States would be granted citizenship. Johnson took issue with this as it would only grant federal citizenship, leaving citizenship at the state level to be decided. Johnson goes on to say that if citizenship was already granted based on the constitution as Congress was arguing, then there was no need for an additional law. If, however, this was not the case, then was it a good idea to allow "our entire colored population and all other excepted classes" (Johnson, 1866) (as already mentioned, gypsies were listed as an excepted class) to become citizens without the consensus of all states. He posed the question, "Can it be reasonably supposed that they possess the requisite qualifications to entitle them to all the privileges and immunities of citizens of the United States?" (Johnson, 1866). He goes on to suggest that the laws already protected "foreigners" (Johnson, 1866) (here calling those who have been born on U.S. soil foreigners) and grants them civil liberties leaving them little need for the granting of citizenship and that given time they could perhaps go on to prove themselves worthy of citizenship.

Johnson then carries on for quite a while, largely concerned with the recently freed population of slaves though in his summary he again includes the "excepted classes" (Johnson, 1866). He discusses at length the problems with creating in "one piece of legislation" (Johnson, 1866) equality between Whites and Blacks in rights, criminal proceedings and otherwise. As previously stated, while the piece of legislation and subsequent note highlights the struggle of the Black community toward citizenship, at its footnote is the right to citizenship for a handful of previously unrepresented groups and among those are gypsies. By grouping them in with those recently freed, President Johnson was declaring that gypsies too did not have a birthright to citizenship, that the value of gypsy personhood and potential contribution to American society was in question and that gypsies should not be considered on equal footing with Whites (U.S. House of Representatives, n.d.).

The presence of Romani in government documents, in legal proceedings, congressional speeches or otherwise is regularly accompanied by the dark shadow of crime, "othering" or mystery. A depiction of Roma in the federal writer's project from 1920 labeled "tricked by gypsies" tells the story of a woman who was suffering from rheumatism and was promised help by a group of gypsies. Rather than receiving the help she was promised she lost money, quilts and two hams. She described them as dressing in stereotypical costume and the writer identified them as the "despised gypsies." (Federal Writers' Project, 1920). This narrative exemplifies so well the thread of "otherness" woven almost invisible to the eye throughout Roma history in America. Roma become painted as one-dimensional characters, bereft of their own narratives of family, faith, love, hope, existence, patriotism, pride or work. They are most often without mention in the history of the United States unless mentioned in a pejorative context. One may not explain away each claim of Roma crime or deception but, should any group in America be painted as their mistakes rather than their contributions the narrative of America in its entirety would be much different. It is little wonder that Roma in fictional media are portrayed most often in a one-dimensional manner as in reality they have historically been portrayed in as the very same.

For American Roma, the choice of assimilation or nonassimilation upon arrival in the United States and even into the present day has been strongly influenced by this history of marginalization and the simultaneous desire or necessity to remain separate from the outside world. As discussed in chapter 2, Roma in America have historically encountered prejudice and discrimination. Though less overt today Roma continue to encounter prejudice in various forms. It was important to understand the Roma experience with prejudice and racism in America before delving further into the lives of Roma today. Because historical, or even current, prejudice plays such a major role in the decisions of Roma, one cannot understand their lifestyles and practices without grasping the reality of prejudice as a part of the narrative of the Roma people.

In chapter 3, I begin by building a theoretical framework of assimilation theory. This framework will help to better conceptualize the lives and decisions of Roma in the United States by providing both a language and set of constructs to reference as we discuss Roma lives.

ASSIMILATION THEORY

In 1964, Milton Gordon proposed his classic assimilation theory in which he outlined the process by which immigrants or marginalized groups become part of the host society. Gordon's theory proposed that immigrants follow a single trajectory in their journey of assimilation. Gordon proposed that this journey begins with structural assimilation in which members of the minority are able to enter into close relationships with individuals from the host society followed by large scale entering of institutions (i.e., marriage) which would eventually lead to the ending of prejudice and discrimination toward this group (Gordon).

Some scholars felt that Gordon's work was flawed, citing that this ease of assimilation occurred mainly for groups which already closely resembled the host group and that assimilation also requires the acceptance of the host group in addition to the willingness of the minority group to assimilate (Brown & Bean, 2005). Early immigration groups such as the Irish, Italian and Germans were able to successfully assimilate within three to four generations, this has been attributed by some to be a privilege of their "Whiteness." More recent immigrant groups in the United States who are less likely to resemble the host population are finding assimilation a much more complex and lengthy process (Alba, 1997).

Total assimilation was once seen by some scholars to be the ultimate goal of immigrant groups in the United States (Gordon, 1964). Today, however, American society shows a different mindset among its immigrant groups. These groups have elected to explore different routes for relating to the host society (Alba, 1997). Berry's fourfold model of acculturation rejects Gordon's single trajectory model and instead, identifies four options for relating to the host culture (1997).

Berry proposed that some groups may follow Gordon's route of classic "Assimilation" in which individuals give preference to the norms of the dominant culture over their culture of origin. Others may choose "Separation" whereby they immigrate into a cultural enclave and largely reject the influence of the dominant culture. Other groups may choose "Integration" which involves integrating parts of the host culture into their already existing culture, creating a dual identity. Finally, individuals may find themselves in the category of "Marginalization" in which they are being marginalized by the host culture and unable to assimilate (Berry).

In her work, "Accommodation without Assimilation," Margaret Gibson (1988) proposed that some minority groups may be able to accommodate the dominant culture without entirely assimilating. This would enable the minority group to maintain strong roots within their community while benefiting from the resources held by the dominant culture. Individuals who were able to do this were observed to be more successful overall and were able to gain greater access to upward mobility. Those individuals who were unable to achieve some congruence between their own culture and the dominant culture, particularly between home and school life, fared far worse than those who were able to reach a congruent state between the two. However, minority groups often became resistant to schooling or occupations that were believed to lead to complete assimilation.

The American Roma is one such group. American Roma continue to be a largely unknown and unacknowledged minority within the United States. Scholars such as Herbert Gans might describe their ethnicity as symbolic, due to the ability of many American Roma to easily slip in and out of the dominant culture unnoticed, however, this is not true for all due to both complex cultural issues and simplistic ones such as the dark, Middle Eastern features that many Roma possess which may categorize them as non-White. Like those groups discussed by Gibson (1988) many traditional Roma have become masters at accommodation without assimilation in order to access resources from their environment and are resistant to influences, including education, that would push Roma children toward complete, structural assimilation. Many choose a life of "separation," as outlined by Berry's (1997) model of acculturation while others find themselves propelled into full assimilation out of economic necessity or the desire to live a more settled life.

Margret Gibson (1988) identified a life for immigrants in which mainstream practices could be accommodated into traditional ways of life rather than succumbing to assimilation. While this life of integration seems ideal for groups such as Roma who so highly value their heritage, the ability to live such a life has been stifled by the marginalizing behaviors of the gadje. As Berry (1997) identifies in his model of acculturation, in order for a group to become assimilated, the group must desire to enter into the culture of the mainstream society and that society must invite them in. For Roma, the mainstream culture has often been an unwelcoming presence, pushing generations of Roma to hold tightly to their lives of separation least they find themselves more marginalized than they have already, historically, been.

ROMA LIVES

In chapter 2, I explored in-depth prejudice and discrimination as a normal part of the Roma experience, a countering image to the one painted by mainstream media and beliefs. It is important, beyond situating Roma within a challenged state of existence, to have a basic understanding of the life of the American Roma, both those living "traditional" Roma lives and those who have largely assimilated with the mainstream culture. Those living "traditional" lives are often defined by their transitory lifestyles, independent means of employment and somewhat insular nature of their relationships. While I found in my interviews a wide variation of Roma experience in the United States, I was also able to find many common threads within each narrative. The common threads included a desire to preserve Roma heritage, a mistrust of outsiders and the role of education in pushing many Roma toward full assimilation.

What was clear from the interviews is education has played a significant role in the acculturative decisions of the Roma and their relationships with mainstream society. As a result, I focused on attitudes toward and achievement of education in my interviews. Historically, both men and women have been faced with choosing a life within traditional Roma communities or pursuing less traditional occupations and higher education. In present day, a shift is occurring in which a greater number of Roma, particularly those who have lived historically "traditional" lives have begun to place a high value on higher education for their children, perhaps enabling fewer Roma to be faced with the choice of choosing assimilation and separation from their families and traditional values in order to become educated, some preferring instead the route of accommodation without assimilation or integration.

Most respondents believe that the traditional ways of life that made engagement in the mainstream systems difficult are becoming impossible to maintain, encouraging them to engage with more mainstream occupations and lifestyles. Though practically, the cultural norms of many Roma may be changing, the values and attitudes passed down often remained consistent among older and younger respondents.

To better understand the current cultural norms among Roma families, I felt it was important to involve the norms encountered by older generations of Roma. Without extensive literature that would provide a historical basis for this line of inquiry among Roma in the United States, I felt it was important to establish a historical anchor from which I could determine if evidence

for a cultural shift exists and, as I followed the life trajectory of each generation of Roma, I could determine just how much assimilation played a role in
the lives of the respondents.

In order to determine the course of Roma acculturation historically to the
present day, based again on both Gordon and Berry's models (1964; 1997),
and to learn more about the daily lives of Roma, I identified multiple factors.
In my interview guide, I posed questions asking respondents to identify if
they possessed friends outside of their Roma communities, if they had married non-Roma, if they would be okay with their children marrying non-
Roma, if they belonged to a church or other social organization that was
largely attended by non-Roma, if they ate at the home of non-Roma and if
they had non-Roma to their home to eat. I will identify the outcome of this
line of inquiry along with the answers to the questions already posed by first
exploring the experiences and cultural norms encountered by the older generations of respondents interviewed in order to provide a historical anchor from
which the lives of younger Roma can be considered.

OLDER GENERATIONS OF ROMA LIVES

"Mama and Papa Were Different . . ."
— Viewing Stationary Lifestyle as Exceptional

Peaches, in her eighties, grew up in a time when the majority of her family
members had what is considered to be a very traditional way of life for Roma
families. Peaches' parents worked as fortune tellers, influencing them to
move often. She described how her parents would set up their business each
time they moved to a new town:

> They [told fortunes], that was their thing. Papa did all the advertising in the
> papers, he put the ads up and had it published in the papers. He would go out
> what they called carding, they had [fortune telling] cards with the name and
> address and whatever and he would go out into the neighborhoods . . . White
> people didn't like you to throw cards out in their yards. That's how we made
> our living . . .

This type of lifestyle was common among many Roma of their time. Though
Peaches and her family moved somewhat frequently throughout her childhood, it was not as often as many of her Roma family members:

> We did not move very much growing up, we were in places for like 4,5,6 years
> at a time before we got tired of it and moved somewhere else. Mama went to
> school, she didn't get to high school, they travelled, like back when they were
> growing up they traveled like every year so they moved around. . . . I can only
> remember maybe ten times when we moved in my lifetime.

Often, the traveling lifestyle of the Roma prevented assimilation as much as their desire to remain separate from the gadje. Peaches viewed her parents' ideas surrounding interaction with the gadje as different from other Roma: "Mama and Papa were different . . . we had gorja friends and they would come and spend the night. We had gorja friends and we had Romanichal friends."

In those times, it was rare even for gadje women to work outside the home but necessity forced Peaches and her sister to break with cultural norms for women and begin working. Peaches observed how this brought about a major cultural shift among her family members, specifically the younger ones:

> I think my sister and I . . . were the first ones that started working among all of our cousins. Their mothers told fortunes and their fathers did the advertising. . . . the girls stayed home, they didn't work. [My sister] and I were the first ones that started and this was the best thing that could have happened to us because mama and papa both got to where they couldn't take care of us you know so we worked and took care of them. . . . That was the Romanichal way, the younger ones taking care of the older ones . . . That's the way it was.

Cultural norms defined many of the decisions that Peaches made however, necessity required her to make choices outside of what was culturally normal. Despite this departure, Peaches' behaviors were acceptable given the role that she filled within her family as the oldest sibling, when her parents were unable to work. Her family members responded positively to holding a mainstream occupation and soon began to follow suit:

> Ever since then, everyone saw you know, they've got money and they're not working but like 8 hours a day and we work day and night [telling fortunes] and that's when the Romanichal started their children working . . . A lot of Romanichal didn't work because they traveled a lot, they just wasn't in one place enough to work. Then, in modern times they bought houses and sold land and they was able to work, they were in one place you know.

This shift among her family members changed the cultural expectations regarding women and working. Roma women were no strangers to work, as Peaches describes, supporting the family often involved both the mother and the father. Authors such as Gropper (1975) and Sutherland (1975) also provide evidence that Roma women historically served as main income earners for many Roma households. Working, however, among the gadje in jobs that required education and training was altogether new for many Romanichal. Though cultural views on working experienced a shift, many Roma resisted engagement with the educational system because of the extent of interaction with gadje that was required. In addition, the traveling culture of these families, often prevented them from engaging with the educational system.

Peaches's youngest sister would go on to college while she and another sister continued to work. Though, in both friendships and working, Peaches entered into the world of the gadje, in many ways, she remained unassimilated. Though she would have certainly met the criteria for Gordon's first level of assimilation, assimilation stopped there. Entering into social institutions of the gadje, such as marriage, at the time, was certainly out of the question, even for parents as liberally minded as Peaches's:

> Papa and Mama let us date, I dated gorjas. At one time, I was engaged to one.
> It was different in every Romanichal family, some were staunch against it and
> some were ok. Some didn't want anything to do with the gorja.

As discussed in a previous chapter, Peaches knew that when the time came for her to marry, she was expected to marry Roma, no matter what her dating experience had been. Peaches could be defined in terms of "integration" in which she would integrate some aspects of gadje life, work and friends, within the confines of her Roma world. Peaches went on to marry a Romanichal and, though she had some gadje friends, as she aged they became less and less, preferring to stay in contact largely with her Roma relatives.

Peaches's description of her life and the life of many found in her day painted a picture of a lifestyle that prevented settling in one place and was a barrier to both education and working a steady job. For Peaches's generation, which is arguably the oldest current living generation of Roma, it would seem that Roma lifestyle and cultural norms did not allow for large scale assimilation among Roma.

Al, in his mid-seventies, from the Southwestern United States paints a different picture of life around the same era as Peaches. Al was not born a Roma. Instead, he married into a Roma family at a very young age. Having assimilated into Roma culture over sixty years ago, Al is able to shed light on a very insular sect of Roma both as an insider and an outsider. Al moved away with Roma from his town when he was only sixteen years of age. While he was able to become a part of their community, it was not without initial resistance: "Some of the older ones didn't like outsiders and you just kind of have to win them over." Al identified that though he was able to win them over by marrying into their family and working alongside of them, their attitudes toward outsiders, even to this day, have hardly changed:

> The Gypsies have always been an insulted community and they were no differ-
> ent, they didn't talk to that many people outside their own group you know . . .
> It's the same even now but probably more so [in the past].

Al acknowledged that he had joined a community that remained largely insular from the outside world. Unlike Peaches, he and his newfound family preferred to remain separate from those outside the community with the exception of their working lives.

Al was already working by the time he joined the Roma community, having dropped out of school at the age of sixteen. He describes the communal effort of Roma at the time to bring income into the family while unlike Peaches, holding to traditional means of working:

> You do whatever you want to do at the time. We'd go around and pump septic tanks, in that day just about everybody was doing that, we'd paint houses and barns and do a lot of work. Just traditional jobs you know, at the same time. At the time you know even the women, everybody in the family worked, not like it is now, the kids didn't go to school they worked too, they'd peddle baskets or flowers or whatever it is you know.

Al identified even further back, in his father-in-law's time, men would trade horses or fix wood-burning or coal stoves and women, like Peaches's family, would tell fortunes and "drab" selling medicines and herbs. They were always nomadic, necessitating close relationships within their community but few if any outside. Al continues to work today, still maintaining independent employment, more skilled and less nomadic though, as Al points out, they have always been a nomadic people.

Marilla, ten years Al's junior, from the Northeast, observed many of the same cultural norms that Peaches encountered among her own immediate family. Like Peaches, Marilla was able to make friends outside of the Roma, most likely because, outside of her immediate family, Marilla was not connected with other Roma. Despite being largely disconnected from the community, her traveling life still prevented her from maintaining non-Roma friendships. Marilla recalled:

> We travelled a lot and I was permitted to have male friends outside of the family but we didn't stay in one place for very long . . . in second grade I went to 9 different schools . . . one place would have taught you multiplication and you go to the next place and you hadn't learned it yet so you were always missing out.

Though Marilla, at times, saw herself outside the Roma culture, her parents held views known to be traditionally held by other Roma outside the United States (Silverman, 2012). Marilla identified the expectations for her life as a Roma woman held by her parents:

> I would get married and have children and serve a man. . . . As much as my mother said you will not marry this girl off for money, lo and behold, wouldn't you know that is exactly what [my father] tried to do, marry me off.

Marilla's parents' plans for her life did not work out as they hoped. Marilla resisted the traditional life she felt she was being forced into:

> I saw so much ugliness in misogynistic feelings toward women in that family and I knew early on that I had to escape, that is how I felt, I had to escape it. Even my family, I had to escape.

As will be observed throughout many of the interviews, the cultural expectations of women marrying and caring for their home has been a major cultural barrier for many Roma women in the United States. Many Roma women, especially from older generations, have been unable to successfully accommodate aspects of mainstream culture as education or work beyond traditional jobs was often viewed as unnecessary to the future of Roma women. These barriers were certainly observed in Marilla's life. Marilla identified that although she graduated from high school, it would be fifteen years before she went on to pursue a college education. "A lot of that was the fact that I eventually got married and had a child and I wanted to focus on her first or at least that is what I thought I was supposed to be doing."

When it came to people outside of her family, though she was allowed to have non-Roma friends, she was taught to fear the outside world, a practice not uncommon among many of the Roma families represented in the interviews I conducted. Fear was a mechanism utilized to maintain separation between Roma and the world of the gadje and to maintain traditional roles and cultural norms within the family. This fear was not unwarranted, and was in many respects protective. Marilla's father represented perhaps the most extreme picture of one who used fear to instill a desire for traditional Roma roles in his children. She described these experiences with deep emotion:

> We were encouraged with fear. [My father] was a tyrant, you didn't think for yourself, he made all your decisions, you only spoke when you were spoken to. He really didn't allow us to have our own life experiences and would criticize us when we didn't have the skills to master something . . . I was just a woman you know, meant to cook and clean and spread their legs and do what they are told. He had a real hard time with any woman that opposed him on that.

For Marilla, the oppressive, patriarchal nature of her upbringing filled her with the knowledge that following traditional practices were not bringing her the life she had hoped to have. This feeling influenced her to begin looking at how others, in the mainstream, had come to have the life she hoped for herself. She recognized that to have the lifestyle she desired, she would have to assimilate:

> I saw people who lived much better than I did, how they lived their lives, people I admired. They had nice homes, they were modest, loved their chil-

dren. I saw that was what I wanted . . . I wanted that for myself and I knew you had to work for it. The more you are working the more you assimilate and realize what it takes in order to do that.

Marilla followed, what she considered to be the path toward assimilation. Based on physical characteristics alone, Marilla identifies herself as "White" however, she acknowledged that if a "mixed race/ethnicity" category exists, when asked, she often elects to identify herself in that way. The majority of her friends are not Roma. Marilla observed that interaction with non-Roma, in even current times, continues to be unusual among individuals of her generation. Marilla's observation further exemplifies the strong barriers that exist to assimilation among older generations of Roma:

> I still see that [the older generations] are afraid to, not so much in the younger generation but in my own still, they are scared to know anyone outside their clan. . . . everything is very closed minded, even their thinking is clannish. They are very fear based people and a lot of that comes from being on the run for 1000's of years and trying to feed your family in nontraditional ways.

Marilla's observation about why these attitudes against assimilation exist are supported by literature (Hancock, 2002) and by other interviews I conducted for this book. Despite these barriers, Marilla believes that things are changing, that a shift has taken place among younger Roma in which they are not afraid of people outside of their own and that, unlike her own experiences, young Roma today no longer have to choose to be separate from their own community and assimilate to acquire the lives they want, including careers or education. When asked if she believed that Roma women have to separate from their community to pursue these things, she took a very positivistic view of the current situation in the United States: "I think until recently, yes [women had to assimilate], I don't think that is the case now."

Marilla's ideas about the current state of younger generation of Roma fall in line with both Gibson's accommodation without assimilation and Berry's ideas of integration rather than assimilation. Though Marilla takes a positivistic view of today's Roma, a definitive conclusion cannot be made from her case alone. Though other Roma interviewed also took a positivistic view, others possess opposing views that will be explored in later interviews. What can be concluded from Marilla's study is that, in her experience, education and nontraditional career equaled assimilation. Once that path to assimilation was followed, there would be no return to the Roma life of her past.

Like Marilla, Fey is in her sixties. She grew up in the Northeastern United States though she currently resides in the Northwest. Fey shares many values and experiences that Marilla discussed in her interview. Like Peaches's mother, Fey's mother and grandmother were fortune tellers. Fey described her mother and grandmother as strong women, responsible for generating income for the family. As a child, Fey assisted her father in advertising her mother's trade and described the world of her childhood as a "wonderful environment."

As previously discussed, Fey was taken from her community at a young age and forced to assimilate by leaving behind her customs, language and given Roma name. Though those individuals who had taken Roma children from their community cited their need for education as a main motivating factor in relocating the children, Fey's educational prospects were dim by the time she came of age. Fey received her GED and then took an unusual path to eventually obtaining her graduate degree:

> Ok well, I ended up with years of working on the street doing drugs, selling drugs, prostitution, being a real brat. Then I went to methadone clinic in [the city] and there was a sign up at the time saying free room and board for students who would come to this college in [another city]. I went there and it kind of changed my life.

Despite encountering many obstacles following high school Fey was able to pursue higher education when she was presented with an unusual opportunity. She would go on to complete her bachelor's degrees and a master's degree.

Though Fey is proud of both her education and her Roma heritage she identified that receiving her education was, at one time, a sign of assimilation because a women receiving an education in her childhood community was atypical:

> [It was] very atypical. That's why they took us away supposedly is because we are not being schooled. We apprenticed sort of like the kibbutz in Israel, we decided who we wanted to apprentice with and we did. No school was certainly not big but I am old, that has changed.

Fey observed in her childhood community, the preference was to carry on the old customs of passing on a trade. This enabled Roma to live outside of dependence on the gadje economic system, and away from potentially discriminatory and marginalizing encounters. This way of life lent itself to separation from the world of the gadje. The gadje found the chosen separation of Fey's community an unacceptable arrangement. Local government forced the young generation into assimilation and marginalized the elder ones. Despite the attempts by gadje to transform Fey into a "White Girl" she continued to attempt to adhere to as many of the customs of her people as she could remember as she got older. She described herself as "totally assimilated" despite trying to uphold these customs.

For Fey, what started as a life of separation transformed to forced assimilation but, through reconnection with her family and heritage in her forties, she began to live what Berry's acculturation model described as an integrated lifestyle. Fey has friends who are both Roma and not Roma. She belongs to several social institutions within both worlds and identifies that there are multiple pieces to her identity.

Because of Fey's life of integration, she believes it is possible today to be an educated Roma who maintains strong ties to her community. Though in her younger days, education outside the community was not common, Fey sees a change occurring:

> I will not say that Roma communities in this country will not support a woman's education. I think that is changing. I think that is old world. I think the more Roma women who get educated and there is a responsibility to raise women's consciousness . . . to contribute back to their community so I think it's a slow process but I do not think one has to leave their community to be an educated woman.

Though not directly stated, Fey's answer seemed to imply that through integration, or Gibson's idea of accommodation not assimilation, a strategy that Fey herself adopted, Roma today can pursue education with the support of their community. She has observed a shift in attitude beginning to take place, though the process may be slow. Fey was not the only respondent to identify this shift occurring. Gracie also holds similar views regarding a shift in the education, and as a result their assimilation, among modern Roma

Oldest Generations

The five Roma who represent the oldest generation of Roma interviewed present a complex picture. There can be no doubt that they all looked with hope to the future of Roma, however, there can also be no doubt that the cultural norms of these generations presented many barriers for Roma. Rigid adherence to traditional gender roles, a strong desire to remain outside gadje influence, a desire to exist outside of the formal economic system of the gadje all served to make participation with gadje education or careers for many Roma of their day unnecessary or impossible to achieve. The positivistic view that things have changed and would continue to change held by these individuals was not unwarranted. The next group of Roma interviewed, those in their forties and fifties, represented the next generation. There can be no doubt that within this generation, a shift had begun to occur within Roma families and among the many individuals represented in these communities.

THE PARENTS OF TODAY

The largest group of respondents was represented by Roma largely in their mid-forties, some in their early fifties—women and men whose children are beginning to come into their own as adolescents and young adults. The majority of the individuals from this group of respondents possessed a college education. There can be little doubt after hearing their stories, that between their generations and those of Peaches, Marilla, Gracie, Al and Fey, a shift occurred within Roma lives. For some, this meant that the norms of their communities had shifted away from the traditional norms. For many others, this meant a move away from the identity of their childhood and a move toward assimilation.

Survival as a Way of Life for the Roma

Among all the respondents of this group, Louisa was the only woman who did not possess a college education and continues to live a "traditional" Roma lifestyle. She is in her forties and lives in the Midwest though, she identified, she has lived in almost every state in the Southern United States. Louisa is a stay-at-home mom who homeschools her youngest child. In the past, she has gone into business for herself and been successful. Her businesses have been independent work common to Roma families. She readily identifies as "Roma" when asked to identify herself racially or ethnically.

Though Louisa has some non-Roma friends, she stays mostly connected with her Roma relatives, largely due to her traveling lifestyle which she describes as unstable in many respects:

> We don't have a lot of stability, we don't have a calendar planned out for the year, like something pops up like I hate to take any responsibility at church. . . . I never know when I have to leave even though I have home you just never know what is going to happen and then you are going to have to leave you like you got to be able to go at the drop of a hat. Anywhere at any time.

The life Louisa lives is reflective of the life she had growing up. Louisa moved often in her childhood due to her family's traveling occupation. Growing up, she was still able to connect with others outside of her own family largely due to attending church. Even still, there were cultural norms that were upheld within these friendships, norms she continues to adhere to today:

> When I was 8 years old, we started going to church . . . I had some close friends from church . . . and I spent the night with them which was very rare, very rare. My kids have never spent the night over out of our race. They are very rarely with people not in our race.

For Louisa, separation from gadje was a way of life with few exceptions. Even those relationships that were allowed outside her community were heavily regulated. Separation over assimilation was a way of life.

The traveling lifes made it difficult for her to maintain friends with individuals outside of her community. Louisa described her father's work and how this impacted their lives:

> My father would do construction working outside and you could only stay like when the weather permitted if it got cold and it snowed then the blacktopping would shut down and then you would have to move and go south and when you got south you can only stay then when it gets hot and you have to leave or if you are staying in a town and there are too many people, too many other Romanichal working there they work the town out and it's too hard to make money then you have to go somewhere else to make money.

The uncertainty of this lifestyle created much instability in Louisa's life and prevented her from engaging with mainstream society.

Unlike other women in the study, Louisa was prevented from working growing up. Work was another way for Louisa to be negatively influenced by the world of the gadje:

> I never was allowed to work, I always wanted to work at the mall, I was never allowed to work until this day I told them they never let me work they still get mad and holler "Well you had plenty of money, you had everything you wanted." I think, that's not the point, I wanted a job and I think to this day they still cannot understand it.

In addition to encountering barriers to work and a career, Louisa encountered many barriers to her education due to her traveling lifestyle. Louisa left school in seventh grade and never completed her education, a decision she regrets even today. Despite this, she continues to travel, which can often interrupt the schooling of her own daughter who is now being homeschooled.

Louisa is able to recognize through her own regrets about education that her lifestyle is not ideal for the pursuit of education, but explains that this lifestyle is a way of survival for many Roma:

> The thing is it's about trying to survive and trying to make money and it's like so hard in school because even with my kids, my daughter is homeschooled now and my son just graduated and is going to start college, it was hard because White people looks down their noses, "Well how come they missed so many days of school" and I say "Lady I wish you could walk one mile in my shoes."

Louisa identified that many individuals outside of her community look down on the lifestyle she and her family occupy. Many hold beliefs that these individuals are unstable, perhaps even unsuitable as parents due to the constant change in location that these children experience. Louisa sought to provide a greater understanding of why this lifestyle was necessary to the survival of her family, something she believes an outsider would not be able to fully grasp:

> Like if you are out on the road when you get somewhere it is winter time you barely have the money to get where you are going you've got to get up and go to work. We wake up every day out of work like we just have to knock on a door and make it happen. There is no steady pay check. Every day we wake up out of work, so we can only stay somewhere as long as we are working so if we don't have work then we have to go somewhere else and they want to know where you are going and how long it is going to take. It's hard, it's difficult that's the main thing with school. It ain't that we don't want them to have an education, it's just make it very difficult when we are just trying to make enough money to survive.

In order to maintain a life outside of the economic control of the gadje, one that allows for the freedom and solitude that many Roma seek, the type of occupation that Louisa's family is engaged in is required. This may mean going through seasons of little income and harsh conditions while at other times it may bring much prosperity. When faced with these difficult times, however, decisions must be made in the best interest of the family, and this may require a family or even a whole community to move multiple times within one school year, a decision viewed negatively by outsiders, particularly educators.

Louisa knows that many conditions of the Roma lifestyle are not ideal and have certainly left her with some regrets about her lifestyle. She believes, however, that many cultural norms are beginning to change. "Things is changing, and people are working and stuff and like within the last year things is changing. People know there is opportunity before we had no idea that could be our life." From Louisa's perspective, the option to become educated is more open today than in previous years, however, she also acknowledges that younger Roma continue to choose the traditional lifestyle. For these younger Roma, it's a choice of preference rather than survival:

> The boys [go] out and make money and the girls [stay] home and cooks and cleans and watches kids. And they are fine with that, it's not like they are from the 50's. That's what they want to do. They don't want to work. If they wanted to go to work they probably could but they don't want to know.

Though she has lived a traditional lifestyle Louisa's own son has begun college and she hopes the same for her daughter. Louisa's narrative gives one the sense that separation or even accommodation without separation is possible but one cannot help but acknowledge the many barriers to education that exist within this way of life. As with every traditional story told, something has to be given up to obtain educational achievement.

Louisa was the only one among the eight women represented in this generational group who did not possess some college education or a degree and was one of three total in this age group who did not possess a college education. Despite the fact that this group was a largely educated population, of the seven women with a college education, only two completed their degree at a traditional age. The men represented in this age range with college educations completed their first degree within the traditional age range. For most of the women in this group their lives began strongly connected with their Roma communities and they were raised with the expectation of fulfilling traditional gender roles. The cultural practices and lifestyles experienced by many of the women were encouraging of a life of separation over assimilation.

Donald, fifty-six, was one of two men in this age range who lived largely traditional lives growing up. Donald grew up connected closely with his Roma relatives. He speaks the language and moved frequently, stating he attended between 10–15 schools before he reached 7th grade. Donald's dad was a skilled independent laborer who moved for work until Donald was in middle school. Though connected with his Roma family, as his family moved into a settled life and he engaged more and more in his schooling, they begin to assimilate more into the society around them:

> As I was younger it was more my family cousins and other relatives but as I went to school I started making close friends. When we stopped moving around the country and stayed in one place it became more natural to be more close to my Gorja friends than my relatives . . . We assimilated into the folks we were around. My mother was Gorja, I was light skinned, there was no difference between us and anyone else that was around. Nobody had questions, nobody even asked. Every now and then when I looked at my brother and sister I would say something in Rumnis and you know slip up but I would tell people don't worry about it and would go on from there.

As Donald's father's occupation became more settled and he and his siblings engaged in stable education, they began to assimilate, however, as Donald points out, an awareness existed of the time and place for the elements of his Roma identity to exist and with whom they should.

School became a significant part of Donald's life growing up. Though he became more and more involved and successful as a student, his parents, in line with many older Roma, resisted his education and involvement with his schooling. In coming chapters we will discuss Roma experiences of discrimination in education which have contributed to their mistrust. Additionally, Roma have traditionally resisted education because of the necessity of contributing to family income as early as possible and because educational institutions can serve as major socializing forces which teach ideals that may not be in line with Roma norms.

Donald's parents were no exception to this narrative, leading Donald to act in a manner that would be shocking in any community:

> I was forced to go to school for 10 years. Didn't like it, I wanted to quit and go out on the road. My sophomore year we had been in [the same city] from 6th grade until my sophomore year. My freshman year I got straight A's in everything. And everything started clicking. And what did my dad do? My dad decides he is going back on the road and in my junior year I was told if I did not stay and finish out the year that I would not graduate the following year. I believed education was the best thing I could do. I fought my mother and father and my family to go to school. After my freshman year I figure hey I've got only 3 years left and then my junior year I told my dad I only have a year left I am not dropping out. They wanted me to quit in every way . . . my dad was moving from one town to another 25 miles away just for the sake of making it hard on me so I would finally give in and when he did that I had friends in the town and when I was 17 I went back . . . I ended up taking my mother and father to court so I could graduate from high school. They did not like that at all. I was determined I was going to have something underneath my belt to fall back on.

Despite the attitudes his parents held, Donald knew that school was a means to something besides the life of a transient worker. Though he crossed many cultural taboos to do so, Donald forced his parents into court and fought to complete his high school education. Donald's siblings however did not graduate, his sister only completing school through elementary school.

Donald had plans to attend college but his plans were never realized. Unable to finance his education on his own, Donald attempted to apply for financial aid. This proved to be another fight with his parents, one he was unable to win:

> they needed to see tax papers filled out so I could get financial aid to get into college. My parents told me it ain't none of their business and it ain't none of your business and it ain't never going to happen.

Donald went on to careers similar to that of his father until he tired of being targeted by the police constantly and the other hazards of the traveling life. He decided to settle down in the Southwest. Though he has enjoyed the jobs he has held since his time on the road, he still thinks about the life of his father. "It's still there inside of me, it's still bred inside me but it's just the idea, I was forced out of it." Though he feels the traveling life is a part of his identity, he acknowledges that society does not make it easy to exist in the traditional way anymore.

Today, Donald works in nontraditional occupation. He married a Roma woman but is now divorced. He held different expectations for his children in regards to education, his wishes were that they would attend college. He hoped that his daughter would not marry young and quit school as he had seen other Roma girls do. He states that all of his children were brought up knowing their Roma identity, knowing how to speak the language and knowing that it was their decision what kind of life they wanted to live. Donald knows firsthand that this is a departure from many of the attitudes and expectations of older Roma and that his changing attitudes are just one example of many changes among Roma today:

> I think most of the Roma I know now have settled down which makes them defend what they have instead of the way it used to be of everybody working together to make sure everybody was taken care of. Nowadays you have groups in [various locations] then you've got folks scattered in the rest of the country where they will be one or two families . . . they don't have the group mentality anymore . . . we are alone and that's kind of losing it for our kids . . . young men especially, I know there are young women also but most of the young men are stressed out over getting out and making a living for their family and getting more and more. They turn to drugs they are so stressed out. In the past you had a home or a tent, my father was born in a tent, and you wanted maybe a new pickup and you were satisfied . . . today there is so much more technology and competition. I think we are worse off now than what we were before. Everyone is separated now and so I think we are worse off today.

Donald sees the changes for Roma today as significant both for those who are living traditional lives and those who are assimilated. In coming chapters we will discuss how changes in traditional lives have impacted Roma identity. Donald observes how the pressure of the modern day has significantly impacted Roma communities and, he believes, have made life for Roma in the United States more challenging than in years past.

Eddie

Eddie is in his fifties and was the only Roma male that continued working independently and largely adheres to traditional Roma life though he mainly stays in one place. Eddie identifies that his parents didn't have a house until he was in his forties. His parents waited to acquire a stationary house due to the traveling life, a life which took Eddie all over the Southwest United States growing up. Eddie completed the 8th grade and then dropped out of school because traveling would have prevented him from accumulating enough credits to graduate. Eddie was making adequate money by the time he dropped out so he never worried about completing his education. Eddie stated he began peddling as a child. He would make wallets or coke flowers, wicker furniture and bird cages to sell, similar to his mother who would sell corsages to dance goers when she was a teen. By that time he was seventeen, Eddie was skilled in various labor jobs and he made enough to buy himself a new vehicle. In his words he was "doing all right."

Eddie grew up in a very traditional world, where boys can go out and socialize and drink and meet girls in the town but girls "can't do that because first of all girls can get pregnant and we don't want them to get pregnant that's why there is a double standard, that's why there is a double standard in any culture." He identified however that girls often stayed in school longer than the boys though it was often up to the individual. Today, he says that attitudes toward women have changed in that many of his relatives marry women outside of the Roma tradition who are expected to work outside of the home.

Eddie is married to a traveler woman and they have two children of their own. His expectations for his own children's lives in one sense are similar to those of his father. "I told them the same thing my dad told me, no matter what you do you are going to do it better with an education." Eddie is ensuring this, however, by insisting his children complete high school, an attitude that conflicts with his wife's expectations, especially when it comes to his daughter: "My wife don't want to send the girl to high school but I insist that she does because I don't want that robbed from her, it's one of the funnest times of your life and I don't want that robbed from her, she is definitely going." Eddie also states he would like to see both his son and daughter attend college, and thus live a life much different from his own.

Today Eddie lives in one place though he does the same work he did when he was traveling. Unlike other Roma, Eddie sees technological advances as a positive when it comes to the traditional trades of the Roma:

> It's more comfortable because with the internet you can have people calling you and you really don't have to knock doors or anything. My business just keeps growing and growing and growing. With the advent of the cell phone that's the best thing that ever happened to us cause then people could call you and they wouldn't know if you was local or what and they can hold you for their selves. Now the internet is really really super. Things have changed, I am an A+ rated business and 5 stars on yelp. When you stick around people can't say nothing bad about you.

Eddie has managed to integrate his Roma norms and lifestyle with mainstream practices that enhance rather than detract from the life he wants to lead. Unlike Donald, Eddie believes that things have improved across the board:

> I think things are so much better for everybody. There are so many people here now, it's just generation and generation and if you look at every one of them, they don't know how they are blessed. New cars and you know new trailers and a lot of them have houses and properties. It's so much better now than when I was a kid.

Eddie does feel the loss of community among his Roma connections. While he maintains relationship with his family, he also had gadje friends with whom he stays connected. He sees how the connections among Roma have been lost with the disappearing of the traveling life but Eddie is a prime example of the means by which traditional lives can and have taken a step forward, not to fully assimilate, but to integrate the two worlds successfully.

Unprepared for Life's Challenges, Long-Term Effects of Holding to Traditional Ways

Fener currently resides in the Deep South but moved often during her child-hood. Currently in her mid-forties, Fener previously worked as a registered nurse but retired due to illness. Unless she is close with someone she rarely identifies herself racially or ethnically. She is currently married to someone who is not Roma. She attends a church that is largely attended by individuals of other ethnicities. By the standards set forth in the previously established literature (Gordon, 1964), Fener appears to have fully assimilated away from her Roma roots.

Fener's life growing up would have predicted a different trajectory for her future. Fener's family moved often in her childhood for work and to be near other Roma family. Though she would make friends at school from outside of her community, she was encouraged to play and interact with her siblings and cousins. Fener didn't recall receiving any other direct messages regarding the life she should expect to have as a Roma . . . she expected to have the life she observed around her:

> What I've seen in my family is that most of them got married, that's what I thought I would end up doing but you know grow up and get married and have kids. I think it was just implied that's what you were going to do when you grew up, get married and have kids.

Educational achievement was not among the expectations she had for herself, though she enjoyed school. Fener knew that the traveling lifestyle was not conducive to completing education for most Roma girls and often, even if they stayed in one place long enough to finish high school, they would leave before they graduated to work and help their families. This occurred normally around the age of sixteen or seventeen.

Fener followed a traditional path of marrying and having children at a young age but soon found that this path had not prepared her for the challenges she would face:

> I got married just to get out of the house, I felt like that was the only way out. I got married and had two girls. It didn't work out, I moved back home and

realized I needed to do something . . . so I decided well I'm going to go to
school and become a nurse.

Fener did go on to become a nurse and later married again outside of the
Roma community. Fener knew both of these decisions were unconven-
tional for women in her community but, she recognized that the life she
wanted for herself was not conducive to holding on to traditional lifestyle
choices nor would they allow her to give her daughters the life she hoped
for them to have.

Fener raised her daughters to be involved in school providing them with
stability and encouragement. She encouraged them to pursue an education
and career rather than relying on a man. She wanted them to be able to avoid
the circumstances she found herself in after her divorce. Though she stays in
touch with her family today her lifestyle does not reflect the culture of her
childhood. Fener has assimilated and left much of her past behind.

The Challenge of Breaking Cultural Norms

Gertie's life took a similar trajectory to Fener's. In her early fifties, Gertie
also resides in the Deep South though she moved often growing up. Today,
she is attending college in order to complete her bachelor's degree. All of her
friends consist of people outside of the Roma community. She belongs to a
church that is not attended by any individuals from the Roma community.
She has chosen for some time to have little to no contact with her Roma
family. She stated that she thinks about being Roma more often since she has
gotten older but, when asked, she identifies herself as White. Though currently unmarried, Gertie's previous marriage was to a non-Roma, and she is
glad to see her own daughter married to a non-Roma. Like Fener, Gertie has
entirely assimilated into the world of the gadje and yet, her childhood started
on a much different trajectory.

From early on, Gertie was aware that there were expectations she was
expected to fulfill as a Roma woman. Expectations she was not always able
to fulfill:

> My mother didn't really teach me how to interact with other gypsies because
> we lived in a town away from them until I was 13. We lived in another town so
> I didn't really know how to interact with either society. I was kept isolated
> from both. The gypsies have their own norms and mores and negative sanc-
> tions that I was not aware of and it made my life very difficult because she
> didn't teach me those.

Like other Roma, Gertie moved often growing up which sometimes meant
being further away from her relatives, however, eventually her mother decided that being near her family was the best place for her. Gertie was able to

see clearly the expectations for life within her community: "I don't think they ever [thought] about going to school . . . [The women] have the children and clean the house."

Gertie left high school before graduating. It wasn't until Gertie made friends outside of the Roma community that she was influenced to pursue furthering her education:

> I had a friend in bible study that showed me how to get my GED and showed me how to get into college so I actually went to college and my mother was very non-supportive. She wasn't willing to help.

Without the support of her family, however, Gertie quit school and, like Fener, she decided to marry to get away, a decision that did not work out for her in the end. In time, Gertie found herself divorced with children, with few skills to assist her in making a living for her family.

Gertie has had four children and, though she has worked many different jobs throughout her life, she is just now returning to finish her college education. Gertie came to the conclusion early in her adulthood that it was important to separate from her community in order to have a better life for herself and her children. She views the cultural norms she was taught in her community as detrimental to her ability to function within mainstream society, "It took me a while to understand how to communicate and be a part of a normal society as a whole."

Following a path outside of her family's expectations carried many negative sanctions that Gertie described as "being shunned and ridiculed, gossiped about which is the gypsies' worst fear, losing your reputation." Gertie admits however that there were those who chose to assimilate away from the Roma community who still managed to maintain the respect and admiration of their family members. One family member in particular achieved a college education and never sought the acceptance of her community as Gertie had. Gertie saw her family's response to her as significantly different from the one she received when choosing to live outside of the community's expectations:

> I think they were impressed with what she was able to accomplish. She was successful at what she did and also she got married when she was in college. I think if she was a single woman out there I think there might have been some eyebrows raised. She had a husband and family along with her career so that kind of legitimized her decision. Plus they knew her mother had health issues so they probably figure that was the only route for her.

From Gertie's perspective, this family member was able to break cultural norms because (1) necessity required it and (2) she adhered to cultural norms that held greater weight, such as marriage. For Gertie, however, she believed, like Fener and many of the other women interviewed, that the only way for her to achieve the life she wanted was to assimilate. This was largely due to the extent to which her Roma family emphasized separation to a point that was impossible to veer even slightly outside their expectations.

When asked about the lives of other Roma today, if they were choosing the path she had taken, she had this to say:

> I think some of them have assimilated but even the ones that have assimilated into the mainstream society, it still hasn't changed their mindset, they probably still struggle with identity issues. There's a real dichotomy of feeling guilty because you have broken the cultural norms but then you know I think they haven't quite pushed all the way through the door.

Gertie acknowledged that even those who choose to assimilate carry with them an enormous amount of emotional baggage. These individuals may experience guilt regarding the choice they have made to move away from their culture and their identity. In addition, though they may appear outwardly assimilated, many of the traditional mindsights that they have been ingrained with make it difficult to adjust to the new world in which they are trying to exist. Unlike many of the respondents, Gertie didn't view integration as an option in her past though, today, she identifies that she has begun to see that it's possible to "take the good with the bad," preferring to integrate the positive elements into her assimilated life.

Though Gertie and Fener believed the life they hoped to live required that they leave behind the culture of their childhood, others, like Ruby were exposed to both an integrated and separate lifestyle early on and yet, she choose, like Gertie and Fener, a path of assimilation, maintaining the shared belief that this was the only strategy that would enable her to have the life she hoped to have for herself and her children.

When Lacking Social Norms Effects Individual Prospects

Ruby, in her forties, resides in the Southeast where she was raised. Unlike other Roma, Ruby resided in one place growing up. She has recently completed her degree and works in education. She is currently married to someone who is not Roma. Though she maintains relationships with Roma family members, she identifies that the majority of her friends are not Roma. She identifies that she rarely thinks about being Roma and identifies herself as White. In the past she has only belonged to community organizations that were not affiliated with the Roma community. She identifies that she has assimilated, that she is in the "Gorja" culture.

Growing up, Ruby's immediate family was more broad-minded than her extended Roma family. Her parents encouraged education and supported the idea of going to college. She was allowed to interact with non-Roma and go to their homes. Her extended family accepted these friendships but expected she would make a traditional choice for marriage:

> My great aunts and my grandmother wanted me to attend dances and stuff and fly me out to Texas to meet other people within [our community]. That made me really angry, we had a large disagreement about that.

Like many of the respondents, there existed for Ruby a traditional expectation that she would marry within her community. Her parents often deviated from the expectations of her family, encouraging her to obtain an education before marriage. Despite her parents' expectations, she observed the expectations surrounding women in her extended family, the expectations her female cousins could have for their future, and she felt even this was problematic:

> Education is not valued . . . I don't think it is the smartest decision for women to not be educated beyond the 7th or 8th grade. The husbands are not going to live forever, for a woman not to be an independent thinker you know, not being in charge of your own destiny . . . just doing everything your parents say . . . Gypsy girls are so, they're so obedient and subservient, I wasn't raised that way I guess, I was raised to be an independent thinker and to think for myself and I don't know I think they put the limitations on themselves . . . Intelligence in females is not a desired trait . . . I also think that they are uneducated a lot of times and when you have two uneducated parents living in poverty, I feel like for a child there is a lot of factors there working against them, poverty, socioeconomic status.

Ruby felt that many of the women in her family were without the means to live independently, lacking education and social skills to propel themselves forward into success. She views the cultural norms within her family as restrictive to women, leaving many of them without the means to care for themselves should traditional trajectory of marriage fail them. For Ruby this is problematic, something that needs to be addressed if the lives of these women are going to change.

Ruby chose to marry rather than complete her college education. She would go on to work in many fields possessing a high school diploma and a few certifications. Similar to Gertie she found that many of the cultural norms she had inherited did not prepare her for working within the world of the gadje:

> At the insurance company I worked for . . . I would come in and the people thought I was rude because I would not come in and smile and greet them but I was not taught to do that. You speak to people when you enter a room? I had never heard that. I didn't greet people and they started talking about me right away. You know only really what you are taught as a child.

Though her parents encouraged her to achieve goals not traditional for the women in her family, she found that many of the cultural norms she learned growing up did not adequately prepare her for adult life because many were based on a perspective of separation from mainstream society.

Like Gertie, Ruby came away from her Roma upbringing with many negative perceptions of the cultural norms she was taught. Ruby believes that a life of assimilation is the answer for achieving the goals she set for herself and her children. Ruby does not believe that the traditional Roma way prepares women for the realities of life ahead of them. Ruby chose a life of assimilation over the integrated, or accommodated, life of her parents because she continued to see the negative effects of many cultural practices within her own life, even today.

A CULTURE THAT ENCOURAGES ACQUIRING KNOWLEDGE—ALTERNATIVE PERSPECTIVES

Phoebe is one of the respondents who looked back on the traditional disparities of her upbringing with both pride and appreciation. Today, in her mid-forties, she resides on the East Coast and, like her generational counterparts, she lives a largely assimilated lifestyle. Phoebe holds a bachelor's degree and has taken courses toward completing a master's. She does not move often for work and has many non-Roma friendships. She belongs to community institutions that are not affiliated with the Roma. She was previously married to a non-Roma individual and when asked to identify herself ethnically she is most likely to say English Irish or French Swedish. All of these point to Milton Gordon's definition of assimilation.

Despite the choices she has made to live an assimilated lifestyle, she has great appreciation for her cultural roots. Growing up, Phoebe had many friendships with individuals outside of her culture. Her family moved often due to work, which Phoebe viewed in a positive light. She believed that the constant relocation she experienced benefited her personal enrichment and her thirst for knowledge and education:

> My culture allowed me to learn about being in a lot of different places with a lot of different cultures and a lot of different people. I think just the lifestyle of the Romanichal is an education in and of itself in that you are adaptable and being adaptable you have to know a little bit and take in different things about different places and different cultures and take in expectations. You just kind of have that ability to adapt that way. At least that's what I thought, I always thought it was a privilege to experience that and I think I brought these experiences with me to the classroom. It was knowledge to build on top the knowledge I learned in the classroom.

Though Phoebe felt that the lifestyle she experienced contributed to her success in the classroom, she witnessed many cultural expectations that made the pursuit of education obsolete among family members who continued to remain separate from working within the confines of mainstream system:

> Some would barely go [to school] at all outside of elementary school. It was probably more like the guys, like my brother who quit . . . He quit because everyone around him quit . . . The boys from a fairly young age, they will go right in and work with dad and it will become a family business. . . . So the education isn't needed . . . more girls will graduate than guys.

Like Phoebe's brother, many men and women adhered to cultural norms of the community in order to work and establish their family within the approval and acceptance of their community.

Despite what she observed around her, Phoebe received encouragement from her parents regarding education. Phoebe's father died when she was in her late teens. She began college but soon decided that the stress of college and her family life were too much and decided to take a break, going on the road with her family for a year. Following this year, she married someone outside of her community and returned to college to complete her degree. Through her many life experiences, Phoebe has chosen a life for herself defined largely by assimilation and yet, she has left the decision of being a part of the traditional practices of her family up to her children. She supported the decision either to assimilate into the culture of her traditional Roma family or to continue on the path that she has chosen. From Phoebe's perspective, the appreciation for knowledge found within this community can allow for a lifestyle described by Margaret Gibson (1988), accommodating what is needed to survive in a modern economic system without full assimilation. Others, such as Vaidy, shared Phoebe's views on accommodation.

Vaidy, like Phoebe, is in her forties and looks back with appreciation and admiration of her Roma heritage. Vaidy lives in the Northeast, holds a PhD and works as a professor at a well-known university. Vaidy's life consists of a large number of non-Roma, non-White friends but also maintains connection with her Roma family. Her husband is not Roma. Vaidy identifies herself racially as Roma and is involved in much Roma activism. Vaidy appears to be living an integrated lifestyle when her life is examined within the context of Berry's (1997) acculturation model. Given her upbringing, it is not surprising that she has held tightly to her Roma roots.

Vaidy lived in one town growing up. She did not live a traveling lifestyle as many other respondents in the study had. She had many friends from outside of her community. As for the expectations her family communicated to her about her life as a Roma, they were more centered around personal behavior and integrity then on rules for or against assimilation, though themes of separation remained:

> That was a very big expectation, that I should maintain these boundaries. That I should take care of my family and be close with my family and not leave my family. Speaking Roma and I don't know I think that is pretty much it. Devotion, dedication to my parents, to my cousins and maintain cleanliness and maintain the language.

Vaidy did not experience many of the barriers to education that other respondents had discussed. For herself, she was pushed to achieve educationally and given the support she needed in order to do so. Vaidy acknowledged that there are many barriers in place for Roma, even today, to access education but, a push against education was not something she identified with:

> Here I am in my [forties] I would have thought I would see a whole generation of educated people who would come after me and I haven't seen that. So that really tells you something about how many of us are in the US who have access to higher education. or even finishing secondary school?

Though Vaidy has not witnessed this entire generation of educated individuals, there can be no doubt that as a shift for this generation was occurring. This was not only true for Roma women but men as well. Henry and Gilbert are among Vaidy's generation, both in their forties, both possessing a college education. Unlike many of the other respondents from this generation with a college degree they, like Vaidy, were able to pursue education in a traditional timeframe and have lived their lives as white collar professionals, unlike many of their older relatives.

Gilbert, in his late forties, resides in Europe but is originally from the Northeast. He was the child of immigrant parents from Eastern Europe, his mother being Roma. As discussed in chapter 2, Gilbert was not aware of his Roma heritage until a neighborhood kid made a racist remark toward Gilbert. It was then that his mother revealed his heritage and, along with it, the understanding that this was a secretive piece of information. Gilbert's parents were both white collar workers, well educated. Gilbert had friends from many ethnicities and while his parents expected him to associate with individuals of good moral character, they had few other expectations for his social relationships.

When asked if Gilbert's mother had any expectations for him as a Roma man or otherwise he had this to relate:

> Her preconceived expectations were that I would be normal. Being normal meaning that in the statistical sense being normal like everyone else. She didn't want me to be specified or different. But this is something, that's why she didn't tell me for the longest time, she didn't want me to turn out to be

Roma. She married a gadje and that's kind of now safe for everyone else and who needs to know the past.

Given her experiences as a Roma in Eastern Europe, Gilbert's mother hoped that her son would be able to live a "normal" life in America. By all accounts, her hopes were fulfilled. Gilbert recalled few times he was discriminated against in any way in his school years. His parents were involved in his schooling and he went on to graduate high school and college, eventually obtaining a master's degree. Gilbert's partner is not Roma and he maintains relationships with individuals who are not Roma in his life.

Gilbert has spent a significant portion of his professional life living overseas. He is heavily engaged in activism for Roma in Europe but admits he knows very little about the life of Roma in the United States. His impressions of Roma today are that a large variety of Roma exist, that some are very traditional, some very insular and some so assimilated one would have to dig, and know to dig, to find out about their Roma heritage.

Henry, in his early forties, also represents the educated population of white collar Roma workers from the middle age group of respondents. Like Gilbert, his father was also a white collar worker and only one of his parents, his father, was Roma. His father was the first generation of U.S. born in his family. Henry's grandparents were Roma immigrants from Eastern Europe. He states that his grandparents never went to school or learned to read. In his own upbringing, Henry saw college and a professional career as a matter of course, following the example of his father. It wasn't until his teen years he discovered the departure from familial expectations that took place when his father decided to go to college:

> When I was growing up I didn't know as a little kid that my father, to become a professional had needed to challenge his parents and call their bluff when they said they would never speak to him again. That is something I learned as a teenager. Growing up I just assumed they had wanted him to go to school. And when I was growing up my grandparents and my parents were pro-education and I was only vaguely aware that wouldn't have been true if I was born a generation earlier . . . It's not the same across all of my family either, my grandmother had siblings, sisters, that went to school in the US and went to college and so her family really caught on quickly to the American mainstream idea but my grandfather did not and my grandmother didn't really have a voice in the house.

Henry observed the changing attitudes toward education that occurred through each generation. Henry, like his father went on to college and eventually earned his master's degree.

Growing up Henry described his group of friends as diverse for the small town he lived in. He knew of Roma in the town but they did not attend school so his interaction with them was limited. His parents had little expectations in the way of friends and they did not care who he chose to marry. Though Henry described himself as being very much in the closet as a Roma growing up, he still managed to pick up the language from his grandparents, a skill which afforded him the ability to obtain multiple positions working with Roma overseas during college. Today he continues to be involved in Roma activism. He is married to a woman who is not Roma and while he hopes to pass on the Roma language and heritage to his son he admits it's challenging because much of his family is not Roma. By all accounts one could say that Henry is very much fully assimilated and yet, he holds a strong identification with his Roma heritage.

The shift in Roma attitudes toward assimilation, education and professional lives found in this generation has left the door wide open for the generations of Roma who were to come after. The last generation of Roma interviewed were represented by individuals in their twenties and thirties. They represent the latest generation of adult Roma, separated by several generations from ancestors who daily feared being run out of town or worse by local gadje. These Roma are the outcome of the current generation of Roma parents, and their experiences reflected the shift in cultural norms and opportunities for Roma that began with their parents.

AN OPEN GENERATION

Josephine is in her thirties. She resides mostly in the Southeast though she travels often due to her husband's work. Josephine identified that she was taught few lessons regarding the life she could expect to have as a Roma woman but, she stated, "I could easily see that the majority of women were home makers." No different from the generations before her, Josephine observed traditional roles for the women in her life.

Josephine was also taught traditional lessons about cleanliness, lessons described by many of the women interviewed, "As far as lessons, I was taught at a very young age to be very clean and take pride in my things and home. Cleanliness is very important to Roma people." Though her family may have been traditional in the ways of cleanliness and gender roles, Josephine's family was very much open to allowing her to have friends outside of her community, friendships she maintains to the present day. Though she attended public school growing up, she left school to attend homeschool in the 10th grade and received her GED. Josephine identified that her parents were open to whatever would make her happy. No barriers were placed on what she was able to accomplish.

Though in some respects Josephine lives a very traditional lifestyle, traveling and homeschooling her own children, she views herself as someone who has integrated her two worlds in a way that is comfortable, a way that works. By leaving the door open to choose what she wanted for herself rather than forcing separation, Josephine was able to choose a path of integration. Because the option to choose her path in life was left open, Josephine never felt that she had to leave behind her community identity in order to accomplish the goals she had for herself. Josephine lives in what she describes as "The best of both worlds."

From Josephine's interview, it was clear she felt that Roma would not be forced to choose between their heritage and lifestyle if they were met with openness and support from their families. Though women may be raised surrounded by women in traditional roles, these women can pass on many lessons from their own experiences that can empower their daughters to pursue whatever life they choose for themselves. These are the lessons that Josephine conveyed in her interview, providing support for the idea that choices for Roma go beyond assimilation or separation alone, for Josephine, a middle ground exists.

Gayle, in her thirties, grew up in a home that closely resembled Josephine's in many ways, a home that was open and supportive. Gayle remembers that she had many friends outside of her own ethnicity growing up, something she attributes to living largely away from the Roma community and having one parent who did not share a Roma heritage. Gayle was not exposed to the "traditional" Roma community until she was older and became curious about her heritage. Gayle was encouraged to pursue many opportunities and interests, to do what she wanted. She described her mother's approach in this way:

> She kind of already had the opportunity to make choices on her own and so she really wanted that for me too and so she was very encouraging for all kinds of things and all different opportunities which I am so thankful, she essentially said as long as we were doing something safe you know she was encouraging us to do it.

Unlike many of the Roma women interviewed, Gayle was not restricted by being a woman within a traditional community because she resided largely away from them. Gayle was not exposed to the traditional gender roles in her immediate family that most of the women interviewed described. She did not move around growing up, her parents held permanent jobs that did not require a traveling lifestyle. From all appearances, Gayle's immediate family had assimilated even into marrying outside of the Roma ethnicity, the second stage of assimilation according to Milton Gordon's stages of assimilation (1964). Gayle possesses a college degree and partially attributes this success to her parents' encouragement and support.

Despite the benefits of living within a largely assimilated family, as Gayle got older, she became interested in the life of "traditional" Roma and chose to live within one such community for a brief time. While there, she was exposed to a life much different from the one in which she grew up. She began to see gender differences between the men and women and the barriers that existed for the women in these communities, recognizing that the traditional ways of life may not be conducive to the education of Roma women:

> The community I had for a while was very traditionally conservative so there was a lot of things men could do that if women did it would be absolutely called into question but if men were doing it, it was totally accepted. It depends on the community and level of conservativeness . . . I would venture to guess if people were more open to educational opportunities you would see a major shift in men and women's roles because a lot of times if women are dependent or if they are with their families of the men they marry. You don't have a lot of power or agency . . . the only way women have that power in the community is if they are older. . . . it can be very constricting I think.

Gayle saw the life of this traditional community as restrictive and identified that the traditional ideas discussed by participants, like Peaches, in her eighties, are still in existence among some communities even today. Within these communities women are often restricted to the role of homemaker and mother, while for some this is a role they gladly fulfill, for others, this is the only option they are presented with when they come of age.

Gayle sees these traditional practices as largely problematic because this lifestyle prevents individuals from being able to pursue careers or education. Gayle identified the disparities that exist in career and education between those, like herself, who are largely assimilated and those who live within traditional Roma communities, those who prefer an isolated and separate lifestyle:

> I work at a university but the point is I work for someone. I'm not having a fortune telling office or doing driveways or buying and selling cars or something like that which is more on your own type of thing.

Gayle referred to the jobs traditionally held by Roma, jobs that did not require a consistent schedule nor do they require working underneath anyone. Gayle viewed these types of occupations in a largely negative light:

> It lends itself to instability. I mean you might go to an area and have a lot of money and then in winter it's feast and famine. The instability is not contributing to an environment where you are going to send a kid to school. If you are on the road in the summer there are a lot of practical careers but there is a lot of getting back to what people in the community think it is also a form of control and people being scared to let go of what they know. It is the fear of the

unknown. I think older people especially are weary of that because they see a lot of erosion of some of the traditional things they value.

When asked if she thought women who live within Roma communities must leave their community and assimilate, Gayle answered passionately:

> Well if the people or culture are going to force them to make that choice then yes but part if it is not having any support from your community that is some of the biggest issues. Some of the people haven't even gotten past 5th grade I mean, forget about high school, high school is wow. I think there are ways people can access education but the barriers in their way are so great . . . sometimes they don't have the support and they don't have the resources.

For Gayle, Margret Gibson's (1988) idea of accommodation without assimilation is a real possibility if communities could take hold of it. Gayle sees assimilation as unnecessary to education but only if communities will choose to support Roma in pursuit of it. Gayle identified that the lack of support was one of the greatest barriers to receiving an education in Roma communities.

Though Gayle believes that traditional values and practices can largely be preserved, even when community members choose to pursue education, she, like others, also believes that there are some aspects that will and should be changed:

> I think that there are aspects of traditional Roma culture that are not that good you know so I don't think getting your daughter married at 15 or 16 is a good thing. Is it traditional? Yes. Is it good? No. I don't think when you talk about tradition of what's cultural you have to live up to this gold standard that it's everything that makes community so great because I think there are a lot of things that are not so great and I think that is one of them. There are things outside the culture that could be good. It is unfortunate that [we] are trying to tell somebody you have to make the choice between being a gypsy or being educated, that's wrong. I don't agree with that. I think if [we] want to preserve our culture and our language then being educated is a way to do that . . . it's just we have a certain mind-set about what education could or might do and it's a lot of fear.

Gayle views the lives of Roma living traditional lifestyles, resisting education, as a culture in decline within the context of their social situation. As society and technology advance, these communities are being pushed further and further toward the margins of society, making traditional means of generating income almost obsolete. This creates even more barriers for education and work for women as well as men. Gayle believes that things must change in order for the state of the Roma to change. While she believes it is possible for these changes to take place, she acknowledges that these changes must take place from within the community itself:

> I don't want to sound like a pessimist but I want to be realistic and I don't think the situation will get better till we do something about it and no one is going to come along and say yeah you know, I really should help Roma people. No one is going to do that unless we do it for ourselves.

She expressed tapping into an understood idea that Roma are invisible under-served minority in the United States. She believes passionately that because of the invisibility of the Roma and the marginalized treatment they have received worldwide, Roma must bring about change on their own if they hope to see a shift in the trajectory of future generations.

From Gayle's perspective, a life outside full assimilation is possible for Roma communities without eliminating them from an educated life. The pursuit of educational achievement is not possible, in her eyes, with complete preservation of the traditional lifestyle. Like so many of the respondents within the study, Gayle believes an integrated lifestyle is possible, and potentially economically necessary, but only if change comes from within Roma communities themselves.

Of those from Gayle's generation, Rachel was the youngest of the respondents, in her twenties. Rachel was raised in the Northeast, close to her extended family in an area where Roma are widely recognizable. Like Gayle, growing up she had, and continues to have, friends who are from many different ethnic backgrounds. She identifies that though her immediate family is okay with this, her extended family is "somewhat confused" by this choice. She believes that her extended family would probably much rather that she had only Roma friends. Though hesitant to say with 100 percent confidence, she identifies that she probably would have greater connections with non-Roma friends if it weren't for her family. Growing up, Rachel did not move often as many respondents have reported of themselves or other traditional Roma. Rachel is engaged to a non-Roma man, a decision her family had to learn to accept at first, they have since come to happily embrace.

Though Rachel possesses many ties outside of her Roma community, including her college education and work experience, she discusses that she thinks about being Roma often:

> [I think about it] a lot, especially now. I think about it a lot and I try to be proud of it and I try to think, you know, what am I doing that is stereotypical and what is not stereotypical, am I being a good representation of my community? I think about that a lot.

Though much of Rachel's lifestyle points toward assimilation, it was not difficult to see, as she told her story, that her family and heritage play a significant role in her life. Though her path has differed from other women in her family by going to college, their influence still directed the path she would take:

> I wanted to join the military actually when I was in high school and I know that even my parents [didn't like] that, it wasn't something appropriate for woman to do. You would bring you know shame on our family if you did that. I just remember everyone was in an uproar about that so needless to say . . .

Even among a more liberally minded set of parents, rules of separation and appropriateness continue to be enforced. Rachel described how cultural norms have played out in the lives of other Roma relatives, "You know all of the other women in my family have not gone to college at all and they had kids very young and only one of them actually works outside the home."

In spite of Rachel's description of other women in her family, one might say that she and her parents are far more assimilated and nontraditional than her family but, for Rachel, this depends on who she is being compared with. She believes she may appear more assimilated when compared with some of her traditional family members while to others she may be seen as far more traditional. Either way, there is evidence in Rachel's life that to some degree, assimilation, or at the least integration, has taken place. There has been a separation from the traditional ways of her family in order for her parents and herself to become educated and yet, she has not left the old ways or her identity behind. Like many other women and men in the study, Rachel's life exemplifies that Roma can maintain strong ties to their identity and become educated and, though not all Roma ways of life are conducive to education or mainstream occupations, one can still integrate these ways of life into behaviors viewed as "assimilation."

Teddy

Like Rachel, Teddy has found that he too can maintain strong ties to his Roma identity while living a life very much assimilated beyond traditional practice. Teddy is in his late thirties and grew up in a small farming town in the Midwest. Teddy's father is a Gorga and his mother is a Romanichal. Growing up in such a small town, Teddy did not have many friends of diverse backgrounds and, aside from his family, he maintained close friendships with the largely White population of the town. Teddy identified he felt privileged in the life he had growing up and in those relationships though there were times that people assumed his family were Native American and associated many negative connotations with his family.

Teddy believes that his parents represented a departure from the attitudes and ideals of his other relatives:

There was always a strong emphasis from my family to get an education. They had high standards for me and it was a lot different from my growing up than many of my cousins who I grew up with who didn't have any expectations in their own households of going to school, of finishing school. You know, sticking with it and getting an education. You know it really was the opposite. The boys were going to help with the family business and working on the road with their fathers and uncles and those sorts of things. When compared with my Romanichal family, I really had an exceptional experience in terms of higher standards of expectations to do my best and get an education and picking out a career, it was whatever I wanted to do.

Though we have identified many Roma narratives that recounted similar experiences to Teddy's these are often seen as the exception rather than the rule in many Roma families. As we are discussing, a shift is undoubtedly occurring in many Roma families and communities in the United States yet, traditional thinking and ways of life remain.

Teddy described life for his Romanichal relatives and how many of these attitudes and expectations of traditional lives have been passed on:

My grandfather had 9 brothers and sisters and then my grandfather got saved and was a pastor and he settled down his family. He was born in a tent and grew up traveling around. My mom and aunt were born on the road and you know traveling trailers that didn't have toilets because it wasn't clean and sanitary. When my grandpa got saved, he settled down and all his brothers and sisters and their kids, my cousins, they all traveled and hit the road but they would come back to where I grew up living. So my cousins would come in and out of school there sometimes, maybe 3rd to 6th grade, they didn't go higher than 8th, some of them did but they passed through.

While Teddy's grandfather chose a much more assimilated life, and thus passed this on to his daughter and subsequently Teddy, much of his extended family remained on the road. He observed the difference in their lifestyles, as well as their education and the expectations for their future.

Unlike many of his Roma relatives, Teddy's parents were very engaged in his education. His parents expected him to attend college and encouraged and supported him in that decision. "I was sort of an odd duck when it came to that because I had support system from my family, from my parents, not like my cousins had, they didn't have the support system you know family pushing them and challenging them to do their best from an education standpoint." Out of all of his cousins, Teddy identifies he is just one of a handful of family who made it into college. Despite this, Teddy maintains that familial ties remained close, he too hit the road in the summers to work with his family and was always around his cousins, an important tie for an only child.

Teddy went on to graduate college and engage in many different professional careers in recent years. Though he has participated in political and government positions and other successful ventures, he maintains strong ties with his Roma family and roots. He participates in Roma activism and maintains a pride in his identity. By all accounts, Teddy too could be said to be largely assimilated in mainstream society and yet he feels a connected and close part of the Roma community, not just in America but worldwide.

Benny

Unlike Teddy, Benny grew up without much, if any really, connection to his Roma roots. Benny, thirty-one, grew up in the Midwest without knowledge of his Roma heritage until a later point in his life. His family immigrated to the United States from Eastern Europe around the turn of the twentieth century. As Benny identifies, the goal from the start was very clearly to assimilate. Like many immigrant families, they hid an identity that had caused them misfortune in their countries of origin and used their life in America as a fresh start:

> When my family came here, it was very clear their goal was assimilation. My grandparents wouldn't teach any Czech. They would speak to each other in Slavic words but none of my family understood what they were saying . . . They were very clear that no you guys don't know this language, you are Americans . . . even trying to wash away their Czech heritage because simply put they knew it was bad news to be different here in the US.

At some point Benny's mom began to do some digging into their family genealogy and it was only then that the knowledge of their Roma ancestry became apparent. Before that time, Benny saw himself as a typical Midwesterner with a family that had worked together at the same factory for generations. As his mom began to dig into the family history, they begin to see and observe that many of their customs and norms within the family aligned with those of his Roma ancestors. Benny has sought to make connection with those roots since that time and, in many ways, regrets the loss of the ties to his heritage that have been hidden for so long.

Despite his lack of early ties to his heritage, Benny too saw his mom's encouragement toward education as exceptional. His mom wanted him to go to college and get a degree and didn't place as much emphasis on working as many of the other males in his family experienced. Benny was raised by his mother alone and observed her making many sacrifices to ensure his future could be what he wanted it to be and could be one that would enable him to comfortably support himself.

Life for Benny's mother, coming from a family of immigrants, was challenging:

She had a father who wasn't in the picture much, he was an alcoholic. Her mother wasn't there either. Basically she and her brothers and sisters kind of raised themselves. And they had to do whatever they had to do to make ends meet you know a poor family living in their inner city . . . They just had to survive and make things happen. To keep the house you know. In and out of the orphan schools and everything like that, state run facilities and stuff. It was assumed they had to do that which was part of how she raised me and what she expected of me was not to have to go through that. It was do what you have to do you know enjoy life. She started working when she was 16 at the plant. She only just retired and she started there in the early 70's. It was very work and do what you got to do.

Benny saw that the life that his mother and her parents experienced as an immigrant family influenced their desire to assimilate further into American society, to move beyond the challenges they had experienced in Eastern Europe and those they had faced in trying to find their place in the United States. Teddy identified that even those challenges were glossed over in order to minimize their experiences as immigrants. "I think that even if it did bother them or even if it did you know make life difficult they certainly weren't going to show it and they didn't want their kids thinking it was a thing." Benny sees the hiding of his familial origins and their challenges as unfortunate:

A lot of us have changed here they came here from parents who wanted to reinvent themselves and all of their culture was lost. It was completely white-washed . . . there were so many of us that live here . . . and it is a big family secret, so a lot of us think they're Hungarian or German or something like that. The culture has been erased.

In this statement, for many Roma in America, we see a departure from the lives of those in Europe. Had Benny's family remained in the Czech Republic today, they would likely have faced significant discrimination as Roma, where today they have entirely assimilated into the mainstream America. This too is unfortunate to Benny who observed that many people came to America with the hopes of being able to get freedom from the prejudice they experienced in their home countries and still be themselves. Yet, as many have identified in their narratives, they were "pushed out of work and society and couldn't be who they were . . ." leaving them with no choice but to assimilate. The narrative of Benny's family is not an uncommon one. This is a narrative leaving many young Roma such as Benny with the desire to proudly and loudly connect with his Roma heritage and incorporate as much of this identity into the life he leads today.

CONCLUSION

Historically, cultural norms emphasized voluntary/involuntary separation from the gadje, this meant creating occupations that would allow them to exist outside their economic control. These occupations made gadje education obsolete or difficult to achieve given their traveling lifestyle. Other researchers highlight that historically Roma engaged in traveling because it proved to be more lucrative professionally than sedentary lives. Traveling Roma may have also engaged in tinplating, wage labor and artisan craft. At one time, 77 percent of Romanichal stated they were involved in horse trading. Some anthropologists believe that the large shift of Roma women in the 1930s to fortune telling kept many Roma from urban poverty during a trying time for the United States (Chohaney, 2012) and that much of their success or ability to survive economically has come from filling labor needs as they are observed.

As years progressed, and the traveling lifestyle became less common, attitudes toward gadje influence remained the same, unsurprisingly given the continued prevalence of discrimination against Roma discussed in previous chapters. As a result, separation was widely emphasized and formal schooling, an institution of the gadje, was not. Because many parents did not hold education beyond middle school, it was not emphasized for their children. Traditional gender roles made education an unnecessary achievement for many women.

Over time, occupations and traditional roles for women have begun to shift as more and more women have begun to acquire education out of necessity. Seeing the economic and personal stability that came through education, many women shifted their cultural values and began to pass them on to their own daughters. These daughters today believe that a much more open attitude toward education exists, and for women, an emphasis on education has emerged.

While suspicion and a wish to remain separate from the gadje remains prevalent among many Roma, many now see that the accommodation of gadje practices into Roma ways of life is possible. Though an entirely conclusive answer cannot be reached given the variation among Roma families and communities, one can hypothesize, based on the narratives of this study, that even among those living the most historically traditional lifestyle today, formal education is valued and encouraged.

Though the life of the American Roma, to some, may appear disconnected from what Roma face internationally, I did not find this to be the case. Most of the respondents' lived experiences mirrored the lives of their Roma counterparts worldwide in some form. The narratives collected for this chapter exemplified the impact that structural oppression has on marginalized individuals regardless of the country in which they reside and also exemplify what Roma have been able to accomplish by empowering themselves with education.

Throughout this chapter many barriers to Roma lives were discussed, often coming from within the Roma community itself. In the coming chapters, I wish to delve further into the barriers Roma encounter from those outside of their community. In previous chapters I discussed prejudice and discrimination as a normal part of the Roma experience. In this chapter I identify how this has led to many Roma seeking separate lifestyles. In the coming chapter I will explore the further effects of the prejudice and discrimination on Roma access to social resources, working and living conditions and their ability to decide independently their methods of acculturation.

Chapter Four

The Price of Roma Prejudice

Structural and Personal Marginalization

As discussed in a previous chapter, in 1970 a Chicago newspaper featured a "settled" Romani family purported to be living the American dream. The article paints the life of a settled Roma as an ideal one in sharp contrast to the lives of migratory Roma who live an existence portrayed as crowded and constantly at odds with the law. Janko, thirty-seven, the father of the featured family and his mother Ti-Tha were able to provide a look into the Roma experience, one that opposed the depiction of an idealized settled life, one that underscored the reality of Roma existence:

> Don't think its ever going to change, Its like if you're Italian, you're automatically a member of the mafia: we evoke a negative image . . . There are a lot of Gypsies who won't admit it. I can tell you about lawyers, police officers, real estate people. . . . They all lead normal lives. The don't want it known. There's nothing you can do. Janko, thirty-seven. (Yuenger, 1987, D1)

> I really made a mistake. If I had to do it over again I'd raise my kids 100 percent Gypsy. Gypsies believe in family. Children respect their parents. These non-Gypsy kids you see today, what does all their book learning get them? I'll tell you one thing for sure. They're prejudiced against us. We're targets, there can be a million gypsies leading normal lives but you never hear about that. Everybody is against us, the politicians, the press, the government even the churches. Boy it's a good thing you don't have to go to church to go to heaven. Ti-Tha. (Yuenger, 1987, D1)

Both Janko and his mother formulated a negative view of Roma interaction with society. For both, no matter how assimilated the Roma has become, there would always be those in society who viewed them as outsiders. These narratives highlight the prejudice they face daily and perhaps idealize the separate lifestyle as one that allows for insulation from prejudice (Yuenger, 1987).

For American Roma, prejudice may most often take on the form of inter-personal prejudice in the present day, though evidence of structural prejudice in America is certainly in existence. In the 1880s laws were passed barring Gypsy entrance into the United States. Two articles from that time highlight the prejudice with which gypsy immigrants were treated at Ellis Island and the tragic experience of those immigrants turned away. In 1909 a group of Gypsies from South America was denied entrance at Ellis Island because they were gypsy. While they were able to prove they had ample wealth with them they were denied access based on their identity (*New York Times*, 1909). The author is somewhat sympathetic to their plight stating they are preferable to the American grown hobo; however, he places the onus on the group for coming out as gypsy proudly rather than identifying themselves as common tradesmen. He goes on to say that the commissioner was right in denying them access because, "We have too many unproductive nomads now and people who come here from foreign lands are expected to do their share in developing the industries of the country and becoming good citizens."

Another bizarre article from the same time highlights the case of gypsies who were not allowed entrance into the United States, had their weapons taken at Ellis Island, were deemed "undesirables" and, in the article, were said to have used their own children as weapons, seeking to bludgeon the inspectors by flinging their children at them (*New York Times*, 1909). Many articles of the time highlighted the undesirable nature of gypsy immigrants and their violent or bizarre response to being deported as evidence of their being unfit to enter America. Many gypsies seeking asylum from the perse-cution of their home countries were denied access simply because, as gyp-sies, they were unwanted. These articles exemplify just one example of the structural oppression Roma have faced in America historically, structural oppressions that continue to impact many today.

In present-day Europe, prejudice takes on extreme forms of structural and personal oppression. In February of 2016, French police evicted over 350 gypsies (Roma) from a shanty town constructed on an abandoned rail line. Gypsies, having no alternative, constructed over 130 makeshift homes, which were evacuated and destroyed during the police raid. Gypsy presence is widely resisted in France. *The Express* reported that the prime minister of France has declared that gypsies "cannot integrate" into French society suc-cessfully and has identified gypsies as "foreigners." (Perring, 2016). Gypsies in France not only struggle to find the most basic of necessities for them-selves and their families, they are met with resistance from mainstream soci-ety in many countries throughout the world. The resistance they encounter increases the level of negative outcomes they experience, significantly im-pacting their physical health, mental health, social mobility and economic well-being as well as their identity development, a factor which should serve as a buffer against the effects of discrimination.

In previous chapters, I discuss prejudice, commonly defined by attitudes toward a group or specific individuals within a group, comprised of many individual and social components (Stangor, 2009). This prejudice, at the individual level may look like hostility, rejection or strongly held negative beliefs that take on behavioral forms. At the societal level prejudice most often results in discrimination, unfair and unequal treatment, and looks like social stratification, resistance of mainstream groups to the presence of minority groups and widely accepted discriminatory practices toward immigrant or minority groups (COA, 2007).

Outcomes related to the experience of prejudice and discrimination are poor (Karlsen & Nazroo, 2001). The experience of prejudice has been closely associated with increased rates of poverty (Crandall & Stangor, 2005). Life satisfaction is decreased. Social support and resources are far scarcer among those who experience prejudice on a consistent basis. Williams (1999) identifies that racism and discrimination have a negative impact on SES, increase negative health outcomes, decrease overall social mobility and limit opportunities to improve one's SES. Liebkind and Jasinskaja-Lahti (2000) identify that the experience of discrimination is closely connected with poor psychological outcomes among immigrant groups.

In the previous chapters I identify the resistance that Roma encounter to their attempts at assimilation, or engagement with mainstream culture, in the form of prejudice and discrimination. I then discuss what assimilated, integrated or separated lifestyles look like for Roma in the United States. As previously stated, it was important that I establish prejudice as a normal part of the Roma experience and that I give a broader perspective on Roma lives in the United States involving more commonplace things such as education, work and family structures and expectations.

In this chapter, I identify the impact of this resistance by examining how Roma in the United States and Europe experience prejudice and discrimination and how this impacts Roma both socially and psychologically. I found it impossible in this chapter to exclude European Roma from the story I am telling for reasons discussed in the introduction of this book.

I examine in this chapter how Roma encounter barriers that make it impossible for them to own their acculturative choices. Petrova (2004) asserts that there are many misconceptions surrounding Roma acculturation, many do wish to integrate but are often pushed out by mainstream society's prejudice and the Roma's unwillingness to entirely relinquish their culture. Many Roma find it difficult to secure occupations outside their traditional ways of making money and are resisted when they try to reside in permanent homes due to racism (Apelseth, 2013). This type of resistance to Roma assimilation and their subsequent encounters with discrimination and prejudice has many negative outcomes for the individual socially, emotionally and psychologically.

IMPACT OF RESISTANCE TO ROMA ASSIMILATION

A case presented by Ureche and Franks (2007) involves a young girl's complaints of stomach problems, weight loss and feeling tired when faced with returning to school. She reports she often feels scared and isolated at school. She is symptomatic of anxiety and/or depression and a direct link between these symptoms and the bullying she has received at school exists. She identifies that boys have been following her to the bathroom, calling her names and telling her to "go back where she came from." The resistance of those in the dominant group to her participation in a major social institution, school, has resulted in an experience of significant negative outcomes. The resulting symptoms and resistance to returning to school are evidence of the effects on her psychological well-being. A Roma professional from the United Kingdom who participated in the Children's Study identifies what many Roma children encounter at school:

> Our children go to school from a low age up to ten years old. They come out of school and they can't even read. Why? What are they doing? They put them at the back of the class and take no notice of them. (Kathleen, professional, Yorkshire, 32)

School is not the only place where Roma, seeking to engage with the dominant group, are turned away or isolated. Roma report discrimination in school, on the street, as they seek employment, in restaurants and local pubs. When they are able to secure work they are often underpaid or exploited (Lane, Spencer & Jones, 2014). Roma who seek to become "housed, living in permanent homes, are also exposed to racism from their neighbors and this has a negative impact on their well-being" (Lane, Spencer & Jones).

Though, as Berry points out (1997), the individual must choose the method of acculturation they wish to follow, they must also be allowed by the dominant group to follow this course of action. Without some form of permission or acceptance, a minority or immigrant group will not succeed in fully or even partially assimilating. Widely criticized for their unwillingness to engage with the societies they inhabit, Roma are met with reluctance as they seek to fully or partially assimilate. This reluctance by the mainstream has resulted in Roma experiencing distress which mirrors that of the young girl reluctant to attend school.

In addition to the emotional impact of assimilative resistance in the form of prejudice and discrimination, Roma who encounter an increased resistance to their attempts at assimilation have shortened lifespans (Lane, Spencer &

Jones, 2014). Roma are two times as likely to experience depression and three times as likely to experience anxiety as those in the dominant group (Lane, Spencer & Jones). Data exists to support that Roma in Europe experience resistance to their assimilation, and its resulting affects, in their daily lives but the picture in America is much harder to piece together.

AMERICAN ROMA AND RESISTANCE TO ASSIMILATION

In Fey's narrative one is easily able to identify resistance to the Roma way of life. As previously related, Fey was a part of a forced assimilation program. In a rare occurrence, the dominant group sought to forcibly bring Roma children into the dominant culture, forcing them to leave behind their cultural roots:

> Fey: No, when we were in the orphanages we were punished for speaking Roma which was the language, our main language.
> *Interviewer: So they essentially didn't want you to have any connection with that part of your life at all.*
> Fey: My name was changed, it was (name omitted). My name was changed to (name omitted). I was a white girl.
> *Interviewer: Did you feel like that's who you were?*
> Fey: Never. I was only a kid but never. Which of course you know was a problem . . .

Fey was faced with the situation of having to choose one culture over another. This dichotomy of identities, the pressure to choose between cultures felt from their communities and the outside world was not unique to Fey. Peaches, a woman in her forties in the Southeast, describes it this way: "But for the most part, my life was divided into two sections, I was Romanichal but I was leading a Gorja life you could say." Peaches adeptly describes the experiences of living in a state of double consciousness.

Research has shown that living in a continual state of double consciousness, facing pressure from multiple directions can have significant impact on one's identity, self-esteem, self-concept and core beliefs about the individual's group (Lyubansky & Eidelson, 2005). Of the American Roma interviewed, more than half identify an experience of "Double Consciousness" at some point in their lives as they sought to navigate their identity as a Roma and their participation in mainstream society. The stress and subsequent consequences of this state of double consciousness can arguably be said to be the resulting impact of assimilative resistance by the mainstream.

Others among the Roma interviewed emphasize the resistance they have encountered in America and their comments convey a feeling of discouragement, despair, fear and, a hopelessness regarding the ability for Roma to successfully integrate into mainstream society without recourse. Ruby, a woman in her forties from the Southeast, places this in a historical context:

> Well because years ago you know gypsies were ostracized they were run out of town for practicing fortune telling, dickering, and so, there is also a lot of stereotypes and a lot of non-gypsies, gorjas, believe things like gypsies will steal your children, and you know they will cheat you out of your money, they will steal from you. So, it just it was always something, I think that years ago they lived in fear, so, I think that was just perpetuated from generation to generation.

Ruby identifies that resistance to the presence of Roma has been a historical occurrence in America. She acknowledges that the fear created from encountering resistance has been passed down generationally and continues to impact acculturative strategies of Roma today.

Louisa, a woman in her thirties from the Southwest United States, describes what the situation is like for many in modern America:

> We just knew we was completely different it's like, we're in the same world but we are on a different planet. Everything that happens in the economy doesn't affect us. Were in our own little world, we try not to let anyone know who we are because no one is going to come help us. We are discriminated against if they find out who we are. Like everybody else gots rights, Black people have rights, Gay people have rights, Animals have rights we ain't got no rights anywhere in the world, in any country. And something else, they know the gypsies don't have no education so they know the gypsies don't know what their civil rights are. Like the White people can say, well, I have rights, gypsies don't know they have rights, they don't know they are Americans, they don't know they have civil rights. I keep mine on my refrigerator so that they know that we have rights. But, it's in the book of congress that a gypsy is not allowed to hold a government position.

Louisa describes the despair with which she views her position in the world. The desire to have rights, to exist as others do and the disappointment that not only do Roma lack rights worldwide but they are unfairly targeted and discriminated against. Louisa describes her state of being as a defensive one, demanding that she have the same rights as others in America. Louisa gives evidence that she has experienced distress related to her social position, further evidence that she has experienced forms of discrimination and prejudice in her lifetime. Louisa and others interviewed intimate that their lack of rights is highlighted by the ease with which they are so easily portrayed as racist caricatures on reality television, bringing to the surface the conflict between the desire of some to assimilate and the reality of the mainstream's attitude toward Roma.

MEDIA INFLUENCE ON PROCESS OF ACCULTURATION

Research on minority portrayals in entertainment media overwhelmingly identifies that negative portrayals of minorities influence negative attitudes of the majority group toward the minority group. These portrayals also influence the treatment of the majority group toward the minority group, influence minority groups' willingness to interact with the majority group and impact the minority group's ability to successfully navigate social spaces. These barriers increase the challenge of acculturation for minority groups within the United States (Esses, Medianu & Lawson, 2013; Fryberg et al., 2008; Leavitt et al., 2015; Mastro & Greenberg, 2000; Schemer, 2012; Schlueter & Davidov, 2013).

Research shows that the dominant group's perception of minorities or immigrants, often impacted by attitudes disseminated through the media (Mastro & Greenberg, 2000), has a significant impact on the minority's / immigrant's ability to decide what acculturative strategy they will engage in. A study by Croucher identifies that among Western Europeans, those that feel threatened by immigrant groups are less likely to believe that immigrants desire to assimilate, thus increasing their overall resistance to immigrant presence and alternate acculturative strategies. Rojas, Navas, Savans-Jimenez and Cuadrado (2014) show that Spaniards who have greater prejudice toward immigrants prefer full assimilation in the public and private lives of immigrants. Those who hold less prejudice are more open to immigrants choosing integration in their public and private lives. Among immigrant groups, those who hold less prejudice toward the majority are open to public assimilation and integration in their private lives. Those who experience greater prejudice are more likely to prefer that they integrate publicly only enough to meet their needs while privately they prefer to remain separate.

Negative portrayals have a significant impact on the way majority group members treat minority group members, influence minority groups' willingness to interact with the majority group and impact the minority groups' ability to successfully navigate acculturative preferences (Esses, Medianu & Lawson, 2013; Fryberg et al., 2008; Leavitt et al., 2015; Mastro & Greenberg, 2000; Schemer, 2012; Schlueter & Davidov, 2013). Among those in America and Europe who are engaged in the challenging process of navigating social spaces within the acculturative process and who are simultaneously combating the effects of mainstream media, are the Roma.

In October 2012, *The Guardian* reported that the airing of the widely popular *My Big Fat Gypsy Wedding* (MBFGW) of the United Kingdom had reportedly led to a significant increase in physical and sexual assaults, hostility and bullying motivated by racism and directed toward Roma in European schools. The consequences of these racially motivated behaviors included an increase in Roma withdrawals from public schools and documented emotional damage to Roma children (Plunkett, 2012). These discriminatory actions directed at Roma pushed against the strides they have made in the United Kingdom toward successful assimilation.

Oskana Marafioti, author of *American Gypsy: A Memoir*, and an American Roma has been loudly verbal regarding the harm that the portrayal of Roma on *MBFGW* could cause. An article penned in 2012 by Marafioti details her encounters with the producers of the show. Initially excited about the show, once she understood the angle producers hoped to take, she came to recognize quickly the danger that such a show could pose to the American Roma community. Her first reservation came when she recognized she was not what the producers were looking for:

> As a college graduate, a classically trained pianist, and member of the film industry, I did not fit the bill of the "real gypsies" he was interested in meeting; everyone he had been interviewing resembled me far more than the tambourine-jangling caricature he had in mind.

Marafioti recognized that she was not what producers were hoping for and that her efforts to encourage a direction that would portray Roma in a more positive and realistic light went unheeded. In her article, she discusses what she had hoped to communicate:

> a show like this can harm a group of people already under scrutiny, people who also have families to watch over. Being a Roma isn't a way of life or a cult. We aren't Gypsy by choice or calling. No one can decide to become a Gypsy one day. We are a race of close to 10 million, with a culture that spans centuries and across continents. It is one thing to present a willing group of people in a negative light, but quite another to represent an entire race of people as a niche stereotype. This is particularly dangerous since people know so little about us and yet think they know so much.

Marafioti is cognizant that negative portrayals of Roma have historically damaged Roma in the eyes of the mainstream. Marafioti hoped to convey that Roma and their lives are more than just an entertainment concept or troupe and that to portray them in a stereotypical way has real-life consequences for the Roma community.

Many Roma are in agreement with Marafioti's premise. Fener, a Roma woman in her forties from the Southeast United States, identifies the embarrassment that *My Big Fat American Gypsy Wedding* (Herman, 2012) has caused her personally:

> Yeah, you see this stuff on TV like *My Big Fat Gypsy Wedding* is there . . . to me that is embarrassing, I am embarrassed. We have gypsies that are Dr.'s attorneys, represented in the UN now and you try to break away from what people seem to think gypsies are. Fortune tellers and you know, out stealing

off people. And well they'll steal your children from you. I heard that one growing up . . . I can't stand that, they make us look like a bunch of idiots and again it's all for TV. They get paid they get money for being on this reality TV and it's all a big lie . . . but feeds into the stereotypical thing of what these people believe.

Fener conveys a personal sense of frustration and embarrassment toward the way Roma are being portrayed and acknowledges that it is a further confirmation of stereotypes about Roma that have been held for generations. Others, like Ruby, have mixed feelings regarding the show though she admits it has brought shame to her personally:

> Well I feel like with the advent of TLC (laughs) [The Gypsies] become famous or infamous I don't know and I feel like it has brought wealth and that it, I don't know, its brought shame in a way to some of us that don't want to be looked at like that . . . in a way it's a thing of shame . . . It's a lot of mixed feelings.

Ruby acknowledges that for those on the show, wealth and notoriety have come, but it has also exposed the identity of Roma who wished to remain hidden.

My Big Fat Gypsy Wedding (Herman, 2012; Poppelwell, 2012), in both America as well as the United Kingdom has already impacted the lives of the Roma. Plunkett (2012) identifies that the mistreatment of Roma in the United Kingdom has significantly increased and that this mistreatment has been tied directly to the show. What has been identified by experts as "measurable long-term harm" has been observed within Roma communities. This includes physical and sexual assaults, racist bullying, hostile questioning, damaged self-esteem and removal from school due to bullying. These outcomes have all been linked with the airing of this *MBFGW*. Posters for upcoming seasons tout, "Bigger. Fatter. Gypsier." causing many within the Roma community to protest the flippant way their plight as a marginalized group has been considered by the mainstream and by television networks. One Roma interviewed by the reporter, seeking to contextualize the problematic language of the show posed the question, "Supposing the posters had sad 'Bigger. Fatter. Blacker'?" (Plunkett).

The harmful impact of *My Big Fat Gypsy Wedding* (Poppelwell, 2012) in the United Kingdom prompted a complaint from organizations within the Roma community (Bohan, 2013). The complaint claimed that negative stereotypes endorsed by the show encouraged prejudice toward Roma. The complaint was rejected and no further action was taken. The commissions dedicated to ensuring appropriate content failed to acknowledge the significant impact that *My Big Fat Gypsy Wedding* was having on its citizens. One Roma woman recounted the impact of the show on her life and her children (Bohan):

> We want the children to get an education but there is a lot of prejudice espe-
> cially since the 'My Big Fat Gypsy Wedding' programme. We pulled them out
> of school while that was going on. It was a bad thing, they posted up all over
> the place, it was disgusting.

This Roma woman quoted in *The Journal* gives evidence to the very real way
that Roma have been impacted through current negative media portrayals.
Taking her children out of school in order to avoid the prejudice that resulted
from these portrayals significantly impacts their ability to successfully navigate relationships with those outside of their communities and to obtain a
competitive education.

It would perhaps provide some clarity to both the Roma community and
mainstream society to know how the stars of the show themselves feel about
the way they are portrayed or the feelings that other Roma have toward them
as a result of their involvement in the show. Based on their contractual
obligations, however, many are unable to speak out regarding their roles. I
connected with one of the stars of the show to determine if this person could
be interviewed. While she acknowledged her interest in taking part, she
indicated her contractual obligations meant she was not allowed to take part
in any interviews or photo ops of any kind, effectively preventing her from
having any say outside of what is orchestrated within the program.

There can be little doubt that the portrayal of Gypsies/Roma on American
television as well as Europe is problematic. Again, this is in no way an exhaustive account of television portrayals but is meant to characterize television portrayals of Roma worldwide. These accounts are also meant to highlight the
response of the Roma community to these portrayals. Consistent themes emerge
through television portrayals leaving Roma to feel inaccurately portrayed, marginalized and othered. Despite the protests and critical reception of these shows,
they continue to be popular with the mainstream and producers continue to seek
opportunities to capitalize on the American fascination with Roma. A recent
Facebook (n.a., 2016) post by one such producer read as follows:

> A UK TV production company is looking for the REAL gypsies of the USA!
> Are you a newlywed moving in with your new Prince or Princess? On the hunt
> for the perfect daughter-in-law? We want to hear from you! Message me if
> you're the REAL DEAL . . .

This advertisement leaves little doubt that the desire to capitalize on the
American appetite for outlandish Roma lives is still very much alive. The
only response to this obnoxious plea came from a Roma woman who simply
responded: "Please go away."

Many Roma I interviewed expressed dismay and concern over the role
of Roma portrayals on the quality of Roma lives. Donald, fifty-six, expressed Roma media portrayals have done "a lot of harm" and that he was

"at one time willing to go to congress or wherever we needed to go to start bringing some kind of plan up for Roma, for Gypsies." Like many other Roma, he expressed concern over the way Roma are portrayed and sees a need to actively work against the harm that these portrayals may have caused or may cause in the future.

Some I interviewed, such as Teddy, forty-six, has personal connections with the individuals portrayed on Roma reality shows. Teddy recounts his attempts to change these portrayals for the better:

> I did try to reach out to them and say hey you have a platform on television which a lot of the family doesn't approve of but you can really take the opportunity to shed light on the persecution issues in Europe. There is some good that can come out of this too. It just never came about . . . it sets us back a little.

Teddy has recognized both the harm and the potential for good found in these media portrayals and yet, as many others have experienced and reported, his attempts to use the platform for the good have been fruitless so far.

Gilbert had quite a bit to say about the harm of media portrayals on the lives of Roma both in America and Europe. He acknowledged that media portrayals in Europe affected Roma lives "a lot" where in America he is unsure entirely how Roma are being impacted:

> In Europe, I think that it's like a big deal, people expect less of you, they expect you to be less intelligent. There is this genetic intelligence kind of thing that plays a role. People think you aren't smart enough or aggressive enough. I think that is definitely something that is here in many many areas . . . there are definitely low expectations. In America, for most people it doesn't mean anything, its an exotic fictional character or just something people don't understand.

Gilbert, who lives at this time in Europe, has observed firsthand how negative media portrayals have created barriers for Roma in their occupations and in society. Though he has not observed this firsthand in America, he acknowledged that American moviemakers and writers have the potential to impact Roma worldwide, including those in America:

> I fear, I fear the potential misuse of Roma characters in Hollywood because they don't know what's happening in Europe and they don't care. They could completely take something and make an innocent mistake and it could have horrible repercussions . . . Right now with the Romas that are coming to California from Mexico it could be a problem, again I am worried about it. They are refugees. If they start getting blamed and coming across the border as "these gypsies" it's like a ticking time bomb. I don't know what's going to happen . . . we have to be proactive to protect and I don't know how.

Gilbert exemplifies the fear that many Roma, whether in the United States or overseas have of the repercussion of media portrayals, real repercussions that may set Roma back or make their lives and attempts at any form of acculturation challenging at best and impossible at its very worst.

The Impact of Media Portrayals on Gender

One cannot dissect Roma portrayals without making some note of the gender disparities that exist within these portrayals. For Roma women, their true experiences are almost entirely left out of media portrayals. Roma are presented in a homogenized manner and media representations fail to identify the intersectional experiences of Roma women who encounter discrimination as a result of their ethnicity as well as their sex and, oftentimes, impoverished conditions (Oprea, 2004). These realities exist for portrayals in both the United States and Europe. Though shows such as *My Big Fat Gypsy Wedding* (Herman, 2012: Poppelwell, 2012) focus largely on Roma women, they fail to adequately portray the challenges and roles unique to Roma women within their communities and situated next to mainstream society.

A recent feature on BBC's *Women's Hour* (Murray & Starkey, 2016) provides a much more accurate portrayal of the life of a GRT in Europe. Rather than focusing on ancient tropes and outlandish behaviors (as the popular reality series do), they portray a realistic look into the daily life of the "traditional" Roma woman who devotes her day to supporting her family through work inside or outside of the home. She owns the land she is parked on and discusses the lessons she is passing on to her daughter. She identifies themes of cleanliness, modesty of dress and manner, and hard work, themes which are important within the GRT community and not reflected in current popular media. She discusses reality shows, how they are "meaning to be shocking" and "not typical of gypsy people." In addition, she identifies that the women in the shows are "not as modest as most gypsy girls are expected and desire to be." The interviewee discusses being turned away and targeted in local pubs and marketplaces and identifies how things have changed from past days: "We didn't feel that different [then], we felt like a much more valued part of the community." The program, though a mere 20 minutes, is a positive step forward in recognizing the unique voice of Roma women and in providing those outside their communities a more realistic look into their lives.

An article written in *The Guardian*, a U.K. newspaper, provides another realistic look into the lives of actual Gypsy women (Bindel, 2011). The article, titled "The Big Fat Truth About Gypsy Life" identifies the lack of accurate information presented by shows such as *My Big Fat Gypsy Wedding* (Poppelwell, 2012). Bindel identifies that the show overlooks the poor health and poverty that many gypsy women face. The show paints a picture of women able to afford lavish weddings and designer gowns when this is not a reality for the majority of the community. Some worry that this will influence mainstream viewers to believe Gypsy women are merely conning the government and living off assistance they don't need, leaving Roma women to worry that they may lose the little help they have.

Bindel (2011) relates that many women within the gypsy community are victims of domestic violence, a widely prevalent occurrence in GRT communities throughout Europe. In addition, Roma women face a significant number of miscarriages and SIDS-related deaths due to lack of clean water and proper access to health care. They routinely experience evictions. Illiteracy among these women is disproportionately high. All of these factors are overlooked as they do not play into the spoiled and outlandish narratives in mainstream depictions. In addition, Bindel interviews several Gypsy women who were significantly bothered by the way they have been portrayed as Gypsy women:

> The programme didn't show the real way we go on. All my friends are asking if it's true what they show on telly and I think they've done different [toward me] since it was shown. (Mary, 15)

> The way us women come across in the programme is a disgrace . . . It shows us nothing but slaves to men, only good for cooking and cleaning and always being available to open our legs to the men . . . We don't want that for our daughters. (Helen, woman in her twenties)

Again, news articles such as Bindel's along with programs such as BBC *Women's Hour* are bringing a countering image to negative portrayals of women and are providing a realistic look into the challenges that Roma women face.

Undoubtedly, media portrayals of Roma, whether they are American, European, men or women, negatively impact the lives of Roma in many ways. Most certainly, media portrayals impact the level of resistance Roma encounter from mainstream society toward their acculturative choices. Resistance to assimilation has been encountered by Roma in the form of racism and prejudice. Portrayals in mainstream media have served as a catalyst, in many cases, for these encounters. In the coming section, I delve even further into these outcomes by exploring the state of mental health among Roma worldwide and draw connections between these negative experiences and the role of the media. Unfortunately, no information was found providing a clear picture of the state of mental health among Roma in America thus I will rely on research conducted with European Roma for a better understanding of how mental health is impacted by societal resistance, racism and prejudice.

ROMA BARRIERS AND INEQUALITIES THROUGHOUT EUROPE

Mental Health

As previously stated, European Roma are twice as likely to experience de-pression and three times as likely to experience anxiety as those in the domi-nant society. Among Britain's GRT (Gypsies, Roma, Travellers), a rise in suicides was found in 2013. Suicides among the GRT are three times the normal population and are found to be most frequent among Roma males ages 25–29 (Zabara, 2014). These statistics compare strongly with those of young Black males in the United States whose third leading cause of death is suicide (SPRC, 2013). Roma in Sweden are found to have suicidality rates seven times the national average among men and six times the average over-all. A study by Civil Rights Defenders has linked this in part to the impact of having to hide their identity from the mainstream and being made to feel "less" than others (2016), an experience all too familiar to Roma in America.

The hiding of Roma identities in schools and workplaces as a result of systematic racism is a significant contributor to poor mental health among the Roma (Smolinska-Poffley & Ingmire, 2012). The Roma mental health advocacy project finds that the powerlessness and vulnerability of Roma to impact their position within the dominant group has resulted in poor mental health (Smolinska-Poffley & Ingmire). Roma are significantly impacted by their lack of control over how they are treated or represented in society. Their lack of social position which limits their control is found to have a significant impact on the psychological well-being of Gypsies and Travellers (Van Cleemput, 2007). Roma are also impacted by the hostility and discrimination they regularly encounter (Zabara). A study by Yin-Har, 2011 explores the impact that social exclusion has on the mental health of GRTs:

> Members of Gypsy and Traveller communities report (personal communica-tion) that they feel their culture and way of life is not valued or respected, but is instead demonized or ridiculed. These cultural threats have a potential im-pact on self-esteem and mental wellbeing.

Yin-Har describes the plight of the GRT community as one that is frequently resisted and belittled by mainstream society to the detriment of their overall stability and well-being.

Roma in Europe experience negative mental health outcomes as a result of direct discrimination. This may come in the form of direct discrimination from the general public but may also occur within institutions that are meant to provide appropriate services (Rechel et al., 2009):

> In general it is very difficult to work with Roma. All physicians say that. Firstly because there are barriers and mistrust, and secondly because they

cannot explain what the [health] problem is. And because they really seek help only in crisis situations, when it is in principle difficult to provide quality care. Of course there is, how to say it, I don't want to call it discriminatory attitude, but it is derogatory [. . .] They [the Roma] feel this attitude and of course they don't like to go there to be humiliated, as would every other human being. (Health care worker, Bulgaria 6)

This Bulgarian healthcare worker sheds light on the reality that Roma are in need of addressing health concerns but, they are often unable to access appropriate services because of the prejudice and humiliation they encounter.

Another study by Rechel et al. (2009) recounts the experience of a Roma parent who lacked trust in the healthcare establishment's willingness to assist Roma. "In the Roma neighborhoods, if there is an emergency, the ambulances refuse to go there. This is widely known. [. . .] There are two reasons. The one is that they really refuse to go there . . ." Roma are widely known to lack appropriate access to emergency medical care due to overt prejudice and yet, the media remains largely silent on the many barriers Roma face.

Studies meant to address potential mental health disparities among Roma children can be themselves agents of discrimination (Lee et al., 2014). A study on the MH disparities between Roma and non-Roma children in Bulgaria found that on parent-reported measures Roma children were found to have high prosocial behaviors and few differences between non-Roma children. When teacher-report measures were considered, Roma children had a higher prevalence of all disorders tested. The authors of the study acknowledged that the Roma parent may have been trying to avoid stigma while the teacher may have discriminatory attitudes toward the children.

Given the literacy rates among Roma in Bulgaria, a Roma parent manipulating a self-report measure to the extent that they would be able to ensure scores among their children were equal to those of non-Roma children except in the area of prosocial behaviors seems counterintuitive. Though mentioned, the study failed to accurately discuss the likelihood that the teachers had bias in their report, making the findings of their study unusable at best and extremely harmful at worst. Not only does this study exemplify the direct discrimination that Roma may experience from educators but also from those within the mental health or academic community themselves.

Roma report experiencing depression or "nerves" (anxiety) and find themselves struggling to cope within ghettos where they work and live (Ceneda, 2002: Zabara). Some Roma have a history of personal or familial trauma that remains unacknowledged and unaddressed by the countries in which they reside (Strauss, 2012). A significant number of Roma in the United Kingdom who were found to be seeking assistance with their mental health issues sought assistance due to issues resulting from traumas relative to their social positions including war, the Holocaust, bullying, racism and rape (Smolinska-Poffley & Ingmire, 2012).

Though many Roma experience negative mental health outcomes as a result of the direct discrimination they experience, there is a resistance to seeking appropriate help for symptoms of depression. A study by Van Cleemput et al. (2007) finds that, among the Roma interviewed, there exists a pride in addressing one's own mental health issues rather than reaching to outside sources. In a study conducted with 269 Welsh Gypsies and Scottish and Irish Travelers, one woman describes her reasons for not addressing depression directly (Van Cleemput et al., 2007), "You can't just sit and let yourself be depressed. You have to get on and do things. I think 'oh my children, they've lost their father and I have to carry on" (208). For this respondent, addressing mental health problems head-on was not an option.

For many Roma, fighting through mental health problems on their own is essential to one's survival, socially as well as economically. Another Gypsy woman from the same study describes her experience with depression:

> If you can't fight it yourself you're dead, you get worse, if you just think you haven't got it, just let go, try and control yourself, it's better . . . try and clean and leave it out of your head, because if you try and think, turn my depression off, you don't think I've got depression. I don't need to see the doctors, I don't have depression love, I say, I'm fine. (208)

Due to their experiences, many Roma believe they should address any problems that arise individually or within their community. The inability to do so may cause additional stress as they may perceive this inability as a failure to retain control over their lives, placing them in a vulnerable position (Van Cleemput et al., 2007).

Roma communities possess a stigma toward mental health services and lack of trust toward mental health providers because of historical precedent of Roma children being deemed mentally disabled and needlessly placed in classrooms for children with mental health challenges (RGS, 2012). A focus group of Romanian Roma participants conceptualizes the stigma associated with mental health in the Roma culture:

> Mental health problems must be hidden. There are two major taboos in the Roma culture, sexuality and mental health. . . . Roma usually do not know anything about mental health problems, they fear mental health illnesses.

The focus groups characterizes the overarching attitudes toward addressing mental health issues in the Roma community, attitudes further exacerbated by their lack of support and available resources in mainstream society.

Roma in Central and Eastern Europe have experienced significant trauma due to their social position leading many to experience negative mental health symptoms. Heaslip (2015) conceptualizes the ways in which the trauma of the Roma's social position has negatively impacted their psychological well-being:

> These feelings of being vulnerable link to an outsider identity within society, perpetuating a feeling in which Gypsies and Travellers feel a lack of belonging within society which they perceive to belong to the Gorgi (non-Gypsy) world. This in turn leads Gypsies and Travellers to continue to self-segregate as a mechanizing of coping with the feelings of hostility from the settled community, in order to retain a sense of belonging, of being wanted which is important for one's psychological well-being. (96)

Heaslip identifies that the social position of the Roma is a direct result of their treatment by society which encourages them to self-segregate as a mode of protection. This limits Roma ability to choose assimilation if they wish and, limits their ability to freely select from the various models of acculturation. Data for the extent to which this trauma has impacted Roma is lacking due to the fact that many Roma are without appropriate access to mental health care (Ceneda, 2002). A study by Rechel et al. (2009) identified that Roma in Eastern Europe have an overall poorer status due to poverty, low education, and lack of access to appropriate services. While there is a lack of data on American experiences, documented parallels between American and European experiences in this area exist.

Access to Social Services

The lack of access to appropriate health services is a significant issue for those Roma who are willing to seek support to address their mental health needs. This also serves as additional evidence of acculturative resistance among the dominant group, preventing Roma from engaging in social institutions and marginalizing their efforts to address the negative effects of their social stratification. Heaslip (2015) identifies that the social position of Roma, exacerbated by their portrayal in mainstream media, places them within a vulnerable context and prevents them from accessing appropriate resources which can have lifelong consequences:

> A core determinant of health vulnerability at a population level is the social status of the group, as social hierarchies promote intergeneration inheritance of social status resulting in a highly systemic and deterministic fashion (Furumoto-Dawson et al., 2007). For example, any material and psychosocial stresses imposed by social inequalities impacts upon healthcare over the entire life trajectory. (45)

Heaslip acknowledges the multiple intersecting factors that contribute to negative outcomes for Roma. He identifies that these outcomes have the potential for lifelong occurrence.

Not only do the psychosocial stresses experienced by Roma due to social inequalities negatively impact their mental health but they also have the potential to impact their physical health over a lifetime and, because of their vulnerable social position, may place them in a position where they are unable to access appropriate resources (Ceneda, 2002; Rechel, et al., 2009; RGS, 2012). The inability of many Roma to access these resources leads them to draw heavily from the resources available to them. Among these are the large amounts of support they experience from their families. Access to this type of support makes the traditional traveling life essential to their emotional survival. Sadly, government regulations and biased media campaigns have begun to erode this way of life for many Roma across Europe as will be discussed in a coming chapter.

Roma are restricted to accessing other resources from their environment in forms beyond social services. Employment and housing challenges are common for Roma due to the prejudice and discrimination held by those in positions of power. Housing especially is problematic for Roma due to mainstream resistance to their traveling lifestyles and encountered discrimination when they seek to live settled lives.

HOUSING FOR ROMA IN EUROPE AND AMERICA

Europe

In January of 2016, Travellers from Ireland were evicted from homes parked at an unofficial parking site (Holland, 2016). Seventy Traveller men, women and children were evicted. Local law enforcement forced the Travellers from their homes and suggested splitting the men, women and children up in order to secure safe accommodation, separating families and requiring children to be separated from their mothers. The evicted Travellers and others from the community feared that the local council may have been seeking to take away their children under the guise of providing help. A spokeswoman for the families had this to say regarding the incident:

> We have heard reports of these kinds of intimidating suggestions being put to Travellers in Co Louth since the evictions and even before. This is an ongoing issue. It has been said to Travellers that if they declare themselves homeless the children could be taken away. These threats to break up families are not acceptable.

The suggestion from local council that GRT families be broken up in order to secure appropriate housing was unacceptable to the community and their advocates. The spokeswoman for the families identified that GRTs felt they were being intimidated to relent to the council's suggestions. This community once again saw themselves the target of behavior that would be considered unacceptable if directed toward any other minority group.

As an American Roma living in Europe, Henry experienced discrimination toward Roma in housing firsthand:

> this has happened to me repeatedly because when they first meet me they don't get the impression that I am a Gypsy then I would come back with a friend or a coworker and they would suddenly realize and they would say I am sorry there is some misunderstanding, I am not going to rent my apartment to you, you are a Gypsy. And I said a minute ago you were dying to get my business, you know everything about me. You know where I work you know what I earn you know how long I have been there. How am I suddenly less tenant worthy? [They say] Oh I'm sorry I just can't have it, nothing personal. How this could be any less personal, you are telling to my face about my racial background, yeah, no offense.

Being American gave Henry no privilege when it came to being Roma in Europe, he found that as quickly as his identity was discovered, attitudes and behaviors toward him changed.

Like Henry, Gilbert was an American Roma living in Europe. His mother, an immigrant from a nearby area, was very specific regarding how he should identify himself and his background when seeking to establish himself. Her fears, based in her own experiences of discrimination:

> My mom told me "absolutely under no circumstances you cannot tell anybody who you are or where you are from, don't even tell them the town I come from. Tell them I come from [another town] that's all they need to know. They don't need to know where I come from which is basically a small gypsy village. They don't need to know where I came from." So basically I listened to her and over the next two years in Prague I saw how people spoke about gypsies.

Gilbert goes on to relate how he was able to "fit in" with the other individuals around him, that he didn't stand out so much and thus was able to hide his identity from those, like the individuals Henry encountered, who would have been inclined to discriminate against him simply because of his identity or the village where his mother's family originated from.

American Housing

Al, seventy-five, can recall a time when Roma in the United States faced prejudice regularly when it came to housing. Though he acknowledges things are different in the United States than Europe, he still identifies a connection exists between the traveling Roma of the United States and Europe:

> there were always signs of discrimination, especially back in the day when we traveled you know. We lived the nomadic life we couldn't get in the trailer park or this that or the other . . . if something did come up or whatever you just moved elsewhere.

Like many Roma in Europe, traveling Roma found resistance to their presence even in places that catered to the nomadic way of life, finding themselves unable to obtain places to park their mobile homes, forced at times to move on in hopes of securing a more welcoming or less discriminatory spot. From Al's perspective, it is the "traveling Gypsies that have way more problems than settled ones."

Contrary to Al's narrative, Benny provided evidence that even within settled neighborhoods, Roma in the United States have faced resistance to their presence:

> it became a thing where they would definitely not be accepted into their neighborhoods by friends or kids like that . . . they talked about how people in their neighborhood started seeing them as hood rats and all that stuff . . . I think there were some people who could read between the lines and sort of see you know due to their backgrounds. They were living in these ethnic kinds of areas, kids of immigrants.

Benny's mother and family were residing in areas where others were able to identify their background and subsequently labeled and resisted their presence in settled neighborhoods. Unlike Al's family, they were not able to just "move on" should trouble arise and were faced with the challenge of residing in neighborhoods with strong prejudice toward a Roma presence.

As narratives from chapter two identified, many of the American respondents have historical knowledge or firsthand experience with being "run out of town." In fact, two-thirds of the respondents identified this occurrence in the life of a relative at some point in history. Some respondents identified being targeted by police, turned away, harassed, vandalized, even in settled homes, threatened and assaulted. For some on the road, this may continue to be a reality, but for many this has changed. Resistance to Roma presence in neighborhoods seems to have declined as settled lives have increased but as this prejudice has decreased, another continues which impacts Roma quality of life almost daily.

RESISTANCE TO ROMA IN OCCUPATIONS AND EMPLOYMENT

Europe

Historically Roma have filled occupations that allowed them the freedom to travel and work independently. Today, many Roma continue to fill these occupations though they have become more challenging to engage in as they encounter resistance to their traditional means of making a living. In both America and Europe, Roma encounter resistance in occupational settings whether in traditional ways of living or in White collar occupations.

Lane, Spencer and Jones (2014) relate the experience of one Roma man in Europe, in need of work who met resistance:

> When I come to the agency they told me don't get no job because It's very quiet. When they go in the office and come back they tell you there's no job. . . . Because looking at my color, you know, that's no for work

This gentleman related his experience in seeking employment. Upon seeking a job at an employment agency, he recognized he was given the proverbial "run around" because of prejudice toward his recognizably ethnic features.

Two of the respondents interviewed have lived and worked in Europe and experienced or observed the discrimination from workers firsthand, though they both worked White collar occupations. Henry described his experiences:

> I never felt that I was personally discriminated against as a Roma person but I think that even though everyone knew I was Roma, it came up every day, they just didn't see me that way, I was American, I was light skinned no matter how much I told them I was Roma. I don't think I felt like one to them. Everyone in my office was Roma from Eastern Europe and looked it. They I think got discrimination from our White colleagues all the time. I think White colleagues would often say things to me about my staff that I found discriminatory.

While Henry found that his lighter skin and American origins provided him some privilege and protections from discrimination, at work he witnessed firsthand how his Roma coworkers were treated by those in the majority. Henry went on to share how he had not only observed discrimination impacting his Roma coworkers but had also witnessed firsthand how prejudice toward Roma impacted Roma resources and organizations:

> At one point I was a very senior manager at a regional foundation and one of the program areas was to support Roma. Everyone I worked with, they all knew I was Roma and that I was the quality control for the grant to Roma. Never the less they were pretty comfortable saying some pretty discriminatory stuff to me about their Roma grant-ee. I had budgets that were for Roma civil society and they kept awarding the grant to friends, White friends, and non-

Roma NGO's who wanted to do "Roma projects." I would say why? Is that the
best possible applicant you can give your money to? If you don't know of any
Roma civil society wanting to do a grant proposal I will hold your hand and
take you to the Roma villages and introduce you to them . . . to me, it couldn't
be more racist.

Henry's experiences are not isolated events. Whether being turned away
from jobs or experiencing daily the negative attitudes of non-Roma coworkers, Roma face obstacles in their employment experiences. Not only can this
impact their ability to successfully provide for families and meet basic needs,
but it can also be a greater barrier to their assimilative choice, particularly if
they desire to become or remain a part of the mainstream.

Gilbert also experienced firsthand the conversations of coworkers who
were without assumption that Gilbert could be Roma. He acknowledged he
definitely stood out among Eastern Europeans due to his darker features and
yet, he was privy to blatant prejudice toward Roma:

It didn't occur to them that I could be a Gyspy because the way they talked
about Gypsies was that they are stupid, they steal, they lie. Things like that, I
would have to listen to it. I would keep it a secret [that he was a Roma] and
didn't tell anyone.

Gilbert's observation, like Henry's, of how Roma are talked about and treated exemplify the ongoing challenges for Roma in the workplace and in
society in Europe.

America

For Roma working traditional occupations in the United States, many barriers
exist. As Henry discussed in previous chapters, those in traditional occupations
in America are much more likely to find that barriers to their employment
opportunities exist than for those working white collar occupations:

Yeah it won't hurt you if you want to be an accountant or like a software engineer
or a political science major or a college professor. I have a hard time believing
anyone like that is going to have Roma ethnicity held against us. But were not
everyone and for people who do certain kinds of work with certain kinds of
clients, yes staying in the closet is effectual. But if you are an independent blue
collar contractor, the word Gypsy is not a good part of your brand.

Many respondents agreed with Henry's assessment of the employment climate. While workers may not be prevented from jobs due to their ethnicity,
many respondents did report they received negative treatment on their jobs
because of it, even among some of the white collar workers. Gilbert related
an incident his mother encountered as a nurse:

> She would be working in a hospital and she would be fixing her hair and there would be other nurses in the hospital and they would talk about I don't know why gypsies have to smell so bad. Maybe they weren't talking about her maybe they were. Maybe they knew who she was but the point is she just lost it and let them have it. She said people are people or how dare you say something like that. People work hard of course they are going to smell because they work hard and people are going to get sweaty. There is nothing wrong with that. She had a couple of bad experiences and she wanted everyone to know but at the same time she wanted to avoid anyone having those experiences.

Whether or not the other nurses working with Gilbert's mother knew her origins, their words and open distaste for Roma they had encountered negatively impacted his mother. When Gilbert related this and other stories he began by telling me that his mother didn't want him to turn out to be Roma, she wanted him to be "safe" and "normal like everyone else." Gilbert's mother's experience of discrimination in her home country as well as the United States left her with the impression that in order for her son to achieve what he wanted occupationally and otherwise, it was best to leave his Roma identity unacknowledged. For Roma in traditional occupations, this is especially true.

Roma in traditional occupations in the United States have often fared much worse within the context of discrimination and acculturative barriers. While Benny would assert that the occupations traditionally held by Roma may not always seem above board by outsiders "That's just poor people, you do whatever you have to get by to try and make money." Traditional Roma in America have historically engaged in horse trading, boxing, fortune telling, manual and skilled labor, among other things (Chohaney, 2012).

Al, in his seventies, continues to live a traditional traveling life in which he engages in skilled labor designing and installing light systems though his previous occupations range from asphalt paving to car repair. Al understands firsthand the challenges that exist for traveling Roma today:

> If you go off and you are itinerant there are sometimes places that people don't know you and it's easy to get into something. If you live somewhere and you have an address and you get a complaint from someone it's just a civil matter it just whatever. If a gadje goes and does something they will consider it a shrewd business practice but if Romanichal or other Gypsies do something like that it's a felony for the same thing. If you run across that, you can't avoid that. That's a form of discrimination, absolutely.

More and more Roma are finding that their traditional ways of traveling to find work and staying insular within their families have become challenging due to societal attitudes toward Roma. For these, it is becoming increasingly difficult to earn a living as attitudes toward traditional Roma become more and more resistant.

Nowhere do the barriers to traditional Roma occupations in America become more evident than in their interactions with the police. As previously discussed, Roma interactions with law enforcement whether in the United States or Europe are very often racially motivated encounters, finding they are often considered guilty before they are given a chance to prove themselves. Eddie, fifty-six, from the Midwest discussed his transition off of the road due to the constant harassment he faced from the police:

> Oh yes the police would pull you over in a heartbeat because they knew what dad was, my dad was a little darker skinned, they knew what my dad was, what my cousins were from the type of work they did and how they kept their vehicles. They kept their vehicles spotless and that was one of the things that stood out to the police that they keep everything spotless, they don't have paint running all over the side of the truck.

Eddie found that more often than not, the police would be waiting for them when they came to work in a town. They sometimes found themselves unable to work and sometimes unable to find a place to park their campers or RVs. This was challenging. Louisa, in her forties, pointed out in an earlier chapter that life on the road means you wake up every day unemployed, without a source of income unless you are able to get up and knock on doors to look for work. Only then are you able to provide even the basic necessities for your family. Eddie recalls what it was like to constantly encounter resistance to both the presence of his family and their desire to work:

> Even as a teenager after I graduated from high school, and we had gone into the paving business we were asked to leave certain towns. We pulled into RV park and set up and get ready to talk to the cities cause my dad was always on the up and up and his dad taught him not to be fly by night . . . you pull in and get permits and stuff. The police would come out and say we've been asked to have you leave.

Eddie then related a time when he and other family members were on their way to a job they had already arranged in Kansas. They were pulled over by state highway patrol for a routine traffic stop and rather than being written a ticket, their car was towed, leaving Eddie to walk the 8 miles into town. Eddie protested the treatment he received from the police:

> I said I have done nothing, I have broken no laws . . . the police officer told me you can either deal with me . . . or deal with that trooper over there, when I asked him what's his problem he said here about a year ago some fly by nights came through and robbed his mother . . . he's after anybody who is not from here who is knocking door to door . . . I told him you know we got permits and we've got a tax number and we've got a right to do what we are doing . . . He

looked at me without cracking a smile or anything and said I could find as much as a jay walking ticket on you and you'd be going to jail.

Eddie's experiences are not uncommon for many Roma seeking to maintain their traditional lifestyles. These occurrences serve to push them further from mainstream society and make an integrated life, with one foot in each world, even harder to achieve.

Rachel works a nontraditional job where she has also found prejudice toward her Roma heritage. Rachel currently works as a nanny and has encountered stereotypical attitudes not just from the parents who employ her but from their children as well. She finds they constantly comment on her behavior questioning if that is something "you people" do and commenting on her physical appearance: "The [one child] she is always saying you would be so pretty if you would fix your nose." Her employers and their children feel a freedom to say whatever they think and feel about her appearance and life as a Roma.

CONCLUSION

As discussed, Roma who encounter resistance to their acculturative strategies and subsequent discrimination or prejudice do experience negative social and individual outcomes. The result is harmful effects on the social, economic and mental health of the Roma. This not only affects their ability to effectively cope with the challenges they face but highlights their lack of appropriate resources. The experience of American and European Roma mirror each other though more evidence exists to support these conclusions in Europe. One final area of discrimination and barrier for Roma remains to be discussed: education.

In the coming chapter, I will discuss the many barriers Roma face within educational settings both in Europe and in America from elementary and secondary school to college and graduate school, even in their occupations as teachers and professors. Berry discusses assimilation happening in part when members of a group are able to engage with major social institutions, educational institutions being perhaps among the most prominent of important socializing agents. The inability of many Roma to successfully engage with these institutions is due to the barriers they face. These barriers include bias attitudes of educators and administrators, resistance among family members due to historical segregation, bias testing and school segregation. The barriers not only keep them from engaging in preferred methods of acculturation but also handicap many Roma in Europe and America from obtaining an education comparable to others in the majority. This lack of education, as research has shown, may set any group up for significant hardships in their future.

Chapter Five

Roma and Education

In 2014, the European Union released a report on discrimination of Roma children in education. The report cited that education provided to Roma was not only inferior but had exposed Roma children to being disproportionately diagnosed as mentally ill, being educated in Roma-only schools, White flight from schools largely attended by Roma and lack of appropriate books and educational buildings. This report exemplified the educational experiences of Roma worldwide and sheds light on the mistrust Roma parents have historically held toward educators (Euroactiv, 2015).

Among individuals in the United States, studies show a gap between most minority groups and the White majority in test scores, grades and overall educational achievement (Kao & Thompson, 2003). Additionally, even for those who achieve educationally, the payoff, when compared with what Whites are able to gain, is not commiserate with their efforts (Mickelson, 1989). The achievement gap is a long-recognized issue between White Americans and many ethnic minorities. As Kao and Thompson describe, there are two basic theoretical barriers to education among minorities. The first barrier is that ethnic minorities are stratified socially which inhibits their achievement by inhibiting their ability to access resources, social status and quality education. The second is that their cultural orientations can discourage individuals from achieving academically (Kao & Thompson).

As previously discussed, Roma have held a mistrust toward educators and educational settings due to discriminatory practices and historical inequalities (Silverman, 2012). Engaging with the educational system in the United States places the Roma directly in the center of gadje influence exposed to their values that may differ from those taught at home. They may be seen as unclean (Hancock, 2010), undesirable due to their mixing of boys and girls

135

and Roma may experience unfair targeting of by administrators and teachers as well as ethnic insensitivity.

Among Roma who identify as less assimilated, is not desirable that their children spend more time than is necessary being influenced by the morals and customs of the gadje. Those who are influenced by the gadje may be seen in danger of becoming corrupted and of being drawn away from their community (Hancock, 2002). Traditional gender roles and cultural expectations play a part in the lack of secondary education among Roma children (Bhopa). Children may be expected to leave school to contribute financially or help at home. Roma-Traveler children's lifestyles often contribute to inconsistent school attendance (Derrington, 2005). Parents who possess little education are often unable to support their children's involvement in school and may contribute to the ongoing distrust of gadje in school and lack of educational achievement in their children. In addition, historically, traditional Roma culture emphasized vocational and home training over traditional schooling. Home training was believed to more prepare the Roma child for life within their community subsequently, many did not see a benefit of going to school beyond learning the basic skills of arithmetic, reading and writing (Bhopal).

Distrust of the gadje has historically presented a large cultural barrier to Roma education and, as many scholars point out, this distrust is not unfounded (Bhopal, 2004; 2011; Derrington, 2005; Grover, 2007; Hancock, 2002; Levinson & Sparkes, 2005). Roma often encounter discrimination from administrators, teachers and students who hold deep prejudices and do not understand the Roma way of life (Bhopal, 2011). Historically, Roma have been excluded from gadje schools or have been sent in large numbers to schools for mentally ill (Hancock, 2002; Grover, 2007). They are often targeted by teachers and children with bullying, name calling and severe reprimands for defensive behaviors when they choose to retaliate to this treatment. As Derrington (2005) points out, Roma are often left with the choice of "fight, flight or play white."

Hancock (2010) relates efforts in the United States to address these disparities by creating educational spaces for Roma led by Roma. As of yet, none of the spaces have been enduring due to lack of appropriate support from outside the community. A divergence of priories within the community has also impacted their longevity. Thus, those Roma who do not choose to homeschool their children yet are reluctant to be influenced by outside values may find themselves impacted by a primary cultural structure of the gadje and on the receiving end of cultural and ethnic prejudice.

SCHOOL ENCOUNTERS OF PREJUDICE
IN AMERICA AND EUROPE

America

Roma have been widely criticized for their lack of education or involvement in government run educational settings. As modern times have continued to evolve, traditional Roma have become all too aware of their need for an education, either because traditional means of gaining a living are no longer accessible or because an advanced education would assist them in their traditional endeavors. Sadly, schools are among the most difficult environments for many Roma. American Roma tend to fare better than those in Europe though, even in America, Roma have faced prejudice as a normal part of their educational experience both historically and in modern times.

Little research currently exists documenting the experience of Roma in American public school systems. Of the 23 people interviewed, ages 22–80, two-thirds reported some form of discrimination during their school years. Vaidy, a respondent in her forties from Northeast United States identifies that many of her older relatives have been kicked out of school because of their ethnicity. She also identifies that she herself has been bullied and made fun of in the classroom due to her identity as a Roma.

Anne, a woman in her forties from the Southeast United States, identifies that both her older relatives as well as her own children were unwilling to put their children in public schools because of the prejudice they faced:

> No they just said that Gorjas didn't understand them because you know back then, and even now you know my daughter lives in Chicago, even now they don't put their kids in school. They marry young so I can understand why Gorjas felt that way but the older generation just felt that they were being picked on for their ways of believing.

Often reluctant to engage with individuals from the mainstream because of prejudice, their reluctance has been further cemented by encounters with discrimination from teachers and students. Rachel, a woman in her twenties, identifies incidents that she encountered in elementary school:

> I went to an elementary school, a public school. That was pretty good there were a couple of kids who were very antagonistic toward me when they found out who I was. A lot of them were, just said oh cool when they went back to whatever they were doing. I did punch a White boy once for calling me a dirty gypo. I didn't get in trouble 'cause the principle knew he was racist.

Rachel goes on to recount many experiences of micro aggression as well as outright prejudice throughout her school career. This increased as she

entered high school where she became the target of intense, racially motivated bullying.

Allie, a woman in her forties from the Midwest, moved to the United
States from Europe at the age of 26 in order to attend college. Allie used her
experiences growing up in Europe to inform how she should conduct herself
in the classroom:

> I was pretty much on the down low, people didn't know where I was from and
> my accent was a lot less American then and people couldn't place me and I let
> them think I was from wherever I was from. You know they would come out
> with all kinds of things and I was just like uh huh. It wasn't until the end of my
> second year and I was in a class and someone brought up gypsies and some-
> thing in Europe and I commented positively of course and kind of all hell
> broke loose.

When first coming to America, Allie downplayed her ethnicity and hoped to
remain unnoticed by her fellow students. Compelled to speak positively
about those she was closely connected with, she immediately encountered
that which she had worked so hard to avoid.

Allie then describes the lack of understanding that her classmates had
about the reality of being a Roma, who they are and what their lives are like:

> It was the most bizarre experience, most of them in the class didn't seem to
> know what they were talking about and it shocked me a lot because in Europe
> you mention the word Gypsy and everyone has, most people have negative
> ideas and it seems in the United States most people have half romanticized
> idea and half the gypsies in America are hippies wanderers smoking weed but
> the bad gypsies are in Europe. And so it was this weird dichotomy I experi-
> enced growing up to be a gypsy. Everyone knew by your name growing up
> where you were form, you didn't really hide it. It was just a weird experience
> Undergraduate people seemed more interested in learning maybe in learning
> about the reality of it.

Allie identifies the difference between being completely recognizable in Europe and being largely invisible in America. She found that many of her
classmates' negative ideas about "gypsies" were directed at Roma in Europe
where many of them had romanticized ideas about any that may be living in
America.

Though not explicitly stated, one need only to look at the types of media
portrayals surrounding both American and European Roma to draw conclusions about how these specific stereotypes can be directed toward groups.
While negative press related to European Roma exists in excess, the limited
amount of media portrayals directed at Roma in the United States are bal-
anced out by popular songs glorifying the "Heart of a gypsy" (Caillat, 2014)
or Pinterest (n.d.) boards dedicated to quotes about "wandering souls." Anne

believes that, at best, many individuals are ignorant of the lives of Roma and the connotations surrounding the term gypsy while others, such as those Vaidy encountered, carry significant prejudice they are unafraid to express in academic settings.

Europe

In Europe, the educational situation is far more dire and is more easily tied to the ways in which Roma are portrayed in the media. In a study conducted by Lane, Spencer and Jones (2014) with Roma from England, Scotland, Wales and Northern Ireland, it is found that 9 of 10 Roma children sent to school experience bullying and 2/3 report experiencing a physical attack of some kind. Harding (2014) reports that GRT children face significant challenges when compared with their White peers in Great Britain. Racism and bullying are a common part of the Roma school experience and social exclusion frequently occurs with peers at school.

A study by Strauss (2012) conducted 275 qualitative interviews with both Roma and Sinti individuals about the education situation of Roma and Sinti in Germany. One-fourth of the respondents identify they have experienced discrimination in school. Those interviewed who attended school in the 1950's and 1960's identified they experienced a significant amount of dis-crimination from teachers while those who attended school more recently reported a significant amount of demotivation by their teachers:

> and after that, the teacher was just so mean to me that she even badmouthed Sinti in class and said, "the gypsies stink, and they're dirty." And then I didn't want to go to school anymore, because it hurt me so much that I just sat and cried. (Sinti woman in her thirties, 83)

> But on the other hand, there were some who were, who had a bias, a real aversion. It was noticeable, too. True, they didn't say it directly, but you just noticed it. The teacher preferred other students. Then you just noticed that. (Sinti man, age twenty-one, 84)

Former students relate their experiences with teachers from outside of their communities. The Sinti woman respondent identifies overt experiences of discrimination in her classroom while the Sinti man identifies more covert experiences of discrimination.

Other studies in Europe identify that bullying and even violence by other students is a common experience of Roma in school (Russel, 2016). A 13-year-old girl reported that a fellow student threatened to stab her when she revealed her ethnic heritage. She also reported that she had been verbally assaulted and that some students had threatened to come to her house. A study by Harding (2014) identifies that GRT children fare much worse in school than White children and face racism, bullying, and physical abuse at school. Another Roma identifies that the term gypsy was not one they were familiar with until they went to government run schools:

> They put me into school and that was when people first started calling me a Gypsy, smelly and stuff. And I couldn't understand it. I didn't know what a Gypsy was. I really realized that we weren't liked. That we were completely different, different person to what country people were. (Roma Man) (Russel, 2016)

This respondent discovered that not only had they been labeled by an unfamiliar term, but that the label carried many negative connotations, making him a target for harassment.

Another significant issue faced by Roma in Europe without evidence in America is school segregation. An article from August 2016 identifies that Roma children in Hungary continue to be segregated from their White peers (Serdult, 2016.). The quality of segregated schools is said to be lacking and fall short of the quality of schools attended by non-Roma children. Serdult reports this from a Roma father:

> We felt the quality and infrastructure of the school was not good. She had the best possible marks in the segregated school: 5s (the Hungarian equivalent of an A+). Her grades fell to 2 when she moved to an integrated school. The level of education between these schools is not the same, the grades reflect this. She had to catch up tremendously. It was difficult to adjust as she was not well received in the new school. Her marks are now back up to 5s.

Parents and students face inferior conditions in segregated schools but, in their efforts to integrate they face significant resistance from non-Roma parents. Serdult identifies that segregated schools are currently on the rise rather than declining. Other studies show Roma children in Yugoslavia, Albania (Kushi, 2016) as well as Slovakia (Higgins, 2013) attend segregated schools.

An article from 2013 in the *New York Times* (Higgins) relates the struggle of Slovakian schools in trying to integrate Roma into mainstream institutions. Slovakian school officials seeking to conduct this integration successfully have looked to the educational desegregation struggles of the United States to inform this process..In schools already seeking to integrate Roma students, Roma are still treated differently than their White peers. They are placed in Roma-only playgrounds and during lunch they are given bagged rations unlike the White students who receive hot meals. Their parents have, at times, been banned from the schools and classes are chosen based on the ethnicity of the student (Higgins, 2013). Roma children taking part in integration have difficulties trying to catch up after being educated in subpar conditions and many Roma parents fear the integration due to the discrimination they have experienced in the past. Resistance has also come from the teachers themselves, "These people are interested in only two things: money and sex . . . They are lazy and don't want to learn" (Vladmir Savov, English Teacher). The quote from an English teacher characterizes the deeply held prejudices toward Roma that lead many teachers with integrated classrooms to discriminate against Roma students and their parents (Higgins).

It is challenging for Roma to accept that their children will attend subpar, segregated schools. In Norway, many Roma come from Romania seeking a better life. Sadly, they find discrimination as well as extreme poverty. Roma in Norway report being spit on, having their things set on fire and being run over by cars. They often experience physical violence and are frequently told to "go home" presumably to Romania. They are vilified by the press. Despite this, they are hopeful that their children could be a part of integrated schools that would give them an opportunity to have more than their parents:

> If we have to live so poorly, we at least want our children to have better lives. We want them to go to Norwegian schools and be integrated. We want to contribute, earn money and pay taxes. We can do any jobs; clean, pick up garbage and anything else. (25-year-old female in Norway originally from Romania)

Sadly, the hopes of many Roma parents may not be realized while Roma in Norway continue to be vilified by the media, encouraging distrust and contempt for the immigrants seeking a better life (Apelseth, 2013). Kathleen, Irish Traveler, and mother of 6, reports to *The Guardian* the impact that media has had on her children at school (Bindel, 2011):

> Now every week I go to the school and the parents are talking about that [reality] programme. They won't let our kids mix with theirs because they say we stink and don't talk properly. Settled kids won't even play sports with ours in case they touch them.

Because of the negative ways Roma are being portrayed through the media in Europe, Roma children such as Kathleen's are experiencing an increase in discrimination by non-Roma parents and encounters with prejudiced attitudes from parents and children.

Public and governmental opinions have a significant impact on the willingness of the public to allow Roma to receive an equal and integrated education. In the United States, Roma face discrimination from students as well as administrators who hold previously conceived notions about Roma. This takes place not only in primary education settings, but as many of the respondents reported, it also takes place in settings of higher education.

More American Experiences in Education

For some, like Vaidy, in her forties, school, though enjoyable academically, was a place she regularly encountered prejudice. She recalled that kids would bully her when they found out she was Roma. The children would make fun of her and tell her to sit in the back of the class:

> I had friends and then suddenly I didn't have friends anymore, that was probably why . . . I think at that point as the kids got older they realized there was something to make fun of . . . there were a couple of kids in particular who were really mean and rude. . . . They would say that gypsies need to sit in the back . . .

In Rachel's life (twenties) as in Vaidy's, bullying became more prevalent as she got older. She experienced being called a "dirty gypo." Once she got into middle school and high school, a private school, the bullying significantly increased. Rachel recalls that people would start rumors about her, try to get her expelled, spread lies about her father because they knew she was Roma. People would say that she was probably at school on a scholarship or that she likely stole something, all motivated by their knowledge of her identity as a Roma. Even the headmistress at her school had no problem speaking in a derogatory manner about her father in front of her.

Eddie, fifties, recalled that assimilating successfully in school was challenging not only because his family moved frequently but because of the attitudes he encountered from his fellow students and school administrators:

> The girls are curious about you and want to talk to you and the guys get jealous and want to beat you up . . . you just fight every day. I have been to some horrible schools and the stuff the teachers let them get by with is ridiculous and uh you know so there was times it was really, really rough. The teachers hated you and the students hated you, it was just rough. I can remember being in school for a day or two and then being out because they done something to one of us. You get your own prejudice growing up in the school.

The experiences of Eddie and his siblings in each school they attended further confirmed the bias that his parents held about entering the world of the gadje. The prejudice they encountered made it difficult for them to maintain a consistent education on top of the transient lifestyle they were already living.

For others, the recollections of school discrimination were regarded as a trivial event but several made it clear that had they broke the silence that was instilled in them about their identity, there would have undoubtedly been a change in the way they were treated by students and teachers alike. Louisa recalled a time when her nephew was in elementary school and another child was instructed by an adult not to sit next to him because he was Roma.

Unfortunately, these experiences were not isolated to elementary and high schools but were found to be quite prominent within the university setting.

DISCRIMINATION IN HIGHER EDUCATION

Surprising to me during the interviews was the finding that the majority of the stories of discrimination in education came from higher education. These stories were reported by those interviewed who possess a college education and they shed an unfortunate light on the presence of prejudice within higher education in the United States, specifically toward Roma. Despite being in spaces that are considered among the most enlightened in our society, for those who shared their experiences in higher education, they were met with ignorance, indifference and marginalization. These experiences occurred both as students and faculty. A story recounted by Fey describes how she was followed and had beer cans thrown at her by individuals who had attended one of her first lectures on the Roma. While not all prejudice met was as outright as Fey's experience they were just as poignant.

Encountering Ignorance in Higher Education

For some Roma, the ignorance of Roma culture or experience is not as frustrating as the refusal to be informed. Rachel, the interviewee who most recently finished her undergraduate degree, encountered many professors who lacked appropriate knowledge about Roma but refused to accept information that Rachel offered as legitimate. When Rachel would try to offer insight into what might be considered offensive in her community, professors would often respond in a very derogatory way:

> I would try to tell them um that's really offensive maybe you should try not to say that, then I had them be like, "Oh you're not like really an ethnic group" and I'm like ok have fun being an ignorant jerk the rest of your life.

Rachel's attempts at bringing enlightenment to her professors and classmates were met with resistance. As previously stated, few social taboos exist that prevent outsiders from engaging in stereotypical speech or discriminatory actions toward Roma. Rachel described encountering this frequently during her time in college.

Allie, in her thirties, encountered some of the very same attitudes described by Rachel in her undergraduate program. She identified that most students and faculty had negative ideas about Roma that were half romanticized and half pejorative. Despite these negative interactions, she felt that most undergraduate students were at least curious about her background. In graduate school she found herself being singled out:

> In graduate school, people thought I shouldn't be there, most of them had strange tales about gypsy women . . . In my master's program I was the only one who wasn't offered teaching, I wasn't able to publish and my program tutor told me I wasn't that kind of person or up to the task even though I had a 4.0. I can say for certain it was because I was Roma but, I was the only Roma in the class so it seemed weird to me.

As Allie stated, she could not confidently pinpoint her experiences as being the result of her Roma heritage, and yet her experience was not unique among respondents. Like other times in her life, Allie sensed that something was amiss, that there was something different about the way she was treated and compared with others.

Being Told that the Gypsy People Are Not a Minority

Being barred from funding or opportunities in college was a theme that came up with other interviewees. Gayle's story was similar to that of Allie's with a much more positive ending. Gayle, in her thirties, related an incident that happened when applying for funding in her master's program. Gayle applied for a minority scholarship and when she was meeting with the scholarship facilitator she was told that gypsy people were not a minority. Gayle recalled:

> that just lit a fire under my ass I was so angry that she said that I even called my mom . . . at this point I had made connections with Roma people and scholars. I had gotten in touch with [a major Roma scholar] and he wrote a letter of support. . . . I set up a meeting with the lady and the dean and the lady was singing a different tune. . . . I brought books and articles and I was like I am going to educate these people . . . and they allowed me to apply for the scholarship.

Several of the individuals I interviewed recalled experiences of being unacknowledged as a minority group in government settings and otherwise. In educational settings especially they feel they are left without a voice to represent them and often find themselves fighting against those in power for recognition of their experiences in a marginalized community.

For Gayle, the experience ended positively as she later received funding through the program. She identified the moment of receiving the funding as a defining one in her life. That was the moment of being acknowledged for who she was, though it had not come without a fight. For many Roma students, the achievement of something as big as funding or as small as professors modifying their language to more culturally appropriate terms comes at a price that may include loss of opportunity, pressure from faculty or scorn of fellow students. Though discrimination was found among the narratives of students, it was not limited to them as discrimination was also found among faculty.

Being Told that Gypsies Can't Read or Write

Although Vaidy is employed by one of the nation's elite schools, she has encountered the same attitudes and barriers that were encountered by other interviewees at schools across the United States. Vaidy recalled participating in a job talk in which a faculty member, already aware of her background, asked questions in such a leading manner she was forced to self-identify in a very public way, an occurrence, as previously discussed, that is very protected by Roma. Vaidy recalls receiving criticism about being both a Roma and a feminist, with critics stating that being Roma is too patriarchal, essentially saying a choice between her identity as a Roma and as a feminist had to be made.

Previously, it was discussed that individuals rarely possess social barriers that would prevent them from explicitly stating racist or stereotypical statements directly to Roma. Vaidy experienced this firsthand at a conference where she presented a paper:

> These two [professors] . . . were both like "oo the gypsies, do you remember all these rhymes that were very racist" and then went into all these nursery rhymes about the gypsies stealing you and they were very happy with themselves. I don't think they realized it and I was really easy going about it but then one of my students . . . were like really that was so racist and you didn't call them out on the fact that they were being so terrible.

Though easygoing on this occasion, having previously been exposed to the familiarity and comfort with which individuals express racist epitaphs, it could be likely that in some respects Vaidy had to be impervious to it as a common part of her lived experience. It took outsiders to acknowledge the extent of the discrimination she was encountering.

At other times, Vaidy has called individuals out, even her own students, for perpetrating racist stereotypes in the classroom. Vaidy recalls incidences when she has tried to educate her students about Roma scholars to be met with statements like "Ha! Gypsies can't read or write, what are you talking about?" She has faced criticism from administration or faculty who've commented about how she's "still doing the gypsy thing" in relation to her research, discouraging her from continuing down a path that they viewed as novel for a time but unproductive overall.

Being Told Roma Don't Belong to the Discourse

A growing body of scholarship by Roma feminists and scholars in higher education has begun to emerge which explores the possibilities of Roma advancement in career and education. Some Roma women argue that they are able to hold to their traditions while obtaining advanced education (Bitu

& Vincinze, 2012; Brooks, 2012; Gelbart, 2012; Schultz, 2012). Despite this stance, some Roma scholars have encountered feminists who argue that to fully embrace feminism, their traditional identity (Schultz) must be left behind. Roma feminist scholars are told that their cultural values are at odds with feminist ideals and they are therefore excluded from feminist discourse or encouraged to part ways with their Roma identity.

All of these experiences added together paint again the picture that few social barriers exist to protect Roma from outright interaction with prejudice. When met with prejudice and stereotypes, the individuals who present them are unapologetic in their presentation. Among those interviewed, discrimination and prejudice in the college setting was much more identifiable than early on in their education, however, when considered along with the idea that many of those interviewed did not choose to identify themselves as Roma until their college years, this finding stands to reason.

ROMA ATTITUDES TOWARD EDUCATION

With so many negative attitudes and barriers in place, it is no wonder that among many Roma resistance toward education has existed historically. This is certainly not the rule for all Roma but is undoubtedly an acknowledged occurrence within many Roma families, particularly those who have carried on traditional working practices. In chapter 4 I discussed what attitudes and lifestyles among American Roma occur today and that, in part, included education. To explore this further, I wanted to continue the discussion on education as the second part of this chapter. Roma have certainly faced barriers to their education and their ability to successfully assimilate into educational settings. These barriers do not always come from outside the community. Many respondents identified barriers to obtaining an education from within their own families. These attitudes and barriers have often been born of mistrust from the gadje and yet, many respondents, particularly the women, found this to be quite crippling. In the coming section, I discuss challenges to obtaining education that respondents encountered in their own families.

For some respondents, education was neither encouraged nor supported. Just as parents represented in some Roma literature (Derrington, 2005) encouraged their children to remain separate and placed little value on education, so too did these respondents' mothers and fathers encourage separation. Many saw little benefit in pursuing education when it would not contribute to the Roma way of life. Following Berry's model of acculturation, many parents encouraged their children to embrace separation, preferring their sons or daughters to remain attached to the ideals of their own culture. Despite this encouragement, education led to an integration of what they knew at home with the new experiences and ideas they were exposed to at school, often leading to a duality of identity. For many, it was the first time they had been exposed to people outside of the Roma in any significant way.

"Nobody Ever Sat Down with Me"
—Lack of Support for Roma Education

Gertie, who is currently attending college at the age of 54, was discouraged from interacting with non-Roma while simultaneously receiving messages that education was something to be valued. Though her father was outspoken against her receiving an education, her mother encouraged her to pursue education verbally while failing to show her any actual support in the way of obtaining a high school or college degree:

> Well my mom was always different, she wanted me to go to college and have an education but she never showed me how to do that. Growing up she said she wanted me to go to college and then when I got to the age where I could do that she never showed me how or gave me the means to do that.

Growing up, Gertie's mom was not involved in her education. Though her mom encouraged a college education she gave nothing in the way of actual support. Gertie's dad made his expectations clear from an early age. He was against education, he had other ideas in mind for his daughter's future. His expectations fell in line with traditional gender roles of the Roma and touched on a theme of morality that could be found in many of the respondents' recollections:

> He just wanted me to marry another gypsy, he was totally against gypsy women being outside of our roles. He thought it was immoral . . . He wanted me to find someone to marry that would have taken care of me.

Gertie's plans for herself fell in line with her dad's expectations. She floundered without support from her parents or even help from school. Looking back, Gertie wishes she had been encouraged to pursue something different. "Nobody ever sat down with me, including anyone at school and said, hey you know what do you want to be when you grow up? What do you want to be one day?" Gertie felt that she lacked appropriate support to achieve or even set goals both at home and at school.

Gertie had different expectations for her own daughter. She expressed that her desire for her own daughter was to go to college and be whatever she wanted to be and this was the message she instilled in her. To achieve this Gertie felt she had to offer her daughter a better opportunity to achieve this dream by exposing her to people who were not traditional Roma, people who would discuss education as a desirable and beneficial thing, people who possessed education and careers. In Gertie's world, Roma were people without these ideas or aspirations. Her decision to separate from the Roma she knew was one that was often looked down upon by her family members but one that was not an unusual occurrence among the other Roma interviewed.

"That Boy Is the Only One Who Will Go to College" —Gender Difference in Education

Like Gertie, Marilla, currently in her early sixties, was given the expectation early on that she would fill the role traditionally assigned to Roma women. When asked about the expectations she heard growing up regarding her future, Marilla identified clearly the plans her family had for her:

> Yeah basically I would get married and have children and serve a man. When I was a freshman in high school I expressed an interest in going to college and my mother said "There will be no college for you, that boy is the only one who will go to college because he will have a family to support."

Influenced by her family's attitudes toward education, she quit school at the age of 16 and worked in a factory for a year. Her time working in the factory showed Marilla that she wanted more and so she returned to complete high school. Her graduation from high school did little to excite the pride of her family. "It was not a big deal. I felt it was anticlimactic because nobody came."

Marilla wasn't surprised by this reception of her education. She identified that her mom's long held attitudes toward education influenced how she spoke to her daughter:

> My mother hated school so she didn't care whether we liked it or not. My dad only went to the fourth grade and my mother made it to her junior year in high school before she quit. They were not supportive, we were not encouraged. It was such a bad experience for my mom that she was like, "If you don't like it that's ok I understand." At that point she was unaware of the value of education.

Marilla felt that her family failed to give the tools necessary to be a successful adult in education and life. She expressed a sentiment similar to Gertie about the lack of support she encountered, "No one ever empowered me as a girl growing up."

Like other Roma families discussed in this study, the primary goal of Marilla's family was survival. The educational attainment of Marilla's parents was not unusual among many older generation Roma. Without education, they searched for alternative means of survival. This meant obtaining all they could from their environment without assimilating into the world around them:

My families view of being gypsies [was] you just have to take what you can and run with it. [My dad] would say just tell them you have a degree, don't tell them you don't have a degree and didn't go to college. I would say . . . you can't just get out there and say you got it. He'd cheat and I don't think he ever experienced embarrassment.

As Margaret Gibson's research identified, this was accommodation without assimilation at work. Marilla's family was able to accommodate what they had learned about the gadje in order to meet their need for survival while simultaneously remaining separate from society and social institutions.

Despite the many obstacles that Marilla encountered, she was eventually able to obtain a college degree. Because of her negative experiences and the negative expectations of her family, Marilla passed on different expectations to her own daughter:

Well I kept her from that type of lifestyle immediately. She was not aware of who we were or where we came from. I would not permit her to live in that lifestyle. She grew up with the expectations that she would go to school, including going to college.

Like Gertie, Marilla felt that the only way to ensure that her daughter received appropriate messages about education and her role as a woman was to separate her from the Roma way of life. Her daughter received a college degree and Marilla believes she made the right decision in keeping her daughter from the way of life she was exposed to growing up, a life often lacking support, similar to that of another respondent, Fener.

IMPACT OF LACK OF FAMILIAL SUPPORT

Like Gertie and Marilla, Fener, forty-five and a retired registered nurse, also experienced an indifferent attitude toward her education. Many traditional Roma parents encouraged education only so much as it prevented them from being involved with law enforcement and school officials (Derrington, 2005). Fener recalled possessing a love for school that was neither encouraged nor celebrated by her parents:

I loved going to school [my] parents didn't really make a big deal out of it. We went because we had to. I think they knew if we didn't go, the police would come. It was a law you had to go. We went because of that, it's not like they had big dreams of me going on you know for college or whatever. I loved going to school.

Fener recalled that her parents were not involved in her schooling; they never asked questions or checked her grades. For Fener's family, two worlds existed, the world of the Gorjas at school, a world they were forced to be a part of, and the world at home. The two were separate. Like other respondents' families, Fener's family preferred separation over any other acculturation strategy.

Fener identified that her parents' indifferent attitude toward her education left the idea of college up to her:

> It was never like "you're going to college when you grow up, this is what you wanted to do" When they were raised a young girl grows up and gets married you know and has children, that's how they were, that's how their parents were and my great grandparents. I never really talked to momma and daddy about going to college. The subject was never broached in fact, when I graduated from high school it was a really big deal, me graduating from high school. I don't even think it was something they thought about because you know their family before them never did it.

A history without educational achievement and a lifestyle that allowed for the earning of a living without formal education left individuals like Fener's parents and grandparents placing little value on educational achievement for their children.

Like many of the women interviewed, Fener chose to get married at a young age and have children. The marriage did not last and she found herself home with her parents and without the means to support herself and her children. She decided then that she would become a nurse. While her mother's attitude was less than supportive, her father expressed pride in her education. For her own daughters, similar to Gertie and Marilla, Fener hoped to pass on a different set of expectations.

Fener wanted her daughters to value education and go to college because, as she had experienced in her own life, relationships did not always work out. She didn't want them to be unable to support themselves. She wanted them to have options, something she did not see herself possessing as a young girl. Unlike Gertie and Marilla, Fener did not see separation from her culture as a necessity to passing along these ideals. Rather than choosing an acculturation strategy of separation, she saw, and experienced, integration as a viable option for remaining true to who she and her daughters were while pursuing a path which differed from her families' expectations. This conflict between familial expectations and educational achievement experienced by Marilla, Gertie and Fener was no more intense than in the interview conducted with Louisa, a stay at home mom in her mid-forties.

"We Would Be Told to Clean and Do the Dishes"
— Another View on Gender Roles

One of the most poignant examples of the conflict between traditional values, lifestyle and educational achievement and their subsequent barriers was found in Louisa's interview. As previously identified, Louisa continues to live one of the most traditionally Roma lifestyles of all the respondents. At the age of 40, Louisa has yet to complete her high school education.

Louisa's family was strongly against integrating with non-Roma. Like so many others interviewed, Louisa's family ran their own business and were constantly traveling to find new work. This lifestyle alone prevented many Roma from assimilating in any significant way and often interfered with the education of their children. In current times, Roma that continue in the traveling lifestyle choose to homeschool their children however, when Louisa was growing up, homeschool was not an available option.

Louisa's family instilled few ideas about the value of education or the opportunities that education could unlock:

> As a child we was never told, I had no idea that you could have a career and make something with your life something fun, something that you enjoy, like we were not told be what you want to be. It was rare that we even went to school, I would go to six schools a year.

Louisa's experience echoed these respondents close to her in age who found themselves lacking support or encouragement for their future goals. School was not a priority and was given little emphasis. Though little encouragement was given, Louisa recalled that some family members saw education useful in one way, if following the traditional path of marriage at a young age did not work out:

> We was encouraged to get a diploma so when if we got married and our husband left us, we could get a job and like in the old days you could learn to type or be a waitress, just something where you could get a job . . . We was encouraged to make good grades but that was basically it, pass and you done good. We wasn't encouraged you can do better, be all you can be, succeed, none of that. Basically, we would be told to clean and do the dishes.

Again, the expectation of traditional gender roles and ways of life were observed to be a barrier to educational achievement. At the same time, it was fully acknowledged the traditional ways of life did not always work as some women were encouraged to assimilate to the extent of bringing in money for their families. Louisa was both emotional and passionate when she spoke about her lack of education:

> I am still really upset I don't have an education because now I know how dumb and illiterate I am and it's awful, it's so awful. I don't even testify in church and I don't like to speak because I know that I am illiterate and I hate talking to school teachers and going to meetings anything like that. I hate it so bad. It's really bad to be illiterate. Just bad.

Louisa recognized that her lack of education has held her back professionally and socially. Keenly aware of what she believes are her shortcomings in knowledge and social skills, Louisa regrets that she was not encouraged to pursue her education further.

Louisa's dreams for herself are many. At various times, she has attempted to start a business or obtain a job. Without a basic education, it has been an unreachable dream. Other times, working for herself selling various goods, she has been quite successful at making money. Louisa views this success as a sign that had someone encouraged her to obtain an education and pursue a career, she could have been a very successful businesswoman.

Because Louisa lives with so many regrets regarding her own education, she hopes her daughter will have a different future. She would love for her to have an education and sees the value of encouraging her daughter to pursue it. Though she values education, she is also leery of the dangers and negative influences of the public school environment. As a result, she is currently homeschooling her daughter, a choice she did not make with her son, so that she can keep a closer eye on her:

> I don't want her to go to school because I am really scared to death of shootings and robbers. Like the street we live on, the high school. . . . I have two cousins that go to that school and a girl shot herself in the bathroom. Plus, it's on the news here in town where teachers are molesting the kids, it's just scary time for school. [Gypsies] would say that it's not that we don't want the education, it's the environment. Like drugs and girls dating and all the things like being in the environment that we don't like them in.

Louisa's view of public school and her reluctance to expose her daughter to that environment is another example of how many Roma resist full assimilation, resisting Milton Gordon's most basic level of assimilation, failing to engage with social institutions. Verbally or nonverbally this resistance communicates an important message to Roma about their place in the world of the Gorja.

Though the lives of Gertie, Marilla, Fener and Louisa are distinct examples of family traditionally unsupportive of education, other respondents identified that their families were encouraging though they failed to provide little in the way of actual support. This was true for Gracie, Josephine and Anne. All three were encouraged to achieve an education though their parents were not often present to provide emotional support or to actively help with school-related tasks.

NEGOTIATING RACIAL COMPLEXITIES IN EDUCATIONAL SETTINGS

Gracie, who is now in her sixties, possessed a love of school from an early age. School provided an important coping mechanism and escape from a tumultuous home life. Learning was encouraged in her home early on. Gracie recalled:

> I loved school, school for me retreat from my crazy home life. The one thing my father did for me . . . he taught me to read very early so when I went to school I could already read very well. My father loved to read so he took me to the library almost every Saturday of my life even into my college years it was just something we did together. I couldn't depend on him being sober the rest of the week but usually he was sober on Saturday and we went to the library. School for me was the retreat from the crazy home life . . . it was the only place I felt really safe.

From early in her life, Gracie found school to be a retreat. Though formal education was not necessarily encouraged or emphasized it served an important institution in her life, which showed her how valuable it could be to her future.

The historical setting of Gracie's school days was wrought with prejudice against non-Whites. The schools at that time were still very much segregated. Gracie's mother was determined that her children would receive a good education despite being what Gracie identified as, "the kid from the wrong side of the tracks." Gracie's mother fought hard and was able to enroll her children in a school that would provide the education she desired for them.

Despite instilling an early love for learning and fighting against social prejudice to enroll their children in adequate schools, Gracie's parents were surprisingly uninvolved in her day-to-day education:

> They were totally uninvolved in school. That was a good thing my mother fought to get us into that school but I don't ever remember my parents coming to a PTA meeting. I did a lot of public speaking . . . my parents never came. They never came to a concert, never came to a play. I understand that my mother went to fifth grade and my father went to eighth and I think they felt it wasn't their place. It wasn't a place they felt comfortable. My father very much wanted us to get an education . . . [but] they never talked to us about going to college.

Gracie's parents, like many Roma parents of their day, possessed few years of formal education. This had a significant impact on their desire and ability to be actively involved in her education. Gracie observed that her parents' lenient attitude was born of their own struggles with education.

Though her parents never discouraged pursuing a college education, they never talked about college or the means of getting there. Though they were encouraging and supportive of education, they maintained traditional expectations for their daughter:

> They thought I would get married which is what I did. . . . I didn't go to college until I got divorced when I was in my 20's, so yeah they clearly expected me to get married. I think they thought I might work, my mother worked in the mills, but school, never.

Gracie went on to receive a bachelor's and master's degree. Though she understood the traditional expectations of her family, she had also been given enough insight and encouragement to understand the value that education possessed.

Like Gracie, both Josephine and Anne's parents left the decision of school up to them. Anne, in her forties, initially followed a traditional path, leaving school in eleventh grade and getting married, however, she later went on to become a nurse. For Josephine, currently in her thirties, though her parents were supportive, they put no expectations on what she could do. Whatever her decision regarding school was going to be, she was supported.

Both Anne and Josephine passed this open attitude on to their own children, allowing them to decide what they wanted to pursue. Their ultimate goal is for their children to be happy and they do not allow familial expectations to interfere with giving their children the freedom to choose the future they hope to have. No specific expectations are communicated but support is freely offered and pride is expressed with their children's accomplishments, whatever they may be. Josephine homeschools her three children due to the frequent travel required of the family's business. Both Anne and Josephine identify that though they value their Roma roots and are connected with them, they also exist within the world of Gorja. They both identify that they have found a balance between the worlds and view themselves as being largely assimilated.

The majority of the remaining respondents of the study identified that their parents were influential in propelling them toward education. In most of these instances, however, many of these respondents saw their parents' actions and attitudes as a departure from traditional views and practice. Many saw themselves as able to achieve more than their Roma relatives because their parents consciously chose to instill in their daughters and sons the value of educational achievement. Their narratives support the idea that among

Roma, a spectrum of attitudes surrounding education exists and for as many Roma who feel they are constrained by traditional expectations, there are Roma who report that education is a valued part of their community.

SUPPORT FOR EDUCATION AND THE PERSPECTIVE OF BEING AN EXCEPTION

Phoebe, in her forties, was among those respondents who saw their situation as an "exception" to the norm. Surrounded by strong, working women, Phoebe observed a value for education and business savvy from an early age. Her mother and aunt were cloth merchants in the 1950's and 1960's selling imported cloth and furs to high end clientele including movie stars and professors. Her mother had attended a boarding school growing up. Her positive experiences in boarding school and her positive encounters with other educated women translated to a positive outlook on education that she would pass on to her daughter. Phoebe related how her father instilled a love for reading at an early age:

> My father always raised me to read, he's the one that instilled a love of books in me. The first thing we would do when we would go to a new town was to get a library card and get some books. Watching him do that influenced my love of reading as well. There was a high value on learning but maybe not so much on higher education but if I wanted, they were not against it.

Many respondents identified that a high value was placed on the acquisition of knowledge rather than on formalized education in their families. Even the families most strongly against pursuing formal education encouraged their children to acquire knowledge, which, according to Berry's model, would be more likely to place them in a state of integration rather than assimilation. Phoebe herself would go on to pursue formal education, receiving a bachelor's degree in fine arts after taking some time to travel and marry. Phoebe identified that it was both her own motivation to learn as well as the encouragement of her parents to gain knowledge that pushed her to continue her education.

Though the expectations and messages passed on from her parents motivated Phoebe to continue learning, she identified that her experiences were unlike those of her extended family, who held traditional expectations for their daughters:

> extended family, they were sort of set on their children not going because they thought it would take them away from who they are, what their expectations should be. Their expectations were they marry and you know, things are pretty much set. It should be the same as it always had been and if you go to school you are associating more with those who are not your kind and they try to pull you

away from your family. It was looked at as an unwanted threat to the continuation
of you know, our culture. It was a way to keep it untouched and intact.

It was no surprise that Phoebe identified her experiences as "unusual." In her
immediate family, she observed a value for education and a way of life that
involved at least a structural level of assimilation. In her extended family,
there was no place for assimilation, the standards of separation between those
who were Roma and those who were not were strictly adhered to. As the
literature supports (Silverman, 2012), education was viewed as a mechanism
to separate younger generations from family and the traditional ways and was
therefore devalued and, at times, completely discouraged.

Phoebe passed on the same value for education that she was instilled with
to her children. She hopes that her daughter will complete her college education and choose a career that will enable her to be independent. While she is
grateful that her own family held an appreciation for college, she acknowledges that this is not always the case within Roma families, even her own
extended family. She acknowledged that the attitudes passed from parent to
children have a significant impact on the path toward or away from education
that the children will choose to take:

> I think the family and parents have a big influence on the attitudes the children
> have and I think there are some that are more educated than others. There are
> some that appreciate and don't appreciate knowledge and education because
> they want to keep things as they know, the same old same threatened by
> change. Some people don't want change. There is some element of that and
> you know family can perpetuate that.

Margret Gibson (1988) discussed how some immigrant families believed
it could be possible to accommodate nontraditional knowledge, like receiving an education, without full assimilation. For the individuals Phoebe described, this was not an option. To preserve the traditional ways, separation,
again, should be strictly adhered to. Despite this, Phoebe was given a different set of ideas and expectations that have now propelled both herself and her
children forward in education.

"I Was Going to Go to College"
—Changing Expectations among Roma Families

Like Phoebe, Rachel, in her twenties, possesses a college degree. She identifies that the expectation that she would go to college was one that was
expressed very early in her life. Again, the idea of this being a novel attitude
compared with the attitude of her extended family was present in her responses:

> My dad . . . made it very clear to me from a young age that I was going to go to college and that I was not going to get married right away like all of my cousins. The rest of my family are very traditional, they kind of expected that I would get married and have kids right away, like right after I graduated high school all my cousins had [gotten married]. The expectation from the rest of family, they were kind of surprised that I went to college.

Rachel's father was the first person in their family to attend college despite the fact that his parents and siblings hardly possessed a high school education. Because of this, he was insistent that his daughter would go to college and was involved in Rachel's schooling to ensure that she did well. Rachel identifies that her mother was also very involved in her education. It was important to both her mother and father that Rachel would achieve more than a high school diploma.

Rachel stated that if she has daughters of her own, she hopes that they will be independent women who are able to make their own choices outside of the families' expectations. She would like them to attend college but that she will not force them to go. In her own life, she has seen how familial expectations can have a significant impact on educational choices. Despite the support she received from her parents, her extended family had an impact on the trajectory her education took:

> There were expectations that I wouldn't go to college and then when I went to college there were expectations I wouldn't go to graduate school and I am so they are kind of a little baffled as to why I would want to do that because, when I get married, [they assume] I'll be staying home taking care of house and kids and husband. For a really long time, I wanted to be a doctor but I was discouraged from it by my family because it was too ambitious for a woman.

Despite the messages she received from her extended family regarding the appropriate roles for a woman, Rachel was positively influenced to pursue an education and, through the example of her father, she was shown that she could obtain an education and continue to preserve her culture.

HISTORICAL EXPECTATIONS AMONG ROMA

Both Vaidy, in her forties and Peaches, in her eighties, were also strongly encouraged to pursue education. While the messages they received were similar, the path that their educations took significantly differed. Vaidy was able to pursue an education and eventually receive a PhD while Peaches, due to her parent's illness, left school to work and help support her family. Despite the different paths they followed, they both passed on a value of education to their children and an expectation that they would receive a college degree.

Vaidy recalled that though little was ever explicitly stated regarding the expectations she carried as a Roma woman there were a few messages she received regarding education. "I don't think they (expectations) were ever couched in Roma terms expect to say that our people were very hard working and we kept the family together as Roma women but we also worked really hard. I was always expected to get straight A's. I was expected to do well in school." Vaidy was identified as gifted learner from an early age. She received encouragement in her education not only from her parents but her teachers as well. Vaidy's mother encouraged her to pursue a college education at one of the elite universities on the East Coast, and that is exactly what she did. Vaidy was the first and only person in her family to receive a college degree.

Like Vaidy, Peaches was expected to attend and do well in school. She knew from observing her extended family that the value her parents placed on education was a departure from the ideals of her other family members:

> We went to school and it was like you had to go to school, you had no choice. A lot of Romanichal did not go to school, they couldn't read or write because their parents didn't go to school and their parents didn't believe in sending their kids to school to associate with the Gorja. My family was very broad minded. It was a cardinal rule, you didn't miss school unless you were really ill, ill enough to go to a doctor. That was one thing that they insisted upon is that we got an education. All three of us graduated from high school and [my sister] was the lucky one, she got to go to college.

Unlike Vaidy, Peaches' mother was not able to assist her in a dream of attending college. At a young age, both her mother and father became ill. As soon as she graduated high school, which in itself was an accomplishment for a Roma woman living a traditional, traveling lifestyle, she began working to help support her family. Had these circumstances not occurred, the path to college would have been open to her. She recalled that her parents were open to whatever she wanted to do. Though neither of her parents had a high school education, they valued knowledge and emphasized achievement in education. Despite this, the cultural norms of caring for one's own family strongly influenced the trajectory her life would take:

> That's the only thing I regret in my life, that I didn't go to college but I couldn't because mama and papa were sick and I was supporting them and by the time it got to the point where they were well, I could have gone to college but it was not that important to me then. I could see that I was needed more at home than for my personal thing to go to college.

Though their lives took different paths, both Vaidy and Peaches continue to hold on to the value for education that was instilled in them from a young age. Peaches passed this value on to her own daughter who eventually completed her college education. Vaidy has no doubt that her children will go on to achieve a college education given that she has created a culture for them that has already set the expectation of college as an eventuality rather than a choice to be made.

REACTION TO EDUCATION AMONG TRADITIONAL ROMA

"They Will Get Made Fun Of"

Unlike most of the women interviewed, Gayle, in her thirties, had two parents that were college educated. Her parents instilled an appreciation and value for education as well as a love for participating in sports, which would eventually enable her to pay for college. Gayle recalled that both her parents grew up very poor and worked hard to pay their way through college. Her dad was able to go to college on a football scholarship. Because of this, both her mother and father steered her toward sports from an early age as a means of paying for college. Gayle went on to receive a master's degree and considers herself fortunate to have had parents who went beyond the traditional expectations for their daughter.

Though not raised around traditional Roma, Gayle spent some time living within a Roma community where she observed a resistance to formal education:

> It is completely shunned across the board. There is this idea that if you are going outside looking for something you are looking for a source which is outside a Roma source you know. You are going outside the community so automatically you are opening yourself up to it. I don't want to sound angry but that's an idea in traditional communities of ritual purity that prevents easy interaction, like it is spiritually dirty.

Gayle identified that the messages that are often communicated about education involve the idea that interaction with people and ideas outside of the culture bring with it an impurity further solidifying the idea that to remain separate is ideal. Gayle identified other barriers to education for many traditional Roma women. "I think the other thing is there is no precedence for education so people are not sure what might happen if people go out and get an education."

Gayle hopes to pass on the value of education to other Roma by helping them to achieve a minimum standard of education without having to engage with individuals outside of their communities. One way she has attempted to do this was by starting an online GED prep program that provided a Roma tutor. Unfortunately, Gayle found that many individuals who began the program lacked support at home. "They will get made fun of and they will be like oh you want to be like a gadje. People will say look at her, she doesn't want to be like us." Again, more evidence was found that supported the idea that the way the traditional Roma talk to their children about education is often directly influenced by the level of assimilation they are comfortable with their children engaging in.

"Traditional Men Do Not Find That Attractive" —Gendered Views of Education

Ruby, in her forties, was another respondent who received the message that education was to be valued. Neither of her parents had received a college education due to life circumstances and both grew up very poor. Like so many other respondents, Ruby considered her parents different from the norm found among her Roma relatives. "My parents were a little bit different in that they did value education and they did want me to go to college and grow up and be successful academically and financially." Ruby had observed that other family members expressed alternate expectations to their daughters, "They do not value girls getting an education and men, traditional men, do not find that attractive."

Ruby's parents were involved in her schooling and expected her to get good grades. Her parents encouraged her to go to college to study journalism though she had expectations for being a teacher herself. Her parents were not supportive of this decision so Ruby chose not to go to college for many years. She attended a technical school and received a certification and then got married at a young age. She recently returned to college to receive a degree in teaching, an accomplishment that her parents have expressed much pride in. Ruby acknowledges that her parents gave her every opportunity to achieve educationally, opportunities she failed to take advantage of at the time. Ruby has already instilled the expectation in her own daughter that she will attend college and believes she will be able to provide the financial as well as emotional support she will need to achieve this dream.

For Ruby, the consideration of assimilation and its effect on her future was not a factor in influencing her decision to pursue an education. Though extended family members held traditional expectations, her parents were able to effectively communicate a value for education and instill in their daughter the belief that achieving an education was an attainable goal. While many traditional families fear that education may draw their daughters away from the traditional way and therefore prefer them to remain separate, the message that Ruby encountered was that in order to be successful, one had to separate one's life as a Roma from one's existence in the world of the Gorja. This duality of identity negatively impacted Ruby's school experiences and caused her to develop a dislike for school. Ruby's experiences highlight what several respondents encountered. For Roma, it is often the message about the individuals involved in education rather than education itself that prevent women from obtaining a degree.

CHANGING BELIEFS SURROUNDING WOMEN AND EDUCATION IN ROMA COMMUNITIES

Gracie is in her sixties. She possesses a master's degree and has previously worked in a university setting. Today, she promotes her culture through her writing. Though connected with her culture, Gracie spent many years assimilating entirely into the world of the gadje.

Gracie's assimilated lifestyle seemed quite unusual given the upbringing she described during her interview. Her father, like so many Roma from the older generations, held strong ideas about "separation" and "cleanliness." Though in minute ways, this related to cleaning and food, on a large scale, these concepts ensured that as Roma, they would remain separate from the gadje who were viewed as an "unclean" people. In her interview, Gracie recalled the severity of her father's views:

> My father had certain ideas about cleanliness. Food had to be a certain way, food could not touch each other. Everything had to be separate. Laundry had to be separated, the house had to be cleared a certain way. We were not allowed to have dogs in the house, those kinds of thing.

In addition to barriers of assimilation, Gracie encountered gender roles that restricted her and confined her to the realm of home and housework. Though Gracie's mom worked, it was largely out of necessity which, for many older Roma, was the only acceptable reason for a Roma woman to work within a gadje-dominated environment.

Gracie left behind the traditional expectations of her family and not only obtained an advanced degree but surrounded herself with educated individuals, which included both Roma and non-Roma friends. For Gracie, the integrated lifestyle meant incorporating the Roma customs and connections into the assimilated lifestyle she had already established later in life. When asked if she thought other Roma women must assimilate away from their culture to become educated, Gracie had much to say.

Gracie discussed how she currently works as an online GED tutor. Through her volunteer work she strives to help Roma with a desire to be educated to meet their goals at home. Many times, this has been problematic due to the familial barriers and cultural norms that have persisted throughout the years:

> I have tutored Roma girls, whose family, whether or not they showed up to class was very problematic. Usually it was I had to watch the younger kids and

I had to baby sit for my sister. I couldn't use the computer because my father
wanted to talk to so and so wherever. The families didn't make it a priority.
Then I tutored a young man who had never been to school a day in his life, it
isn't only the girls but the girls will have a hard time of it because they think
the boys need enough education to do business in the world but I don't think
they think about the girls.

Despite the many barriers to education that some Roma lifestyles present,
Gracie persisted in believing changes have and will continue to be made to
cultural norms and beliefs surrounding education:

I think there are ways to incorporate your culture into a more educated lifestyle, a more affluent lifestyle but not without struggle probably. Are there
things we have let go of? Yeah. But can you be a proud woman and be
educated? Watch us. . . . I think we probably need to change the definition of
who Roma women are a little bit but we can do that without losing our culture,
without losing the language . . . It will be a struggle.

Gracie observed that holding on fully to traditional gender roles may not be
conducive to a change in lifestyle but she expressed strongly that a life of
integration was possible. Roma women could be elevated through education
while remaining true to their culture and their people in unity with many of
the women who participated in the study. Gracie believes that accommodation without full assimilation is possible. Will it require Roma to give up
some ways of life? Almost certainly but, at least according to these women, it
can be done.

EDUCATIONAL ATTITUDES AMONG MEN

Gilbert, in his forties, found that his parents encouraged him to go to school and
do well. Because of his awareness of the challenges that Roma worldwide face
in their attempts to gain an education, he acknowledged his gratitude for the
education received. "I was lucky enough to grow up in a multicultural society
and I had access to free public education to open the world to me."

Al dropped out of high school and never returned to finish his education.
Al was able to make a living despite his lack of education:

Back in those days education wasn't really a big deal. If you were willing to
work then everyone could get by. It wasn't really big deal like it is now. It's a
lot harder to get by today with no education.

For those Roma resistances to engage with the educational system due to
cultural differences the outcomes for those who were willing to work independently and live a transient life were not significantly impacted. Today,

even those who wish to maintain traditional means of making a living are finding their prospects dim without a proper education.

CONCLUSION

Roma face many barriers in their acculturative practices, among these are the barriers they encounter in their educational pursuits. Whether these barriers come from mainstream prejudice or within their communities or families, Roma are significantly impacted by their interactions with the educational system. For many Roma, these barriers translate to barriers to assimilation. For others, the barriers create a sense that one must choose between pursuing nontraditional occupations and educational achievement or their Roma identity and community. While attitudes toward education within Roma communities have begun to shift significantly among those who once held traditional ideals, many still face discrimination from the outside world as they pursue better opportunities.

In the coming chapter, I discuss two important factors within Roma life that may serve to protect them from the harmful effects of the barriers, prejudice and discrimination that have been discussed thus far. Roma identity and traditional lifestyles have served as protective buffers for Roma in many ways. By discussing the changes that have occurred both in the definition of Roma identity and the decline of traveling lifestyle, I hope to shed light on how Roma have been impacted in significant ways by mainstream influences. Further, I hope to bring understanding to the diversity of Roma definition and identity.

Chapter Six

Roma Identity
and Traditional Lifestyles

Protective Barriers in a Hostile World

For Roma who experience resistance to their assimilation, and discrimination, several factors may potentially serve as a buffer to the stress associated with their navigation of acculturation and the harmful effects of prejudice. The first of these is the lifestyle of traditional Roma who have both their traditional ways and the support of their families to buffer the impact of outside influences. The second, a strong identification with their ethnic identity.

TRAVELING AND FAMILIAL SUPPORT IN AMERICA

Little exists discussing the rise or decline of the traveling lifestyle among Roma in the United States. What is in existence is a trail of laws in many states throughout America that specifically targeted the occupations or lifestyles of Roma who have traveled. In 1915 laws were passed in North Carolina identifying that certain groups must pay a traveling tax and license fee to conduct businesses. Roma (defined in the law as "gypsies") were the only group identified by their ethnicity within the law (Martindale-Hubbell, 2003). Texas Penal Code 607 which stated "All companies of gypsies, who, in whole or in part, maintain themselves by telling fortunes" (Paragraph 7, Article 607), as well as "All persons who advertise and maintain themselves in whole or in part as clairvoyants or foretellers of future events, or as having supernatural knowledge with respect to present or future conditions, transactions, happenings or events." (Paragraph 13, Article 607). These were considered illegal. This was later declared unconstitutional. Laws passed in 1967 in New York stated that individuals caught telling fortunes would be charged with disorderly conduct—many believed this was meant to target Roma specifically (*New York Times*, 2011). Federal law identifies that among groups who cannot be discriminated against based on national origin are Gypsies, though they largely identify themselves by language and ethnicity and are without a home nation. (Perea, 1993). This was a landmark decision made after a man claimed he was fired based on his Roma identity.

Though literature exists identifying that the loss of the traveling lifestyle has meant that Roma no longer see each other on the road (Heaslip, 2015), it is difficult to ascertain to what extent the traveling lifestyle has impacted the strength of identity among American Roma. Of the 23 Roma I interviewed, only four are actively engaged in traveling. During the recruitment phase of my study I reached out to many more but their traveling schedule made it difficult for them to find time to participate. Among those interviewed, several did provide evidence that engagement in the traveling lifestyle provided one close access to family and support systems. Gertie, a woman in her early fifties described her mother's motivation for moving their family frequently:

> *Interviewer: Was there any other reason you moved so much growing up . . . ?*
> Gertie: . . . well my mom got to a point where she didn't want to stay away from her family anymore.
> *Interviewer: Ok so she moved to be near her family?*
> Gertie: Yes.

Gertie highlights the significant impact that the desire for the support of family had on her geographical location, though it may have led to many moves throughout her lifetime.

In the Roma community, as in most, family is important to their way of life not only for emotional support but because of the way in which Roma structure their communities. The decline of the traveling lifestyle has impacted the way Roma not only talk to each other but also the ways in which the elders are cared for:

> you know it was everything to the older generation that families stay close and take care of each other, be there for each other financially emotionally, the younger generation would take care of the older generation when they were sick. Geographically we are spread out now and we don't communicate as much and older people go to nursing homes. (Ruby, forties, Southeast USA)

The loss of traveling together means that what was once a valued part of the community's identity has been lost and the support they once received from within the community is lost to some degree as well.

Donald, fifty-six, discussed the sense of loss his elderly father expresses when he recalls a time more Roma were traveling together:

> That's the thing my father talks about, nobody travels together anymore, nobody is together anymore. There was always kids around, there was always different people around that you were meeting and you might go the next year before you saw them someplace else but you knew who they were and it was like family . . . that's what everyone remembers, including my dad that was the best time in their lives when everyone was together.

While being on the road is not without its challenges, the sense of community and togetherness brought a sense of nostalgia to Donald's father and to many older Roma. Like Donald's father. Al, seventy-five, is among those who feel this sense of nostalgia and loss:

> Everything is changing and I get nostalgic for the past. What I miss about traveling is no matter where you went it was just a mobile community you know and we might move. We used to move on average every four or five days sometimes every five or six weeks. I don't think we stayed anywhere more than 5 or 6 weeks. But no matter where you went at that time you always knew someone who kept up at that time with someone else. You see someone on the road and automatically you would stop and say who are your people? That was how you kept up and that was before you had telephones. No one had a telephone or address so what happened you just had to send general delivery. So how everyone kept up you see some on the side of the road. That's what you do. It was automatic you would stop you know, but not anymore. It's different how people are toward one another.

Al has experienced a sense of loss. He describes the life on the road as a unifying experience, even among those who were not related by blood. Eddie, fifty-one, describes similar experiences and acknowledges the loss of what was once a way of life:

> It used to be you'd pull up to a campsite and there would be a hundred cars and trailers but still if there was just few there would be at least 20 or so people and trailers. It used to be when we pulled together we would pull our cars together and then it got to be where they parked by their own trailers, and now they don't come out to the camps, they have their own homes.

Benny described this way of life as a "fierce bond of who and what we are." There can be little doubt that the traveling life has been significant in the life of the Roma, has been at one time a defining point of identity and a way of life that provided community and safety.

While those interviewed did not state that Roma who no longer traveled considered themselves less Roma, Gertie identified that those who have fully or partially assimilated feel "guilty because you have broken with the cultural norms." Thus, for those Gertie is describing, distress related to decisions of acculturation comes from within. Gertie's own experience with this has made her sensitive to the lives of others:

> I think it makes me more compassionate to people of different races because
> I'm realizing that just because people live their lives and seem to assimilate . . .
> their ways and their culture might be different and it might be hard for them as
> far as understanding American culture.

Gertie identifies that just because a minority group may seem to have given
up their traditional lifestyles and assimilated into the lives of the dominant
group doesn't mean they no longer struggle with identity, miss their old ways
or have trouble coming to terms with their new ways of living.

Phoebe, a woman in her forties from the Southeast United States, has
identified that many Roma today "stay in one town a little more than they
used to. They find their businesses are more settled than they used to." The
impact of this, she identified is:

> they are not as close knit now. I think some things have been lost and some
> things have been gained . . . By staying in one place, I think a lot of the
> extended families and the old traditions, old times, the old ones from way back
> are not as prevalent as they used to be.

The other side of the decline of traditional ways is that as Roma become
more spread out and settled, they become more open to outside relationships
than they would have been had they still been traveling with their families.
Josephine, a woman in her thirties, still involved in a traditional traveling
life, identifies that though she has friends outside the Roma community, she
has less contact with them because her traveling lifestyle does not allow for
consistent interaction.

While Phoebe sees the loss of the old ways as both a positive and a
negative, Ruby identifies that the loss of the old way is not a negative at all.
In her view, Roma are much better off living a settled life with occupations
that are able to provide better, consistent support to their families. "You have
two uneducated parents living in poverty. A trailer park is not a good environment for a child I feel like and there are a lot of factors working against
you." Ruby sees the development of a settled life as advantageous economically and educationally.

Some of the factors that Ruby alludes to are not only the potential for
poverty but also marginalization that comes outside the community. While
government restrictions in America have not impacted the traveling lifestyle
to the extent that they have in Europe, media portrayals and targeting by the
police have significantly impacted them. Louisa, a woman still engaged in
the traveling lifestyle, identifies that the increased profile of the Roma on
television and other media has increased the level to which Roma are visible
at the various sites they try to camp at, leading them to be turned away,
limiting the places they are able to reside. Also, as previously identified,
police have become increasingly wary of traveling Roma and utilize media

sources to warn communities regarding their presence and work which makes it increasingly difficult for Roma to find work in areas they have not built a consistent presence.

Traveling and Familial Support in Europe

The familial structure of many European Roma provides emotional and psychological benefits by providing practical support and security (Lee et al., 2014). Traditional ways of traveling and residing in close proximity to one another provide Roma with a tight knit support system, often as close as their next door neighbors. In a study conducted with German Sinti and Roma (Strauss, 2012), Roma identify the significant role that family plays in buffering the harmful effects of the outside world:

> My family, family, means: safety, trust, being there when things are bad for somebody or being there when things are good for somebody, too. Family is simply sticking together. (Sinti male, fifty-nine, 23)

A strong part of the Roma identity for some in Europe, and a way of keeping families close together is through "traveling," the life of many traditional Roma, who move frequently for work, to avoid discrimination or simply for the freedom of experiencing new places. Additional benefits of traveling were described by Van Cleemput et al. (2007):

> Perceived benefits of a travelling lifestyle also included proximity to extended family members in an otherwise hostile "world." This was felt to be important, both psychologically and in terms of practical support and security. Travelling also allowed the possibility of moving away from potential trouble. Some participants described how they had returned to living in a trailer in order to escape hostility or victimization from housed neighbors. (207)

Van Cleemput identifies that the traveling life provides Roma with social and psychological benefits. Additionally, it gives Roma the ability to resist pressure to assimilate and provides them with significant social support.

The ability to navigate the conflict between the dominant society's acceptance or rejection of their presence and the desire of many Roma to travel within their own communities is a significant contributor to depression, stress and "nerves" among Roma (Doherty, 2013). Many in mainstream European society devalue the Roma's chosen way of life (Heaslip, 2015). The traditional life of traveling and setting up homes in travel parks or other available spaces is not considered equal to other ways of living, leaving many without housing accommodations.

Many changes to the economy as well as laws have begun to erode traditional means of traveler life (Doherty, 2013). In the United Kingdom, Roma are criticized for their unwillingness to assimilate, in newspapers and other forms of media, in reference to their living in nontraditional ways. Once they stop traveling however, not only is their presence in settled neighborhoods resisted but, they may fail to receive protection as a minority. In order to be considered a GRT in some areas, Roma must travel at least three months out of the year. Those who do not follow these guidelines may no longer be protected by law (Broomfield, 2016). Broomfield identifies that the pressure to assimilate into settled neighborhoods or keep up their traveling lifestyles is forcing many Roma to "choose between their ethnicity and their future."

Some Roma are finding that the traditional ways of being are fading and with this loss of the traditional ways, the strength of their identity has also begun to fade. Roma lose their sense of connection to one another impacting the ability of their strong, ethnic identity to buffer the harmful influence of portrayals by the dominant society and the prejudice they routinely encounter (Heaslip, 2015). Roma that choose the settled life often find they are separated from their support systems and the housing they are provided from local councils may be unsuitable for habitation and unsanitary (Yin-Har, 2011). Heaslip's 2015 study identifies the emotional and psychological vulnerability that Roma are faced with when they are forced to make these choices or are restricted through local laws or opinions voiced in local media:

> There was a sense from the community that due to the multiple restrictions on their lives (inability to travel, and restrictions on site) that their ways of living are being eroded with little choice or say to halt the progression. This is moving them further away from living authentically (as they would wish) toward a more inauthentic but settled lifestyle which is resulting in them experiencing feeling vulnerable. (124)

Heaslip describes a situation in which Roma are not allowed by the dominant society to choose their preferred model of acculturation. Instead, though they are resisted by mainstream society, their ability to maintain a separate life is removed, thus increasing their overall experience of vulnerability.

Traditional, traveling Roma resent the interference of the government and/or media in influencing how they live their daily lives. They report lacking autonomy over where they live and how they live and few governments are willing to provide culturally appropriate accommodations (Van Cleemput, 2007). In a study on the health-related benefits of experiences of gypsies and Travellers, one Roma man expresses his frustration at the involvement of governments who seek to change his way of life (Van Cleemput):

> We haven't asked anybody to change their ways. Do you know what I mean? Why should they ask us to change ours? See what I'm saying. And that's what the government's trying to do. They're trying to make you change your ways. (207)

The respondent identifies that it is the interference of the government rather than his own will that is forcing him to choose how he will live among and interact with mainstream society.

Traveling and Roma Identity

Not only does the loss of the traditional lifestyles impact Roma ability to closely access their families and support systems and allows some Roma to insulate themselves from the influence of the outside world, it also impacts their very identity as Roma. The redefining of who is and isn't Roma based on their engagement with traveling lifestyle is another method by which media and the dominant culture discriminate against the Roma.

As already stated, a choice between living a settled or traveling life may result in choosing opportunities for their families or no longer being defined by their rightful identity. These ideas may originate to some degree outside the community, especially through laws such as those already discussed but they may also become internalized. Roma who no longer travel may see themselves as illegitimate gypsy (Toth, 2005). Others are able to continue to take an ethnic view of their identity but find themselves becoming "invisible" to one another as they choose a settled life. Roma who no longer travel together not only lose their sense of community but lose the interaction of cooking on the land or meeting around a community fire (things that have come to be outlawed in some areas) (Heaslip, 2015).

A study by Van Cleemput (2007) identifies that confusion within the United Kingdom exists regarding who is and who is not a gypsy due to the fact that many now live in permanent housing. If anything, this exemplifies that many in the mainstream define Roma by both stereotypical schemas and by their actions rather than their ethnicity, an unfortunate side effect of media portrayals. Those who are able to overcome poverty or low social status, leading them to abandon the traveling lifestyle, are no longer considered part of their group by society or the media (Oleaqu, 2014).

THE INTERNALIZATION OF PREJUDICE

As already identified, media portrayals are among the most influential sources of prejudice. Mainstream media increases the extent to which dominant groups are exposed to prejudice toward minority groups, they also increase the amount of stereotypical portrayals minority groups are exposed to. These portrayals have the ability to significantly impact the identity development of minority groups (Mastro, 2009). This may be particularly harmful to minority groups as minorities may come to internalize stereotypes given enough exposure, even when recognizing these stereotypes as harmful (Manzo & Bailey, 2005).

The internalization of negative stereotypes perpetrated by dominant groups has the potential to impact self-image in a significant way (Jones, 2004; Parham et al., 1999). Mastro (2015) identifies that media attitudes toward, and portrayals of, minorities can significantly impact an individual's self-concept. Studies show that stereotypical portrayals not only affect social attitudes but can impact the individual by influencing self-stereotyping, harming self-esteem, interrupting coping behaviors and increasing depression (Fryberg et al., 2008, Leavitt et al., 2015). Negative social representations have also been associated with poor psychological functioning (Fryberg, 2002). Rivadeneyra, Ward and Gordon (2007) find that among Latino youth, lower social self-esteem was associated with frequent television viewing.

The impact of negative media portrayals is especially harmful as it has the potential to prevent minorities from utilizing identification with their ethnic identity as a buffer against the harmful effects of prejudice (Crocker & Major, 1989). Studies show that those who have a strong identification with their ethnic identity are less likely to be affected negatively by the prejudice they encounter (Crocker & Major) and may be more able to buffer the negative effects of media influences (Rivandanevra, Ward & Gordon, 2007).

The impact of the mainstream media on Roma who no longer travel is not the only way that Roma identity is affected by dominant groups. Another reason Roma experience negative outcomes when encountering prejudice or resistance is the fading of a strong ethnic identity that they may have once held, an identity that has now been significantly impacted by influences outside of their community. Research with American minorities show that an individual's identity may be resistant to the harmful effects of prejudice and discrimination if they possess a strong, ethnic identity. This identity increases their overall sense of self-worth and serves as a buffer against the outside influence of prejudice (Crocker & Major, 1989; Jones, 2004; Parham et al., 1999). While one's identity may serve as an important buffer against the effects of prejudice or discrimination, Roma must contend with many factors that serve to negatively impact their strong sense of identity and thus, reduce the extent to which they are able to minimize the harmful effects of the resistance and prejudice they experience.

Outside Influences on Roma Identity

In the United States, though often invisible to the average person, Roma have a keen sense of the view that outsiders take of them and their existence. This has been highlighted in large part by mainstream responses to media portrayals but is often developed through their own interpersonal experiences. In the United States, Roma identity is largely unacknowledged and therefore little space is left for Roma to have a voice to define themselves. This may be as simple as space on a survey or census questionnaire. With no space to identify oneself as Roma, individuals are sometimes made to identify themselves in a way inauthentic to their identity. In addition, the potential threat for prejudice or the responsibility of educating and explaining to someone who the Roma are or are not also influences the decision to not only remain silent about their identity. It may also lead to internalized feelings of being "othered" as a Roma or of somehow being "less." Allie, a woman in her forties from the Northeast United States, recounts her experiences with identification:

> *Interviewer: If someone were to ask you to identify yourself racially or ethnically, what is it that you normally say?*
> I don't know that's kind of a complex question, most people don't understand Roma or Romani and they kind of give you that look or they say Romanian and then you have to explain you know gypsy but please don't say that, I don't really like that word. So, it really depends on the setting and on any types of census and survey data it's always other because there is no other choice but most of the time now I do identify as Roma but I don't always explain.

What Allie relates is a common experience for Roma who wish to accurately identify themselves, rather than hiding, and are forced to do so in terms defined by the mainstream.

The experience of Allie is the experience of many Roma, including myself. Oftentimes, the only way to identify yourself to the mainstream in a way they will understand is by using a term many Roma consider to be derogatory and one associated with negative stereotypes held about Roma. Rachel, in her twenties, identifies how these stereotypes have impacted the ways that Roma expect to be perceived, "The stereotypes have definitely negatively impacted how we are perceived, what people expect of us." Mainstream expectations for Roma become all the more salient when Roma are forced to identify themselves with a term that carries the weight of mainstream prejudice.

As I have discussed in previous chapters, Roma in America face many stereotypes about themselves that they must combat. These stereotypes have the potential to become internalized and have a significant impact on their identity as well as their belief that they will be accepted by their community or by the mainstream. An article written in the *Harvard Crimson* highlights some of the views held by Americans, views harmful to the Roma community even when seemingly intended to be in their defense (Lacalle, 2009):

> The problem is perpetuated because Gypsies place such a low value on traditional education. Many Gypsies teach their children the traditional music and dance of the Gypsy people, but literacy is not highly valued. This means that Gypsies cannot respond articulately to the negative stereotypes that are circulated in the media of the countries they inhabit. Because of these unique circumstances, both Europeans and Americans should be sensitive to how they treat the subject of Gypsies.

It is not difficult to identify what is problematic about these ideas. Roma are painted as a group completely disinterested in education and without the means to stand up for themselves. These ideas, written at institutions at the top of the American university system, disseminate age-old stereotypes about the Roma.

Phoebe describes the ideas that Americans hold about Roma identity:

> Absolutely, absolutely. I don't think that this country is as much aware even that it's a real culture because I don't think that it's as much noticed here. I don't think that other European countries in Europe around and more of the forefronts I don't think it's much of an issue here. I think that if they believe they exist at all, and if they are real, I think probably the majority have a negative connotation, I think you know "gypsys, tramps and thieves" I think just these old stereotypical thoughts that probably if there were to others to replace then they may have different thoughts but I don't think it's on the forefronts of their minds so much.

Phoebe believes that if people think of Roma at all, it is in a stereotypical fashion. She also believes that if countering images were presented there would be a potential for the mainstream to think differently of Roma, helping to eliminate these stereotypes

Research shows that not only do those who encounter stereotypes about themselves have the potential to experience a significant amount of psychological distress (Jones et al., 1995) but, individuals are at risk of internalizing these stereotypes which leads to damaging effects on one's self-image (Crocker & Major, 1989; Jones, 2004; Parham et al., 1999). This can occur even when the group or individual recognizes these stereotypes to be harmful or erroneous and even when these stereotypes are transmitted through media such as television (Manzo & Baily, 2005).

Gilbert, forty-seven, identifies the ways in which Roma in the United States are not only exposed to stereotypes about themselves, but are also restricted from learning about themselves in an ethnically positive manner:

> To this day I am learning new things, but how is anyone supposed to know this if me with a master's degree looking into different texts and doing different research, this stuff is not readily available, it's not taught in schools just like French people learn French history. American people learn American history in their history classes. What did we learn about Roma history and culture? And it still isn't being taught today and I think that is a crying shame that more of it isn't taught and more if it isn't easily available because Roma people don't learn where Roma people come from . . . there is a real lack of Roma history for Roma people.

Without alternative or countering information, Roma may be more open to believing or internalizing the negative messages that disseminated about the Roma.

Another means of outsiders possessing control over the ways in which Roma identify themselves and the strength of their positive self-identity is in the labels they use to define themselves. As previously identified, while many Roma prefer not to use the term gypsy it is often necessary to use that term to define oneself to those outside the Roma community as a point of reference. One Roma man from Ohio posts on Facebook (2016) his feelings about the mainstream's insistence of using a term many within the Roma community find offensive:

> I think we do a disservice to ourselves when we refer to our family and ancestors as gypsies when talking to others. I mean for one, it's a slur and the longest living misunderstanding of our origin, but also since people don't get what a gypsy is and plenty of bastards are making money off of that between TV and retail, we should make them know what a Roma is. (Roma man, Ohio)

The man from Ohio believes that the use of the term gypsy removes the ability of Roma to choose how they will be defined and relinquishes that power to individuals who profit from it.

Benny, thirty-one, expressed deep frustrations and astonishment at the ways in which Roma terms of identification become appropriated by outsiders. He discussed his thoughts and feelings toward the word gypsy:

> Yeah if this was any other slur, it's a slur. I know many of us own it . . . I am even kind of weirdly proud of it because in my head it has kind of a punk connotation, like we're the black sheep, the don't like us, that's ok I don't like them either. So kind of wearing it with pride but at the same time yeah it's horrible that like even today you can't tell people who we are without saying it . . . You can't even say the N word, I would have guilt the second I let those 6 letters go out of my mouth, but if you were a Black person and you couldn't get people to understand what you were talking about until you referred to yourself as that that would be a travesty. You would be horrified but that is every day for Roma in the USA at least.

In the United States, unlike in Europe, where Roma aren't often recognizable by their features or skin tone, explanations of their identity are often required, much to the frustration of many Roma. As Benny points out, for many Roma the word gypsy carriers with it as many negative racial implications as the N word for the Black community (Cusack, 2011). Often, unlike those within the Black community who lack the privilege of masking their racial identity, Roma must situate themselves within the context of a racial slur in order to bring someone to an understanding of who or what they are.

These narratives highlight the impact of appropriation on the Roma community and their identities. The appropriation of being gypsy though seen as racial slur, is still offensive to many Roma and again, leaves them without the ability to control how they and their communities are defined. This leaves their own identities to be something that comes in conflict with the mainstream's view of themselves. A woman from the United States, also seeking to highlight the impact of appropriation posted the following story on social media (2016):

> There is a store in the town that I'm living in right now that is called gypsies gift shop I decided to stop by because it was something that I haven't done yet I wanted to see what it was like . . . The lady that runs the shop kept asking me over and over what are you looking for what are you looking for I told her I wasn't really looking for anything that I am Roma. I'm what people call a gypsy and I was coming to see what these people are using the name for and she looks at me with a straight face and says oh well we call it that because and I'm going to tell you I'm pretty sure that I was a gypsy in a past life because I just love jewelry. I looked at her for a second I realize that she was serious and I said oh my God what's wrong with you and she looked at me like I hurt her feelings and I said that's strange and not appropriate and I walked out. (Roma woman, USA)

The story described is a characterization of what Roma throughout America and Europe experience when they witness the appropriation of Roma culture. Those who engage in it give little thought to the impact it has on Roma lives and identity.

Cultural appropriation of the Roma identity, even in a stereotypical form, impacts the strength of Roma identity by constantly placing Roma on the offensive and, as previously discussed, reducing this identity to a set of behaviors rather than ethnicity. These ideas which may become internalized by Roma themselves may impact their sense of being a "real" Roma, increasing the overall impact of the negative outcomes they experience. In 2017 many Roma protested the appropriation of Roma culture and the use of the term "Gypsy" in European fashion. This appropriation has continued to re-emerge every so often as "popular" fascination with generic gypsy culture" heightens. In 2012, La Ferla reported on this fascination without a critical voice. Her article "The fortune tellers knew it," celebrates the designers who have turned their "catwalks into caravans" highlighting carnival skirts and midriff baring tops. She points to the success of these lines as the public fascination with those who live "outside the norm" and who do their "own thing." This fascination can lead to many things, appropriation, fetishizing, sexualization but rarely if ever does it lead to true appreciation, celebration or understanding of the appropriated culture.

Outside Influences on Roma Identity Formation Europe

In many ways, the experience of American Roma parallels that of European Roma though significantly more research can be found to support the existence of these experiences among European Roma and the intensity of these experiences is certainly greater among European Roma. Roma in Europe are consistently "othered" by media and interpersonal interactions, (Ceyhan, 2003) placing them at risk, like American Roma, of internalizing the feeling of being "less than." A case study of Roma identity in Turkey looks at 36 gypsy and Roma people, how they define themselves and what impacts their identity. One respondent identifies their experiences with individuals outside of the community, "Non-Gypsies that live in Edirne look at us something like whatsoever, I think, they look down on us, they despise us." (Aynur, Gypsy woman, age thirty-seven, 110). The respondent was all too aware of how she was perceived by those outside of her immediate community.

Another individual involved in the study who was not Roma identifies the treatment that European Roma experience from mainstream society, another example of how Roma have been "othered." "How American people excluded the Black people, we excluded them, so they feel coldness toward us, 'Whites'" (Birol, Roma male, age thirty-six, 142). In addition to being "othered" Roma in Europe face a barrage of stereotypes and stereotypical portrayals in the media that may also impact their identity development and self-image. These include age-old stereotypes such as stealing (Ureche & Franks, 2007), "If you tell the wrong person (you are gypsy) you get a lot of stick. It's always our fault if something gets nicked" (Irish Traveller, 14, 17). These stereotypes also include ideas about Roma being magical. The following is a quote written by the author of a study on Roma women in the Balkans (Kushi, 2016):

> A child growing up in Albania, for instance, is never immune to cultural indoctrination against the Roma population—"the gypsies." No matter how progressive a family may be, they will either implicitly or directly introduce their children to many negative stereotypes the culture throws at the Roma. At a very early age, society warned me to never open the door for a gypsy. Gypsies stole little children and dabbled in evil dark magic, my neighbors would so convincingly tell me.

The magical properties of the Roma were a memorable part of the author's childhood narrative, evidence that these stereotypes were pervasive in her culture.

Roma are often forcibly compared with the mainstream in Europe. The "White" culture is the default culture and Roma identity is situated in comparison to that culture by the mainstream (Heaslip, 2015), even when they define themselves as a part of the dominant culture. The comparison of Roma groups to the mainstream results frequently in Roma being viewed as homogenous. This view impacts their ability to define themselves (Heaslip, 2015). One researcher describes the conflict that exists in wishing to not be defined homogenously, a common assumption of Roma (Jovanovic, 2014), while also remaining somewhat insular from the settled community, which, in her view, perpetuates stereotypes against Roma (Heaslip):

> What was interesting was this expressed wish to be seen as individuals and not a homogenized group, yet this discourse of Gypsy/Travellers is perpetuated especially as the community is a closed community and chooses to stay within its own kind. Therefore a lack of integration between the Gypsy and settled community can only further perpetuate stereotypical, homogenized views. (Heaslip, 2015, 95)

An alternate view is that Roma should be able to define themselves without having to sacrifice portions of their identity for the comfort of the settled community or in relation to that community. Sadly, the ability of Roma identity to serve as a buffer against the harmful effects of prejudice is jeopardized as the struggle to define Roma between the outside community and Roma themselves places identity at the center of their struggle.

In Europe, like America, a struggle exists between the Roma community and the dominant society regarding how Roma are labeled. The majority of Roma have very specific ideas about how they wish to be labeled (Strauss, 2012) though there is no consensus, an issue I discuss toward the end of this chapter. Regardless of the label used, those in the mainstream continue to associate titles with pejorative meanings with Roma, taking the ability to choose and define their labels and placing Roma at risk of internalizing these negative associations. A study interviewed 275 Sinti and Roma (Strauss, 2012), many of whom were able to identify a time when the term gypsy was used against them in a pejorative manner:

> Actually it happened many times. It's almost the same thing every time; people come when they hear that we're Sinti, they say, "You dirty gypsy." (Sinti Male 37, 82)

> Well, they just always said, the "gypsies are dirty, and they steal," and "they never would have thought that I was one," and it was just really bad for me, because I didn't want that. (Sinti Woman, thirties, 82)

> . . . then my teacher said, "You're a gypsy, you won't amount to anything, none of you will ever amount to anything anyway." (Sinti Man, fifty-seven, 83)

One author describes the use of the term gypsy in this way (Beaudoin, 2014): "The word gypsy is often used to reaffirm—by non-Roma—the position of Roma as 'undesirable' outsiders or as people who do not belong."

Another way in which those outside the Roma community can impact the defining of Roma identity is by defining who "is" and who "isn't" a Roma based on arbitrary criteria. One that has already been discussed is traveling but another is based entirely on the way Roma "look." A study completed by a Canadian author about Roma recorded the responses of Roma who had immigrated to Canada from Europe. Study participants related their experiences with the phenomenon of being defined by outsiders (Beaudoin, 2014):

> And many [Canadians] who don't know too much about the gypsy, they ask "But you are White. . . . who can tell you are gypsy?" [In Europe], right away they know. . . . Even if you start to talk, they know, probably by the accent or something. They know. (Elana, New Refugee to Canada, 21)

Roma are expected to be physically identifiable though their looks vary widely. Those without the Roma "look" may be more able to "pass" into mainstream society but they may also be denied their Roma identity by outsiders if they do not look enough "Roma" for outsider's approval.

Roma, like many minorities, are undoubtedly impacted by the defining and portrayals of those outside their community. Not only does this occur on an interpersonal level, but as seen in earlier chapters, is often disseminated through the media. The constant conflict between the way Roma define themselves and how they are defined by the dominant culture is a significant source of stress but, despite this, many Roma are able to maintain a strong sense of themselves. The defining of Roma identity within their own community is influenced by a variety of factors and, contrary to the opinions of those outside the community, is far from homogenous. For many Roma interviewed, a point of discovery occurred before choosing specifically the ways in which they would identify, this time of discovery as well as their interactions with those outside of the Roma community had a significant impact on how they would come to define themselves to the outside world, and themselves.

THE DISCOVERY OF ROMA IDENTITY

Among those interviewed, the point at which they came to understand or discover their identity as a Roma in America was significant. Some interviewed did not develop an understanding of their identity to the rest of the world until they were exposed to "outsiders," often beginning in school. Others found their Roma identity a well-kept secret within their families. In either experience, the individual entered a point of discovery in which they learned more about their origins and decided how they would identify themselves to the outside world.

Benny's family came to the United States from Czechoslovakia. He stated that his family came to the United States with a clear goal of assimilation. As a result, they failed to pass on any significant information about their past, none related to their Roma roots:

> My family came here without any real knowledge about the Roma background, it was discovered over a bunch of genealogy. My mom is really into genealogy and we were able to piece it together. You start to figure out it was kind of a hush hush thing. We all kind of know and accept it and we go with it but it's not an outward thing.

Benny, his mother and Aunt have continued their process of discovery, and now that they have discovered their Roma heritage, hang on to it knowing that it's a significant part of their identity and the identity of their ancestors.

Henry's point of discovery occurred in college. Though he grew up with a knowledge that he was Roma, it was during this time of his life that he began to delve into what this meant for his identity development:

> I had some real complexes growing up, I went to college in the 90's. I started undergrad in 1990 so identity politics and your roots is what everybody talked about excessively on my college campus. So you know exploring my feelings about minority identity was a big focus during my time in college. Unfortunately, being obsessed with that question was normal in college so it made it acceptable for me to spend so much time trying to figure out Roma. Not Roma who attended the same university as me but um I spent a lot of time in college around Roma who were sort of my age who had very traditional lives. And I also had an internship in Europe with Roma NGO. So I had an opportunity to explore my identity in different ways while I was in college. I don't think I really felt Roma growing up. I felt like an American whose ethnicity was something to try and bury and then in college my thinking changed a lot especially as I got to know Rom who I really liked.

Henry's exploration of identity really began in college as he sorted out who he was internally and who he was in relation to the world around him.

HOW ROMA DEFINE THEMSELVES

In the introduction to her research, Velez (2012) shares that coming to an understanding of her Roma identity was a process, in many ways:

> My mother is not my Roma Parent, she has been a major supporter of [my] research . . . in my father's absence she made me aware that my Roma heritage was something important and something to be proud of. It is through my mother's love and encouragement that I was first able to embrace my own Roma identity . . . My father's Romani heritage became a part of my familial cosmogony, my brother and I had an understanding of how we came to be that was as much a creation myth as it was a genealogy.

Her experiences reflect those of other Roma whose embracing of their identity and perusal of its understanding was significantly impacted by their Roma parent whose own grappling with identity provided little in the way of affirmation toward this process.

A major conflict that has the potential to increase negative outcomes for Roma is the way in which Roma identify themselves when faced with pressure from those on the outside. I have already discussed the potential impact that the opinions of outsiders may have on Roma identity. Despite this impact, a strong association with Roma ethnicity still has the potential to serve as a buffer against the harmful effects of discrimination and prejudice. Research shows that the right to self-definition is important, particularly in minority/immigrant groups (Strauss, 2012). A study by Strauss finds that Roma identify themselves in a specific way and are cognizant of how they wish to be defined by those outside the community. Clear rules exist regarding what is and is not acceptable in terms of portrayal and the specific verbiage that is utilized.

The act of "coming out" as Roma is a significant point in the lives of Roma worldwide (Beaudoin, 2014). It is significant to not only the strength of their identification with Roma identity but also to their relationship with those outside their community. Many Roma believe they should have the ability to control when and to whom they "come out" regarding this identity and believe that this control has, to some degree, been taken by stereotypical portrayals in shows such as *My Big Fat Gypsy Wedding* (Herman, 2012; Poppelwell, 2012). These shows have heightened their visibility in negative ways or led some to feel forced to identify themselves as a means of countering negative portrayals (Covert, 2015).

The Definition of Roma Identity in America

Sadly, many Roma do form their identity in relation to the opinions of mainstream society. Though in objection to their stereotypical beliefs, Roma identity is sometimes formed as a response to the isolation they have experienced. Beaudoin (2014) defines how outside influences have impacted the way they define themselves:

> Roma efforts regarding their identities . . . have been influenced by (and in turn influence) governmental and public definitions of self, complicating and challenging the idea that all Roma can/should be designated in a particular bounded manner. (16)

Beaudoin believes that a shared Roma identity does in fact exist but that it is very much informed by the persecution they have experienced, and continue to experience:

> the very idea of making a checklist of attributes that could accurately and comprehensively identify Roma is both impossible and laughable. . . .Yet, a shared identity does exist, one that does regularly exclude non-Roma. . . . With fairly rigid boundaries; often, this identity process relies heavily on shared experiences of persecution. (20)

Beaudoin believes that the binding element of Roma identity is their shared past of persecution. Whether or not they have passed on stories attached to their beliefs, Roma have passed beliefs about their lives in relation to society onto their children, reminding them that they may be a part of the world they are in, but they don't belong.

Henry's father would often remind him of the differences between their family and the outside world, reminding him of the Roma's place within society:

> He would say things sometimes about how we didn't fit in and we will never fit in. You need to remember how different we are from these people. It was definitely part of what was passed on to me that we weren't normal, that we couldn't be.

For Henry, the message of difference came from within his own home. For many Roma, these messages are encountered from the world around.

Peaches, a woman in her eighties from the Southeast United States, conceptualizes her experiences with the opinions of those outside of her community in this way:

> It's weird that it seems like there's such a mystery behind being gypsy and Romanichal and we're just like every other family. I think the difference is there is such a mystery around it, everyone feels like there is some big hidden secret. In the history that I can think of we are the only ones who have been isolated like that, we don't have a country . . . I mean our original country.

Despite the confusion and isolation that Peaches recognizes from those outside the Roma community, growing up, one's identity as a Roma was talked about in a positive light as something to be proud of though it often went unacknowledged in the mainstream:

> We discussed that, being proud of who you are. We are proud of who we are but at the same time, we are no different from anyone else we're just like the Gorjas, But we are proud of who we are. We don't think that that's been recognized as a race, the good parts of it.

For Peaches, Roma identity was "normalized" as being like anyone else in the community, far from the "othering" of Roma that those outside the community have been known to engage in. Donald was also encouraged to be proud of his Roma identity while simultaneously being encouraged to keep it quiet:

> We always knew it from the beginning, we knew we were different from everybody else . . . At the time it was nothing talked about and it wasn't, I don't think it was that we were told that. It was just something that was inside of us. I think it was just something we instinctively knew. As we got older we tried to figure something out but we were told you don't want to tell anyone this, now you can proud of it but people don't like us so . . .

Donald existed in a conflicted space, as many Roma have and do, to be proud of one's identity but to be leery of the outside world and their potential for harm. This most often meant hiding one's identity for the sake of preservation.

Josephine, a woman in her thirties, also identifies that Roma have viewed themselves as people who are proud of who they are and what they value, "They are still a very proud people who put their families first." Fener acknowledges growing up she believed, like Peaches, that despite their differences, Roma were just like everyone else:

> everybody's family is different no matter what nationality you are, Italian Jewish, everybody is different, we have our own culture and as a child you don't know it's any different, and you just understand that's your family.

Fener was taught and believes that there is a "normalcy" to their differences that made them a part of the greater community.

The differences between themselves and others outside their community didn't make for a feeling of otherness for American Roma like Peaches and Fener, instead, it made them feel that their differences were the parts of their identity they could be proud of, proof of a strong ethnic identity that did indeed have the potential to serve as a buffer against the poor media portrayals and prejudice they have faced.

The experiences of other Roma however, have been negative. Many feel they lack the ability to define themselves because of the influence of outsiders. Some believe that Roma lack control over how they are defined and their ability to be offended by racial slurs. A Roma man from Ohio posts online (Facebook Post, 2016) about how Roma are not even allowed to define for themselves what is a racial slur against their community:

> We can't own the word gypsy in the same way other races get to own their own racial slurs because people don't know about Roma, so they don't know it's a bad word or that it's not a lifestyle. (Roma Man, Ohio)

Some Roma remain unsure about whether or not they would like to reveal their identity out of concern for how it will be accepted. Roma have carried with them a belief that their identity is something that needs to be hidden. Many Roma have lied about their ethnic identity at some point in their lives and continue this lie throughout their lifetime, further evidence that Roma are often unable to own and define themselves for fear of repercussions.

The answer to the question, "How do Roma identity themselves?," is that many don't, at least not out loud. Some define themselves as a people who need to stay quiet about their identity. They see themselves as secret and as a minority at constant risk of harm. Henry kept his identity hidden until college, due largely to the influence of his father:

> I was in the closet about being Roma, that was my father's choice you know as he advised, so none of my friends whether they were majority or not had any idea that I was a Gyspy. The fact that I was Jewish or part Jewish made me a minority in the place I grew up so I ended up gravitating toward other minorities but the Roma part of my family I kept quiet about until I was in college.

Despite the fact that he was already very much categorized as a minority in the area he grew up, he still chose to keep his Roma identity hidden until college, preferring not to divulge additional details that could contribute to his role as an outsider. This social position was something he experienced due to his Jewish roots. Henry was not unlike other respondents who hid their identity. Al described the prevailing attitude among many Roma about self-identification simply, "No we certainly don't tell anybody. Some of these younger ones will, the older ones certainly don't tell anyone what you are, you keep your business to yourself":

> Gilbert described his mother's reluctance to divulge her identity even to himself.
> My mother didn't tell me about my Roma background until I'm not sure how old I was, maybe 10, maybe 11 or 12 . . . and it was like a big secret we weren't supposed to talk about. I wasn't supposed to talk about with my father. My thought it was an embarrassment to him. I didn't get it . . . I was a product of an interracial marriage and the attitude my mother felt from my father's family . . . it was an issue of class and race . . . my mother felt it deeply.

Gilbert's mother's identity and subsequently his own was hidden not only because of how she had been treated by the outside world but also, based on his observations, how his father's family viewed his mother. It impacted her thoughts about herself and kept her from sharing this identity with her son early on. His mother maintained a preference that he not share his identity when he moved to Eastern Europe to work and even among his friends in college. "She preferred I didn't tell or was careful about it. I told a couple of friends here and there when I was at college. I wouldn't tell her I told someone." In the United States at least, Gilbert developed his own reluctant attitudes about divulging his identity because of the response he received:

> I would see how they reacted, this was never a big deal because it was America so people doubted me, what do you mean you are a gypsy? How can you tell you are? It was more like I had to prove I wasn't making something up like a Walt Disney Esmerelda trying to be something I am not and that annoyed me . . .

Eddie experienced a similar outcome, when he did choose to divulge his identity, he was often met with disbelief or an accusation of creating a false narrative about himself:

> They can't never figure out what you are. They can't figure it out and you never tell them because if you tell them they wouldn't believe you. Like the kids going to school, I might have told a few of them in a couple of different schools, always end up the same way, they have no idea or they think you are making it up or they would have the wrong idea.

Eddie knew that divulging his identity to those who were curious would have one of two outcomes: either he wouldn't be believed, like Gilbert, or he would face stereotypical attitudes, like Fener.

HIDING ROMA IDENTITY

Many among those interviewed identified that at some point in their life, they have allowed their identity to be mislabeled or misconstrued as a means of protection. Rather than divulge their Roma heritage, they chose to identify with a group that seemed more socially acceptable and less likely to attract discrimination or prejudice from the majority.

Identifying as Native American

Gertie, in her early fifties, recalls many messages about hiding who she was. Gertie grew up in a small southern town where, she recalled, most of the other children had blond hair and were fair-skinned. Gertie, with her black hair, dark brown eyes and olive skin was noticeably different. In school people would often ask her, "What are you?" and most often she allowed them to believe that she was Native American. Her mother, she recalled, shunned the idea of telling others about who she was. The rest of her family encouraged her to identify herself in a way much more socially acceptable than the truth:

They told me to say we were English Irish travelers. Well my aunt did and then my mom never told me that I was anything, she just told me not to say I was gypsy. When I was small I don't think I understood the cultural significance of being a gypsy.

Gertie's appearance and the dark secret of her identity influenced her ability to successfully interact with the world around her. She felt, even from a young age that she was different though she didn't understand the weight of this difference nor what this would mean for her socially. She knew only that to hide her identity was part of her life as a Roma.

"It's Not Something I've Ever Been Proud of" — Motivation to Hide Roma Identity

Ruby's family was especially protective of their identity. Ruby, though in her early forties, carries the weight of her secret with her even to this day. Upon beginning the interview, she identified that had it not been for my involvement in the project she would have refused to even participate in the interview because of how closely she keeps the knowledge of her identity. Ruby recalled:

> it was kind of difficult because I was always told growing up not to tell that we were Romanichal gypsies so I always felt I was carrying around this burden, that I had this secret but yet my grandmother told me it was something to be proud of but I felt like how can you be proud of something yet it has to be a secret.

Ruby felt confused about the messages she received from her family. She was encouraged to feel pride in her heritage and she was given an explicit message that it was important not to tell others about who she was.

Ruby's dilemma was similar to many of the other Roma who participated in the study. Many identified being instilled with a pride in their heritage while simultaneously being encouraged to hide it. Few who were interviewed were able to live with an outright pride in their identity or felt the freedom to share it with their friends. For Ruby, the weight of the secret she carried around made even school difficult to bear as she was surrounded by people outside of her community from whom she must hide her identity on a daily basis. Ruby recalled sharing that secret with a few close friends whom she found to be accepting but she lived in fear that somehow her parents would discover she had revealed their secret. She feared what the recourse for committing such a cultural taboo would be.

Identifying as Italian

Fener's experience with identity confusion was very similar to that of Ruby's. Growing up in the Deep South, she was also instilled with the message that she was to hide her identity from those who were outside her family:

> [we were told to] not let outsiders know who we were. If they did they would think you know we were bad people . . . I always kept close to my family because I was afraid, I was afraid of people who were not my family . . . I hid, I hid who I was. Nobody knew who I was.

Fener carried with her a fear of outsiders, passed down from her family which prompted her to hide who she was. Like Gertie, Fener had very dark features which prompted many questions from the classmates in her southern town. She identified that at a young age she began to lead people to believe that she was Italian, which was much more socially acceptable. She was told never to tell anyone that she was Roma because of the racism that would inevitably be encountered. When asked if she believed she would have experienced racism had her classmates or teachers found out about her identity, she confidentially affirmed she would have. Even into adulthood, Fener maintained to coworkers and other outsiders that she was Italian, preferring to keep the secret she was charged with keeping in her childhood.

Identifying as English Irish or French Swedish

Phoebe, also in her forties, was among the few that were interviewed that lived with a much more vocal and outward sense of pride in her identity. She viewed her identity as something that added richness to her life. She agreed that it was not something that was publicized but something that was taken for granted as an element that made she and the rest of her family unique. Even in a family that spoke proudly of their heritage, the dark shadow of discrimination was present which sometimes led to, if not an outright lie about identity, a lie of omission to prevent unwelcome attention:

> there was always an element of, you don't tell them this because of their negative reactions there would be bias and discrimination and it would affect their ability to make a living so it was something that wasn't always brought up, not that it was something they were ashamed of but it was something they had to do in order to make a living.

Phoebe acknowledged, though she was very proud of her identity as a Roma, it was often the outside world, rather than her family that pushed her to be mindful of self-disclosure. Though she has pride in her culture, she is not ignorant to what pride in one's identity often costs Roma in business and their ability to support their families. When asked what she would say if someone were to ask her to identify herself racially, Phoebe indicated that she often responded by telling people she is English Irish or French Swedish. Which, she emphasizes, she is.

"Wherever I was from"—Hiding Roma Identity in Obscurity

Unlike Phoebe, Allie's acceptance of her identity and decision to identify herself openly was a process. Upon entering college, she felt she had to live on the "down low," never letting others know her true identity fearing the repercussions. She recalls:

> people couldn't place me and I let them think I was from wherever I was from. You know they would come out with all kinds of things and I was just like uh huh. . . . I thought I had to keep very quiet and you know don't speak my language don't wear any kind of traditional dress not mark myself up at all. I just had to kind of be a sheep, follow behind everyone and just keep my head down. I never raised my hand in class, nothing and it would all be good.

Allie was raised in a community that, out of necessity, had to hide their identity. When she entered college, she took these social norms with her, viewing her deception as a means of remaining safe. Since that time, Allie has come to know many strong, Roma women who proudly identify their heritage and this has encouraged her to also proudly identify herself as a Roma. Other interviewees, particularly those who were younger, had similar trajectories of discovering a pride in their identity and a departure from hiding.

Identifying as Hungarian

Gayle, in her thirties, was one of those interviewed who found themselves on a similar trajectory to that of Allie. She grew up in the Northwest in a border town, on a reservation which, she described, was "not a mecca for diversity and acceptance." She recalled that her mom did not want her to identify herself as Roma. Her mom helped her to understand how the knowledge of her identity might lead her to negative interactions with individuals at school or in her community. For some time, she believed it might be better to let others believe she was Hungarian, Native Alaskan or French Canadian, whatever would be more acceptable.

Gayle didn't recall many specific moments where her parents discussed not sharing about her identity but she did recall a sense that people didn't need to know this about her. She recalled feeling some regret about the times that she outright denied her identity as a Roma. In her few experiences of sharing her identity in high school she found that people were less than accepting and found herself being lectured by her mom who reiterated the negative outcomes that were possible if she disclosed her identity.

In college, Gayle continued to allow others to make their own assumptions about her identity. She recalled that many individuals thought she was Arabic because she spoke the language and she passed as Lebanese for some time. She admitted she still didn't want to tell others who she was. Like Allie however, there came a turning point where she was willing to identify herself even knowing what the cost might be:

> I took this class which was a complete life changer . . . it was called women of color in the United States and we had to read all these critical feminist scholars . . . so that was the first time in my entire educated life that I read anything and I could see myself in it. . . . I started to think maybe I should identify myself you know, what could happen?

Gayle came to a realization that to be Roma was something to be proud of. Though discrimination could, and would, occur following her revelation, it had become more important to identify with who she truly was.

MORE ON ROMA IDENTITY IN AMERICA

Some may believe that things for Roma have gotten better in America overall making it easier or acceptable to divulge their identity. Others, such a Fener, a woman in her forties from the Southeast United States indicates she still encounters a stereotypical response when she reveals who she is and as a result, rarely shares:

> I think for the most part I still don't tell people what race I am, if someone wants to know I will say Italian you know cause if you do tell them they don't believe you so what's the use of telling them. I don't know how long it took, I told my husband right away when we first started dating I thought he needs to know if we are going to be serious and I got the same reaction from him. He was like well what's that you know do you dance around the campfire, yeah I'm going to dance around the campfire and then I am going to cast a spell on you, how about that? I put a curse on you. It's you know, craziness.

Fener, who is married to a non-Roma, doesn't appear to take much offense to these ideas as she went forward with her marriage despite her husband holding these views on Roma. Could this be evidence that she, and maybe others, have come to expect that the denigration of the Roma identity is simply an expected part of their experience? Maybe. Stereotypical encounters like Fener's were the experience of the majority of those interviewed, prompting many to continue to hide their identity. Others, like Donald, felt free to live their identity out loud. Donald stated he "never did allow the stereotypes to affect me and since I was 18 I told anyone that wanted to listen."

Many Roma define themselves as a people who must live in two worlds, in a duality of existence. The stress from this double consciousness is the outcome of the resistance to assimilation that Roma encounter. It is the stress that Roma feel when trying to navigate two worlds and successfully fulfill their preferred method of acculturation, still seeking to be accepted within and outside their community. Gilbert describes his experience with this duality of identity:

> I absolutely think I overcompensate way too much. I feel like I have ten times more to prove to everyone despite the fact that I grew up like a regular white boy in the suburbs in America not having to prove anything. I feel the weight of this on my shoulder that I need to be better than everyone else just to be as good as everyone else I need to do it 10 times better.

Even if one is privileged enough, like Gilbert to easily pass in the mainstream, many Roma feel the weight of their ethnic identity and the expectations society has for them inside. Successfully navigating or balancing both experiences can be challenging for Roma. Striking a balance can require significant skill and strength. Phoebe defined this balance and how it has impacted the identities of her children:

> I mean it takes a little navigation and a strong sense of who you are to be able to go back and forth from both cultures without missing from either one. I've always tried to tell my children this: you can have the best of both worlds, you are who you are despite of who you are and no one can take that away from you. It's just kind of interesting path, the best thing you can do is instill that confidence in who they are first and foremost. It's not easy, it's not easy. Everybody feels that they are missing out or they are not as accepted maybe because they don't do one thing or another so they are navigating that path right now.

Phoebe does a great job painting the picture of the life of the Roma who seeks to carry their Roma identity with them as they engage in some form of acculturation. As she identifies, it is not easy and may lead to a fracturing of identity altogether, leaving them without the ability to utilize their ethnic identities as a buffer against the world.

THE DEFINITION OF ROMA IDENTITY IN EUROPE

Like those in America, many European Roma express that their Roma identity is something they identify strongly with and something to be proud of despite outside influences. In a study on the experiences of vulnerability among gypsies and Travellers, one Irish Traveler identifies how his identity has served as a buffer against negative, outside influences (Heaslip, 2015):

> Even though they were bullying me, I fight back and I fight harder even though I'd lose. Every time I got hit I would hit back and I'd fight and I'd try and fight harder. That's the way with Travellers. If they're put down they'll bounce right back up. We are proud people, very proud. Proud of who we are, proud of where we come from. No matter what the outside world says, no matter what they say they will never be as good as us. (Jimmy, Irish Traveller, 92, as cited in Heaslip, 2015, 7)

Despite this pride, some feel that the influence of outsiders on Roma will lead to an extinction of Roma identity eventually (Heaslip), "I think Gypsies will be a bit like dinosaurs . . . dead and gone" (Alana, Roma Woman, as cited in Heaslip, 2015, 131). In saying this, it's possible that the identity of Roma is seen as one that is in jeopardy as more and more people outside the community seek to define or appropriate it.

As I've already discussed multiple times within this book, Roma find themselves lacking control over the way their identities are portrayed, largely through the media. Additional stress arises as Roma are tied to their community as well as mainstream society, just as in America, creating a dual identity and increasing the level of strain they feel in wanting to own and define their Roma identity while also successfully acculturating (Toth, 2005).

One study on Roma youth shows that Roma in Europe have a very strong sense of their identity and how they would and would not like to be defined from a young age (Ureche & Franks, 2007). It is important to Roma that they are able to define themselves and many take an offensive approach when seeking to educate others on what it means to be Roma (Strauss, 2012). Strauss interviewed one such individual who was able to proudly and definitively define who they are, even if it was in opposition to what others believe:

> It's sad and discouraging. I'm sorry, but it's the truth, that's how it is. When I look at myself in the mirror, I'm not white, I'm not black. . . . I'm sorry, that's how it is. And I don't deny it, I'm proud to be a Gypsy, a Roma woman, that's so. (Roma Woman, twenties, 98).

These individuals are able to draw on their identity as a way of dealing with strain from the dominant society while others continue to hide their identity or lie about who they are (Strauss).

One such individual reached the opposite position of the person expressed found pride in their identity:

> I said from that point in time on that never again in my life would I say I'm a Sintizza, and I've stuck to that to this very day, because I simply don't want to admit it, for me it's something really bad. (Sinta Woman, thirties, 98)

The experience of this Sinti woman mirrors the experience of Roma in America and Europe who have encountered enough prejudice to decide they no longer wish to be publicly identified with their true identity.

Again, just as in America, Roma identity becomes something that should be kept secret and is potentially harmful in that it may put them at risk for further marginalization. That is not to say that those who hide their identity are not proud of it, but part of their identity has evolved as a result of mainstream society's treatment. One cannot place all responsibility for the inability to draw confidentially on ethnic identity to buffer the effects of outside influences. Another contributing factor to this is the lack of cohesion within the Roma community which leaves some unsure of how they should be or are defined and if in fact they meet this unknowable standard.

THE IMPACT OF INTERGROUP CONFLICT

The idea that Roma communities are homogenous whether in America or Europe is a fallacy. There is much disagreement within the Roma community regarding how they will be defined and in what way they will make these definitions clear. From family to family or group to group it is somewhat unclear who is "in" and who is "out" though there is consensus across the board that those who are seeking to appropriate Roma culture for their own gain and based on behaviors and lifestyles instead of ethnicity are definitely out. Some individuals as well as some researchers may define those who no longer participate in "traditional" Romani culture or those who have assimi-lated as outsiders or even Gadjo (Minahan, 2013).

One must acknowledge there is no consensus on what Roma should or should not be called. Some might argue this point but, having read hundreds of studies on Roma worldwide, I can definitively say that who is defined as Roma, Sinti, Gypsy, Travellers etc. varies geographically, by family, based on media and historical influences and for a myriad of other reasons. I have throughout this book changed on an almost paragraph by paragraph basis the adjective I used to define the group I was talking about because the studies I was referencing referred to themselves using a specific term. At times, I was referring to differing factions of Roma but many times I was not, and yet I tried to be respectful of the term they chose to utilize. One may say that the term Roma is all encompassing, as I have used it, and gypsy is pejorative but, as we saw from the previous section, some strongly identify with the word gypsy and will not allow themselves to be told within or outside the Roma community that this is unacceptable. One woman from the United States describes her views on the matter online in this way (Facebook Post, 2016):

> I try to be politically correct by saying I'm Roma but everyone thinks I mean Romanian. I have no problem saying Gypsy because I'm proud to be one and I want people to know what ethnicity I am. (Roma Woman, USA)

Others might say that Roma does not represent their history. One scholar may clearly lay out what each term refers to and another scholar will lay out definitions reversing what was then established. Disagreement regarding when or if these Roma identities should be revealed, particularly within media portrayals, also exist (Jovanovic).

I asked each of the respondents how they would identify themselves should they be asked to identify themselves racially or ethnically. I wanted to know, would they say Roma or Gypsy? Would they say White or something else altogether. Would they simply check "other" or "multi-racial" and move on? For much of Gilbert's life, he identified himself as a Slovak American, it wasn't until he moved to the Czech Republic and became involved with the Roma civil rights movement there that he began to be proudly and fully out as a Roma man. Donald stated that he was largely assimilated in the world around him growing up so he didn't identify a specific term by which he referred to himself though he did reference Roma, Romanichal and gypsy within the interview. Al identified the family he was raised in as both Romanichal and Dutch gypsies. Henry also identified himself as Roma.

As previously discussed, Gertie identifies herself as Jewish, though at times she will say Roma. Others identified they would say anything but Roma. One stated, "I wouldn't want to publicly admit, I'm just being honest." Four of the women interviewed stated that Roma was the first term they would identify themselves with.

Though they may exist, Oleaqu (2014) identifies that Roma are often unaware of the goals they share in common. Gayle, a woman in her thirties from the Northwest United States, identifies the lack of unity that is sometimes found within groups:

> There is really a lack of unity between groups there was a guy I think from the group [the interviewer was] from and he was trying to organize this education thing and it was the first time there were a bunch of different groups from [various places], Spanish gypsy people and it went to hell in a hand basket, it was horrible like a crash and burn part of it was because even though I think he did have the best of intentions, he was not a very good manager of people and the other thing was people started getting suspicious of everybody else's intentions and I remember thinking God this is so gypsy of everyone you know it was really frustrating.

Not only did Gayle use the term gypsy in the interview, she clearly identifies that a lack of unity and common efforts can occur. Unfortunately, voices of criticism within the community are often quieted or unheard according to one study (Oprea, 2004), leaving some to feel as if criticizing things such as the lack of cohesion within the Roma community is anti-Roma. It may also lead one to feel that they have been placed on the "outside."

Some Roma, facing the stress of acculturation, whether through full assimilation, by accommodating the dominant culture or through other means, are left without a clear idea of where they will or do stand in their communities once this process is complete. Those Roma in Europe who are deemed successful beyond what is considered "average" for Roma by the mainstream may no longer be considered "Roma" by those outside and/or within their community (Toth, 2005).

In order to gain acceptance by the mainstream, many "pass" as White or engage in behaviors and customs common to the mainstream, leaving them to feel they have perhaps left their communities behind. For these individuals, though they do not wish outsiders to appropriate the Roma identity by simply "living the life," it can be hard to continue to view their Roma identity through an ethnic lens alone. The need to feel "Roma enough" may keep some Roma from drawing on their identity as a means of coping with the conflict they experience when trying to acculturate. Rachel, a woman in her twenties from the Northeast United States, identifies her struggles with feeling validated in her identity:

> I think that is a problem for me (feeling Roma enough) because even though I am Roma, I always feel like oh, I'm not enough you know what I mean but I am enough and I just need to, I feel better about it but before there was a period in college when I would kind of stay quiet about it but not anymore.

Rachel identifies her struggles with feeling that she measures up to the unknowable standard of being truly "Roma." She also acknowledges that she has now made the conscious choice to allow herself and her ethnicity to be defined only by her own standards.

Teddy described his own struggles with identifying himself as Roma given his understanding of the many struggles Roma worldwide have faced and his own positon of privilege:

> I kind of grew up again one foot in each world but I guess I don't come right out and say I am a Roma America, just sort of say I am a Caucasian male. I think about discrimination and how much opportunity I have had is the opposite of discrimination living in America and having been afforded the opportunities to be educated and lived a good life here. Seeing how much people in other parts of the country and parts of the world don't have I really feel like it's a relative thing. I pick and choose how I identify myself depending on the situation.

Though Teddy is very proud of his heritage and is in constant contact with his Roma family, from his perspective, his ability to live seamlessly and privileged in the mainstream removes some of his claim to the identity of Roma. It would seem that Teddy feels that along with a claim to this title is the implication of the struggle of Roma, a struggle which Teddy denies he has experienced. Just as Rachel described, it is his own understanding of what it means to be "Roma enough" that may stand in the way of fully identifying as Roma.

Benny too knows Teddy's struggle as he too lives in a world where White carries privilege and being Roma is largely unknown:

> I will say I am Roma. I don't like to identify myself as being gypsy that is so wrong and I try not to say that out of gate. If I don't think someone is going to pick up on what I mean by being Roma and I don't feel like explain it in that moment I just say ah I'm white. I still identify that because I have that skin color and no one understands what it means for someone to be Roma in this country. I sometimes feel weird taking ownership of this background because it's never been a thing that my family has outwardly discussed, I feel weird taking pride in something that is not a part of my upbringing or what my family identifies myself by. At times you know I am hesitant that way but at the same time I think it is so important to talk about this stuff.

As previously discussed, Roma are at times without the ability to truly own their identity because of their invisibility in the United States and it is this invisibility of identity that often makes them question their right to openly claim it. Benny is out and proud about his identity and yet he has encountered the frustrations of Teddy, the frustration of being misunderstood and the realization that by default, in America he is White.

For Gertie, her struggle with identification came from within the community itself. When asked if she felt the gypsy stereotypes or outsider views on Roma have affected her identity, she identified that it was in fact the Roma community that impacted how she viewed herself:

> Gertie: The way my own people see me has affected me.
> *Interviewer: And why do you think that? How do your own people see you?*
> Gertie: I think they kind of see me as a rebel
> *Interviewer: So in that way your identity has been affected just by how the community views you. So do you think that shaped your identity during childhood?*
> Gertie: Oh yes, definitely
> *Interviewer: So when you say they view you as a rebel, are you saying they view you as someone who didn't conform to the norms of the community?*
> Gertie: Right because my mother didn't teach me the norms so I was the rebel, the black sheep . . . But still one of them you know, like "she's a black sheep but she is our black sheep" (laughs) You know, like that.

Like many other respondents, Gertie found herself stuck, in a sense, between two worlds. Today she identifies herself outside of the community, never feeling that she was truly accepted by her own people due to her lack of understanding of their norms and yet still having a sense that she was claimed by her own people. Gertie too lives with the sense of not being quite Roma enough for the true Roma, something she feels cost her much throughout her life.

I begin this section by trying to answer the questions, How do Roma define themselves and how do the opinions of dominant cultures impact this definition? And the answers to these questions are quite complicated. Roma define themselves in a variety of ways and, at times can lack cohesion. Not only do the opinions of the dominant culture impact this definition but opinions or rules within the Roma community impact the defining of identity as well. Once again, I could not end this chapter without identifying how women are uniquely impacted by this struggle because they must not only address the conflict of being between two worlds but must also identify how their gender is placed within those worlds.

ADDITIONAL STRUGGLES AT THE INTERSECTION OF GENDER

Roma women face a myriad of difficulties and they are often on the receiving end of marginalization both within and outside their community because of their gender (Ceneda, 2002). Ceneda identifies the struggle that Roma women endure and the stress placed on them from multiple communities:

> She has few advocates and is the target of constant hostility. She is marginalized within her community because of her minority status and within her family because of her gender. . . . these women live at the crossroads of gender and racial segregation. (12)

Just as many Roma struggle with their lack of ownership over their identity, some Roma women struggle with the lack of ownership over the intersection of their ethnic identity with their gender. The Roma community has critics from within who state that though there are Roma initiatives led by women (discussed in the conclusion of this study) many are led by men, largely in Europe. These initiatives fail to address the issues unique to women unless they fit within the overall agenda of the community. Roma women's issues of being fetishized and demeaned may go unacknowledged and progress meant for Roma women is often situated within their ethnicity more than their gender (Jovanovic, 2014). Jovanovic believes that many Roma women's movements take on an "us and them" tone, catering to small factions of the community and making it unclear who is considered in and who is out, leaving many to feel marginalized.

Other scholars identify that efforts to discuss the issues unique to Roma women can be seen as questioning the very identity and culture of Roma, leaving some to feel as if Roma identity has little room to include Roma women. They may also feel as if the plight of the Roma women is overlooked for the "greater good" of all (Ceneda, 2002). As I discuss in the previous section, criticism of the community may be silenced by those who feel it will place the efforts for progress at risk, thus silencing those who wish to address the issues of Roma women or the exclusion of Roma women from the greater conversation (Oprea, 2004). Many policies addressing Roma needs have been criticized as "gender blind" and Roma women are often faced with a lack of needed education, involvement in human trafficking and a lack of reproductive healthcare (Kushi, 2016).

CONNECTION TO ROMA IDENTITY

With so much variation in Roma identity and those living in and outside of traditional lives, it was interesting to discuss how connected those inter-viewed are with the Roma community. I looked at things like the acquisition or preservation of the language, norms and customs they observed in their families, how often they thought of being Roma and if they felt connected with other Roma outside of their families.

Teddy stated that he thinks about being Roma every day. Much of this has to do with his close connection with his Roma family:

> I'm in touch with them all the time and I live a more gorger life. I mean really. Even though my family background is different. My cousins and aunts and uncles and grandparents they live a different life I mean a totally different life than I lived and I think about that every day. The reasons I think about it every day is because I am in touch with my family every day in some way . . . It is a daily awareness for me.

Henry states that being Roma comes up for him, "every damn day." Because he has dedicated at least part of his life to working for Roma rights, his Roma identity is close to his conscious thought continually. Through his work he maintains connections with Roma and hopes that his son too will maintain this connection. Eddie identified that though he is half-Roma, he has always felt assimilated closely with his Roma people, much more so than the other part of his family:

> Even my gadje relatives didn't feel like family, didn't feel like the closeness I had with the Romanichal family. I was raised but my mother in the tradition so I am raised by the Romanichal. I really don't even acquaint with the gadje's even though I have half-gadje blood within me. It's strange to see your own grandfather and it don't really seem like your own people.

Gilbert admits that though he is very much aware of his identity and is connected closely with many Roma in Europe, due to both his current residence there and work in Roma organizations, he is not closely connected with Roma in America. He admits that he doesn't know many Roma in America and doesn't know much about their lives as a whole. Teddy identified however, that many more similarities between American and European Roma exist than one might realize, perhaps making acquaintance with one an introduction to the other:

> I went to school in London for a semester in 1998. There was a couple in England . . . I don't remember how I knew about them or got in touch with them but I did and it turned out their son came to stay with my family a little bit and that was a few years before I went to study in England. I went to visit and saw their family and it struck me that [the couple] who didn't go to school or know much about the USA and then my family who didn't go to school and didn't much England they could switch it out and live in opposite places, they had the same lifestyle, they talked the same way. It blew my mind how similar they were to my grandparent's back in the USA. It was just the way they lived their lives.

Benny also found that among his older relatives that immigrated to the United States and those remaining in the old country, there remains "some traditions and customs and things that did . . . it was just kind of obvious." Others interviewed acknowledge their family, even among those with little knowledge of the Roma heritage or those who chose to hide it, had norms that continued to be passed on. Ideas about cleanliness, washing your hands and food preparation were norms expressed in many of the interviews.

Among the women interviewed many said they think often about being Roma. Some stated that the current state of Roma lives, the loss of older relatives or their own aging has increased their awareness and conscious thought about their Roma identity. Despite this awareness, many also stated that they do not have connection with other Roma in their lives, friends or relatives. Some stated they never think about their Roma identity at all, actually expressing a preference not to think about it. Fener expressed her own experience with thinking about her Roma identity. She indicated she maintains contact mostly only with family or other Roma. When asked if she thinks about being Roma she says, "Not all" but then adds, "It's just who I am." For Fener, being Roma is simply who she is without effort or thought.

Another element tying many Roma and their identity to the grater Roma community is the language. Many Roma interviewed identified they spoke or were taught the Roma language growing up. For some, this opened up opportunities overseas in their occupations and college years. The language they had learned growing up translated to Roma communities in Europe. Donald and many like him acquired the Roma language through informal instruction:

Growing up I didn't know that much. I was taught a lot of Rumnis from listening, it wasn't that someone sat me down and told me what it was. It was just part of growing up and what you were hearing.

People like Teddy didn't understand that Rumnis was not English until he started school:

You didn't know these were Rumnis words, you thought they just might be English. I grew up with my family really playing down their identity and I didn't know what was going on and what was different about my family and no one explain it to me. I'd find out in school that words I would say in school I thought were English words . . .

Others, like Henry, make a concerted effort to learn the language in his adolescence:

I could speak it if I wanted to I could practice it and I could learn it whenever I saw my grandparents. I couldn't practice it every day but made a point of learning it. I spent a lot of time in high school with an exchange student so I was living places where there were Roma around so I made it in junior high and high school to try and auto didactically learn it and practice it as much as I could.

People like Donald worry that language, a binding and connecting part of the Roma identity, may be disappearing with new generations of Roma Americans:

I try to teach my kinds and they use it as much as possible. Today it is mostly just used as slang. Its something that if it isn't captured its going to be gone.

The loss of the language for many Roma signals the loss of a vital part of the Roma identity, one that separated them from outsiders for many generations and, within its own vernacular, created an understanding of identity and position with the rest of the world. Eddie describes the function of the Roma language:

Nobody else has a word for anybody that is not one of them. So we got gadje, that's anybody that's not one of us. The only other people that's got that word is the Hebrews and they have the word gentiles for anybody who is not a Jew.

Language is an important part of the Roma identity for many Roma, and like the decline of traveling life, many fear that Roma are losing the language.

CONCLUSION

When seeking to answer the question if Roma identity can serve as a buffer against negative media portrayals and other prejudice from dominant cultures, it can be hard to answer in the affirmative. The intersection of gender with Roma identity is often a greater source of stress within and outside the Roma community. Many challenges are faced by women Roma scholars who are either left out of feminist discourses or, are told they must essentially disavow their Roma heritage due to the perception that it conflicts with the ideals of the feminist narrative. Many Roma women scholars resist this idea and believe that a Roma woman has the capability to have a strong identity as both a Roma and a woman. Despite this, Roma women seem to be caught at the intersection of several variables. They face double the challenges of navigating resistance to assimilation and relying on their identity to buffer the effects of discrimination with so many factors stacked against them.

Bringing visibility to the lives and history of Roma, according to Gracie, is the only way that a change can occur in their lives and in the mind-sets of people and nations who are actively opposed to the Roma and their ways of life. Even the smallest act of acknowledging one's identity of being Roma can make a difference in raising the visibility of Roma. As discussed throughout this study, this smallest act of acknowledging identity, to Roma, can be a difficult task, steeped in fear.

There is a deep pride in identity as a Roma that exists in America and worldwide. Though this pride is intermixed with complicated emotions, questions and expectations, it has served as a buffer and barrier between Roma and the harmful effects of those outside their communities. In the final chapter I highlight the many strides that Roma advocates, activists and scholars have taken to positively impact Roma worldwide. Through their actions, positive visibility, countering images and people other Roma may look up to, have emerged.

Chapter Seven

Roma Activism and Final Thoughts

I decided to spend some time in D.C. taking advantage of the historical data the Library of Congress could offer me and to enjoy a change in scenery as I wrapped up the remaining research for this book. While most of my time was spent doing research I took a break to take a capital tour, my first ever though I had been in Washington many times. The tour guide asked each of us where we were from, only two of us out of the entire group were from the United States. He made it a point to note each country and pointed out the contributions that individuals from these countries had made to the founding of our country, to the architecture, to the intellectual ideas that helped form the Constitution. And they were proud, as they should be. But it did not escape me that in that discourse, Roma were absent.

It didn't escape me that they were absent because he mentioned every other people group; it happened because I had spent days pouring over historical texts, newspapers, legal journals, and meetings from Congress spanning hundreds of years. Each mention of Roma or gypsy I found in America was like a tiny bread crumb, a small trace that they had been, that they had existed, buried within the narratives of others. But every mention was negative. Another Roma accused of some crime, another law enacted against them, another stereotype disseminated by the news, by Congress, by whomever. I hoped for one, just one, positive mention; just one representation of the positive contributions that Roma had made to America.

I found instead that I was learning more than I had planned to ever learn about the gypsy moth in North America. In researching Roma, I often searched for the pejorative gypsy knowing that most historical records would have used this term to define the Roma of the time. The gypsy moth regularly appeared in my results. As I sorted through the data, annoyed, I found myself reading more and more about this pest that had wreaked havoc on the forests of America. Accidently introduced into America in the 1700s it is listed as one of the most destructive species in the world (Tobin & Blackburn, 2007). That it was called gypsy did not surprise me. In those moments of scouring U.S. history for the contributions of Roma, the Roma were presented in no less a negative light. Through the lens of government documents and legal disputes, Roma are often portrayed as people accidently introduced to America, feeding off their hosts, causing damage, wreaking havoc wherever they go. But that is not the Roma, today or historically.

For too long Roma narrative and history has been defined by those on the outside, and a poor job has been done. Whether this narrative has been negatively presented or absent, the representation of Roma in the United States and their place in the overall narrative of the country is in need of rewriting. Today Roma within and outside the United States are fighting for this very thing, addressing the myriad of issues facing Roma that have been discussed in this text and the countless others unmentioned. It is these advocates, allies, activists who are rewriting the Roma narrative, giving an accurate voice to their experiences and paving the way for other Roma to take their place in history.

ROMA ACTIVISM

In January 2018, the European Roma Rights Centre was awarded the Raoul Wallenberg Prize. The prize is awarded for extraordinary achievements in the field of human rights. The awarding of this prize highlights the extraordinary work that has been accomplished by the EERC on behalf of Roma justice (COE, 2018). They continue to fight for Roma to access basic human services and hold governments accountable for their treatment of Roma.

In 2016, 93 Roma activists, all a part of the European Academic Network on Roma studies signed a letter in criticism of the language utilized by the Council of Europe in its inclusion plan for Roma and Travellers. Roma studies (2016) reported that the language insinuated the many issues plaguing the Roma community, such as begging and domestic violence, were "inherent" rather than situating them within the broader understanding of Roma marginalization. The activists believe the council is ineffective and is engaging in "victim blaming" rather than finding legitimate means of addressing these issues. Some within the Roma community are in opposition to the letter of protest because the council is seeking to address issues directly impacting women however, much support for their protest still exists (Roma studies). In either case, Roma activists have been able to take a strong stand in defense of themselves and their communities.

Petrova (2004) identifies that it has been the Roma's lack of power above all else that has impacted their social position in the world:

The single most important concept that helps explain [anti-ziganism] is weakness. Roma would not have been ignored, resented, insulted, humiliated and repressed if they had power.

While this may have been largely true historically, today, Roma have a strong and growing voice in defense of themselves and their community. Roma have begun to identify this change for themselves, though they still see room for improvement. One respondent from Beaudoin's 2014 study situates the discussion of activism in the past and the present:

It's when people don't have a voice; when they're terrified to have a voice, because they're told, "if you speak, you're dead." And that goes on for generations and generations. To develop that voice, it takes generations to start changing things. For example, right now, we're getting a more powerful voice, but it's not nearly enough. (Roma women, 203)

This respondent identifies that Roma have moved from a defense position in to an offensive one but acknowledges there is still work to do.

Though there are still many strides to be made, 2016 alone saw significant steps forward for Roma worldwide. As of August 2016, the Czech government was seeking to rectify an affront against Roma that has been in existence for 46 years. A pig farm was built on what was once a former Nazi camp, a place of remembrance for the hundreds of Roma who died there. The Czech government announced that it was seeking to buy out the pig farm as a first step in honoring what occurred on the grounds (AFP, 2016).

In America, Roma continue to be represented on the Holocaust Memorial Council. In 2016 a new representative was appointed by President Barack Obama to the U.S. Holocaust Memorial Council. Ethel Brooks, an associate professor and Roma scholar and activist at Rutgers University, now serves on the board as a voice for the Roma's place in Holocaust history (Rutgers University, 2016). The continued involvement of Roma with the U.S. Holocaust Memorial Council is important as Roma continue to fight for equal recognition of the horrors and genocide they too faced during this time. In 1986, Roma leaders and members of the U.S. Holocaust Memorial Council gathered together in acknowledgment of the Roma/Gypsy lost during the holocaust. The *New York Times* presented this as the first occasion of its kind in America specifically recognizing the involvement of the Roma in the Holocaust. The United States government has since routinely acknowledged the existence of International Roma day with a statement from the Secretary of State acknowledging their commitment to the equality of Roma worldwide. While the recognition of Roma and their presence in America is a step forward, much work remains to be done.

The fight for Roma acknowledgment continues to the present day. In 2014, Bailey-Mershon, Raeesi and Matache along with a host of other signatories released a statement calling on leaders worldwide to accurately depict the involvement of Roma in the narrative of the Holocaust:

> It is our moral duty and right to preserve the memory of the Roma victims who lost their lives on this day and throughout the war. Thus, in memory of the victims, the signatories call upon governments, international organizations, museums, and commemoration ceremony organizers, as well as scholars, activists, and the media, to accurately refer to the Roma victims of the Holocaust and to reject the description of Roma victims of the Holocaust as being part of an isolated genocide.

Organizations such as the Foundation for Roma Education and Equality, the American Council for Roma Equality, and Voice of Roma, among others, continue to speak on behalf of Roma in both America and overseas who lack appropriate representation whether in organizations such as the Holocaust Memorial Council or the United Nations. The Initiative for Roma Music at NYU focuses on promoting Roma culture through the arts and scholarship and gives voice to the Roma in the United States. Academic studies such as those found at Florida State University, University of Texas at Austin with Dr. Hancock and organizations such as the Gypsy Lore Society which produce the *Journal of Roma Studies* through Project Muse continue to bring scholarly voices to the conversation.

In the 1970s a delegation of Roma activists from the International Roma Union petitioned the UN for recognition of the Roma people. The council was granted membership as a nongovernment organization, securing a voice for the Roma within the UN. While greater strides and organizations have been established, much of it lacks official documentation that is easily accessible to the public, a reality which in and of itself needs to see a shift.

Roma activism worldwide continues to grow and while the list of names is too numerous to identify individually in this space, it is important to note that Roma are not simply passive participants in the way they have been portrayed or treated. In his book, *Gypsy Movements*, Nirenberg (2014) details the continued rise and organization of Roma activism, its reach across Europe and its push toward change at the local and national level. There can be no doubt among Roma activists that there is a need and desire for Roma to speak on their own behalf.

One Roma woman from Beaudon's 2014 study identifies the importance of a Roma voice speaking for Roma:

> I'm really not interested in what non-Roma culturally have to say about Roma, because I think we haven't reached a point yet where we can be relaxed about that, because Roma are still an object, Roma are still not ordinary people. (Roma woman, 199)

Activism occurs for Roma on a large scale through movies that counter mainstream stereotypes (Traveller Movement, 2015) and through music, including rap and dance that counter racism (Imre, 2003). Roma have also begun to utilize mainstream media sources, such as newsprint and social media, a tool historically used against them, as a way to resist prejudiced media portrayals, government actions and individual prejudice (Mago, 2016; Plaut, 2012). Activists have begun to draw attention to topics the mainstream media once shied away from and are increasing the overall amount of Roma being quoted and highlighted in mainstream publications (Plaut).

Though these forms of resistance occur on a grand scale, many Roma emphasize the importance of acting individually. One Roma man from Ohio identifies the first steps that individuals within the Roma community can take toward making a difference:

> One person educating whoever they can probably isn't going to affect the overall understanding of who and what we are . . . but if enough of us casually talk in a friendly and informative manner, it'll get the ball rolling. (Facebook post, 2016)

This man believes that taking the initiative to begin conversations can make a significant difference. Roma women interviewed in America report ways they have found to make a difference individually:

> And that's my role in this culture in that you guys gave me an education and I'm going to use it to educate people against everything you put out. That's what I do, I do talk. Last week I did a talk at the senior center, I had a class come over. That's my main thing now is to just let people know the truth. There are some things from our culture you might not agree with but you know what, it's our culture, it's not a stereotype to sell TV. (Fey, sixties)

Others speak with excitement about the ways in which new voices within the Roma community can make a significant difference:

> I tended to not talk about being Roma to outsiders so I never intended to do that but I think there are a group of us now who believe that if we don't do that then things will be bad. So I mean if you let TLC interpret who you are then that's who you are to the public. That's why I think it is important to encourage our young people to do whatever it is that they have a mind to do. That's why we are so excited about people . . . getting advanced degrees and will hopefully do research and teach. (Gracie, sixties Southeast U.S.)

Many of those interviewed have become actively involved in advocating for Roma both in the United States and in Europe. Gilbert described his entrance into Roma activism that has spanned several decades:

It was in the 90's and early 2000's where I got a little involved and was disappointed with how slow things are moving and how there is not enough action or reaction. I felt I didn't know how much value I could add. I started to watch from the sidelines until I moved to Canada and ever since I have been involved in Roma organizations.

Gilbert is involved in activism, advocacy, blog writing and "anything I can in my spare time." As Gilbert puts it, "I've gotten more and more involved and once you get a little bit involved you get pulled in. It is almost like an addiction. You can't stop." Teddy works with the U.S. state department and other organizations and individuals who are passionate about Roma issues. He is passionate about fighting Roma prejudice worldwide and believes it is vital for Roma to organize and speak out about the discrimination they have experienced both historically and today. Henry discussed his position as a board member for a European Roma organization. He sometimes works as an interpreter for Roma immigrants in the courts. This is especially important to him as he states, "anyone asking to be allowed to live here is on the grounds that there is a dangerous level of discrimination back home." He is involved in writing about Roma and other areas of Roma activism. Most of the other men interviewed involve themselves in Roma activism by taking an active role in educating others in person and in writing, by encouraging their fellow Roma to be proud of their identity and to help others take an active role in Roma causes.

Among the women interviewed many were also actively involved in promoting and advocating for Roma. Several of the respondents stay active in their Roma communities and participate in advocating for Roma rights through various means. Vaidy, Gracie and others have publications about Roma in various mediums. Both Fey and Vaidy have taught at the university level on Roma topics. Fey is the curator of a Roma museum in the United States. She and Louisa, among others, have actively participated in interviews about Roma with various sources. Gracie and Allie have worked as GED tutors online for Roma youth. Many of the women interviewed hold impressive roles in the Roma community, in the United States and worldwide. To protect the anonymity of all of the participants I cannot list here all of their work and positons but wish to relate that many interviewed as well as countless others beyond those I have interviewed represent a strong population of Roma activists that exist today.

Roma organizations exist internationally that address the disparities faced by Roma daily and to speak out the structural oppression they encounter. Organizations such as ERGO (European Roma Grass-Roots Organization), the Roma Education Fund, the International Roma Union and the European Roma Rights Centre are just a few of many. These organizations are bringing Roma and Roma advocates together to fight inequality, identify unfair legislation, create opportunities and meet the basic needs of Roma. Though Roma organizations may be difficult to identify, many Roma create informal groups or small councils to support the local and international communities, share information and encourage identification with Roma identity. Their goals, among other things include policy development, local and community assistance and educational support.

With so many Roma internationally raising their voices against the structural oppressions they continue to face, many countries have begun to take note of their plight. As previously discussed, the decade of Roma inclusion, ending in 2015, was declared as the decade in which European countries would end discrimination against the Roma people (Decade of Roma Inclusion Secretariat Foundation, 2012). The United States' part in this initiative was to serve in an observer status, doing little to acknowledge that these same individuals reside and experience a difficult plight within their own boarders (Aggler, 2012).

Worldwide, April 8 is celebrated as International Roma day, meant to celebrate the culture of and bring awareness about the Roma people. August 2nd is Roma genocide remembrance day, a day set to commemorate the events that occurred on August 2, 1944, at Auschwitz in which mass numbers of Roma were exterminated as part of Hitler's final solution for the Roma people (European Youth Campaign for Society, 2010). While in the United States, Holocaust Remembrance Day is certainly a day that is widely acknowledged, Roma are often left without a voice in the remembrance, thus a day was created to acknowledge the loss of so many Roma lives.

Yearly, individuals gather at the United Nations in New York City to pay honor to those who were killed in the Holocaust and yet, yearly, Roma have struggled to have representation in the remembrance. Gracie, a respondent in her sixties, described this yearly battle with those who would not wish to include the Roma:

> We have such struggles at the UN for example and every year we have lobbied them to include us in their Holocaust remembrance and its every year, [Roma scholars and activists] have burned themselves out trying to change things here and they are immensely resistant and I feel strongly one reason they are immensely resistant is because they have a very European view point of who the Roma are. You know, these poor terrible people who are often thieves and beggars.

Even in seeking to remember the atrocities committed against their own people, to be included in the narrative of atrocity and hope, they are often excluded because of the deep prejudice held against the Roma. Once again, the voice of this marginalized people is silenced.

Despite the attempts by those who wish to rid their countries and narratives of the Roma people there are those who acknowledge the plight they have faced. Gracie believes that Roma must continue to speak out and raise awareness in places such as the United Nations. She recalled an event from a Remembrance Day she recently attended:

> I made a point of introducing myself as Roma and I had some interesting responses you know. That was the year that [a Roma scholar spoke] and she was a total magnet because all these people, they did not know and they didn't have a clue because they didn't understand. I watched one older man come up to her, he was very old, he came up and took her hand and he said, "I was at Auschwitz and I want you to know I remember the cries of the Roma camp." There wasn't a dry eye in the place but this is something we battle every year. This is the UN, they should know better, for them I have no pity. We have to pound them until they get the message.

Whatever role one takes within the grander conversation of Roma resistance and education, it is clear that many Roma are no longer passive actors or individuals in hiding. The purpose of this study, in one respect, is to fulfill the wish of Roma such as Gracie, excited for a growing generation of young Roma scholars and activists who are looking for individuals with the social power and the knowledge to become a part of the international conversation.

THE ROMA LIFE: PRESENT AND FUTURE

While advocacy across Europe is on the rise, little is seen within the United States for Roma in America. In order for a life free of prejudice to be a possibility for Roma, the social climate of the United States would need to see a significant shift. Toward the end of each interview I asked respondents about their current understanding of the lives of Roma in the United States. Among respondents, several answers continually emerged. Respondents identify that in America today, Roma continue to face discrimination. Roma are far more visible due to stereotypical portrayals on reality shows which increase their vulnerability to prejudice and discrimination.

More and more Roma are finding their traditional ways of working and living harder to maintain, making it difficult to support their families or, at the very least, remain separate from the oppressive influence of the gadje. Respondents agreed that the Roma struggle in America pales in comparison to that of the international struggle that is occurring but also acknowledge their struggle often goes completely unacknowledged, making it difficult for others to see them as a marginalized minority.

I asked respondents to identify if life for Roma in the United States has gotten better or worse. A fourth of the respondents indicated that things, for many, have gotten worse. Gertie, whose story revealed she has largely assimilated, had this to say:

> I think it has gotten worse for the ones that still have the traditional mindset. I don't think they really know how to assimilate real well and it's very difficult for them because they don't know how to make a living.

Generations of Roma passing down messages to their children about remaining separate from the gadje have ill prepared them for assimilating into their world and made many fearful to do so, fearing the possibility of what they may encounter. As previously stated, some respondents believed that things have gotten worse due to the rise of stereotypes disseminated in U.S. media and little to no information to counter these stereotypes. Herein lies a motivating factor behind my completion of this work, I hope to give agency to those individuals who wish to counter these stereotypes through the power of their own narratives.

Some respondents identified that most Roma fare the same today as in the days of their ancestors. Many respondents continue to face threats of violence, restricted access to work and resources, discrimination and social stigma. Respondents identified that Roma remain misunderstood and largely uneducated due to social and structural barriers. Others identified that little is done to help the plight of the Roma in the United States which has contributed to the lack of change in their situation. Like Roma worldwide, they face a plight that is either unacknowledged or placed on the shoulders of the individuals rather than the historically rooted structural barriers that have influenced Roma lives today.

About half of the respondents believe that things overall have improved. Some identify that stereotypes have declined while education is on the rise. Others see that Roma have lives free from much of the racism that exists worldwide which provides them with greater opportunities to be socially mobile. Finally, these respondents believe that Roma have a greater understanding of what mainstream society requires of them and are more open to incorporating these things into their communities and lives.

A PART OF THE CONVERSATION

As discussed when I introduced this book, the information and narratives collected here are meant only to be another voice added to the conversation surrounding Roma. They are not meant to be exhaustive nor fully representative but, are meant to bring a modern voice to the already existing scholarship of Roma in the United States.

When I first began this work, my goal was to investigate the lives of Roma in America, to discover how they compare with Roma in Europe and to gain a sense of their unique story. Beyond that, I hoped to delve further into how these lives play out across screens and on paper when compared with those in Europe. Much Roma scholarship, even from American scholars, focuses almost entirely on Roma overseas. This is understandable as, observed even in this book, their plight is significantly more dire and the information relating to their experiences is much more widely available than for Roma in America, though even in Europe it continues to lack in many ways.

I consider the synthesis of so many narratives, collected from so many places, some found within the electronic crevices of the online world, to be a significant step in presenting this research to those familiar with it and also to those outside the world of the Roma scholar and the Roma activist. It is my hope that the breadth of information and the narrative of Roma life running throughout this book can not only significantly inform those within the Roma community who may be living their lives with little knowledge of the greater community they are part of but, to inform also those on the outside. Having struggled to find other studies that brought together so much of the American Roma narrative, it is now my hope that the breadth of this research will become a repository of information for those wishing to further scholarship about Roma or to become more acquainted with them.

I believe this book has the potential to be a significant part of the ongoing conversation happening among Roma worldwide. Within it I inform scholars about the plight of America Roma. With so little understood about Roma in America, I believe it is important to not only provide countering information but to provide any information to the mainstream and specifically to scholars within many disciplines about the lives of Roma in America and overseas.

Undoubtedly more activism needs to take place, particularly in the United States, to combat the stereotypes that have run rampant on screens across America. Individuals, at minimum, can refuse to participate in the appropriation of Roma culture by refusing to watch or purchase anything that engages in appropriation or marginalization through their portrayals. Further, countering images should be created to balance out the stereotypical images that are currently being disseminated. Beyond scholarship, films, music, television and books need to exist to counter the images available and to replace them.

There were many areas I was not able to address given time and information constraints but these are also important to the understanding of Roma life and narrative. Though I haven't discussed them, I believe that there is a need to explore them further. These include Roma views on faith, religion and spirituality, a topic particularly relevant to Roma in the present day as Pentecostal Christianity spreads rapidly throughout Roma communities worldwide (Antanasov, 2012; Persaud, 2010). This also includes Roma ideas surrounding sex and sexual identities, themes which texts such as "Gypsy Sexuality: Roma and outside perspectives on Intimacy," (Nirenberg (ed.), 2011) discuss at length. Roma mental health, health and addiction issues are also areas that need to be explored further. I believe these are all topics that make up a part of the Roma collective narrative and hope in time to see further study on these areas in a way that is respectful of Roma culture and life produced by trusted sources for the right reasons. Research that highlights the negative impact of popular stereotypical images and mechanisms for stratification against Roma in the United States would serve the community well.

As with all research I complete regarding the state of Roma in the United States, my hope is to provide a platform for Roma to join the global discussion regarding Roma exclusion, to expand Roma scholarship and to highlight the social, economic and mental health needs of minority and immigrant Roma groups in the United States and in Europe. The narratives I have presented are meant to be a window into the world of American Roma and, with hope, a catalyst toward work and change among many Roma and Roma advocates who are willing to look inside.

References

Abed-Santos, A (2013, Oct 3). "The problem with 'The Avengers' casting Scarlet Witch as a blonde." *The Wire*. Retrieved from: http://www.thewire.com/national/2013/10/avengers-made-scarlet-witch-blonde/70159/.

Acton, T. (2004). "Modernity, Culture, and 'Gypsies': Is there a Meta-Scientific Method for Understanding the Representation of 'Gypsies'? And do the Dutch Really Exist?" *The role of the Romanies. Images and Counter-images of 'Gypsies'/Romanies in European Cultures.* Liverpool: Liverpool University Press.

AFP (2016, Aug 3). "Czech government to buy out pig farm on Roma holocaust site." *The Times of Israel*. Retrieved from: http://www.timesofisrael.com/czech-government-to-buy-out-pig-farm-on-roma-holocaust-site/.

Aggler, B. (2012-June). "U.S. government became observer to Rom a decade of inclusion." Presented at Embassy of the United States in Skopje, Macedonia.

Alba, R., & Nee, V. (1997). "Rethinking assimilation theory for a new era of immigration." *International migration review*, 826–874.

Albert, G. (2011). "Forced sterilization and Roma women's resistance in central Europe." *DifferenTakes*. Retrieved from: https://dspace.hampshire.edu /bitstream/10009/925 /1/pop-dev_differentakes_071.pdf.

Amnesty International (2016). "Slovenia: Constitutional right to water 'must flow down to' Roma communicates." Retrieved from: https://www.amnesty.org/en/latest/news/2016/11/slovenia-constitutional-right-to-water-must-flow-down-to-roma-communities/.

Apelseth, F. H. (2013). "The Roma people: The effects of discrimination on living standards, a case study of Kristiansand, Norway."

Asher-Perrin, E. (2011, May 19). "Homeless for the holidays: 'You know what happens when you dance.'" [blog post] tor.com. Retrieved from: http://www.tor.com/2011/12/19/qyou-know-what-happens-when-you-danceq-sherlock-holmes-a-game-of-shadows/.

The Ashland Tidings (1916, May 11). "Gypsy Holdups caught and fined. *The Ashland Tidings* (Oregon)." Retrieved from: http://chroniclingamerica.loc.gov/lccn/sn85042399/1916–05–11/ed-1/seq7/#date1=1836&sort=relevance&rows=20&.words=gypsies+Gypsy&searchType=basic&sequence=0&index=10&state=&date2=1922&proxtext=Gypsies&y=0&x=0&dateFilterType=yearRange&page=5.

Asov, M. (2012). "Gypsy Pentecostals: the growth of the Pentecostal movement among the Roma in Bulgaria and its revitalization of their communities (Doctoral Dissertation)." Retrieved from http://place.asburyseminary.edu/ecommonsatsdissertations/10/.

Atanasov, M. A. (2008). *Gypsy Pentecostals: The growth of the Pentecostal movement among the Roma in Bulgaria and its revitalization of their communities.* Asbury Theological Seminary.

The Atlanta Constitution. (1887, July 24). "A gypsy encampment." *The Atlanta Constitution*, 13

The Atlanta Constitution. (1897, August 18). "Kester Talks of Gypsies." *The Atlanta Constitution*. Retrieved January 12, 2018, from: Library of Congress Archives.

The Atlanta Constitution. (1920, January 24). "Citizens Complain About Gypsy Camp." *The Atlanta Constitution*, 4. Retrieved January 12, 2018.

The Atlanta Constitution. (1929, November 22). "Haywood District Officer Arrested in Gypsy Slaying." *The Atlanta Constitution*, 7.

Bailey-Mershon, G., Raeesi, K. & Matache, M. (2014). "The Holocausts forgotten victims." *The Daily Beast*. Retrieved from: http://www.thedailybeast.com/the-holocausts-forgotten-roma-victims.

Beaudoin, J. (2014). *Challenging Essentialized Representations of Roma Identities in Canada* Doctoral dissertation, The University of Western Ontario.

Belton, B. A. (2005). *Questioning Gypsy identity: Ethnic narratives in Britain and America*. Oxford: AltiMira Press.

Berry, J. W. (1997). "Immigration, acculturation, and adaptation." *Applied psychology, 46*, 5–34.

Bhopal, K. (2004). "Gypsy Travelers and education: changing needs and changing perceptions." *British Journal of Educational Studies, 52*(1), 47–64.

Bhopal, K. (2011). "'This is a school, it's not a site': Teachers' attitudes towards gypsy and Traveler pupils in schools in England, UK." *British Educational Research Journal, 37*(3), 465–483. doi:10.1080/01411921003786561.

Bindel, J. (2011, Feb 25). "The big fat truth about Gypsy life." *The Guardian*. Retrieved from: https://www.theguardian.com/lifeandstyle/2011/feb/25/truth-about-gypsy-traveller-life-women.

Bissell, K., & Parrott, S. (2013). "Prejudice: The Role of the Media in the Development of Social Bias." *Journalism & Communication Monographs, 15*(4), 219–270.

Bitu, N. & Vincze, E. (2012). "Personal encounters and parallel paths toward Roma feminism." *Journal of Women in Culture and Society, 38*, 44–46.

Bohan, C. (2013, November 5). "Watchdog rejects Irish Traveller complaint about Big Fat Gypsy Wedding." Retrieved January 22, 2018 from: http://www.thejournal.ie/complaint-big-fat-gypsy-wedding-1159850-Nov2013/.

Bosch, T. (2012). "The Gypsies are coming to America." *Slate*. Retrieved from: http://www.slate.com/articles/double_x/doublex/2012/05/my_big_fat_american_gypsy_wedding_on_tlc_reviewed_.html.

Brooks, Ethel C. 2012. "The possibilities of Roma feminism." *Signs 38*(1): 1–11. *PsycINFO*, EBSCO*host*.

Broomfield, M. (2016). "The Tory war on Roma, Gypsies and Travellers." *Vice.com*. Retrieved from: http://www.vice.com/en_uk/read/tory-war-on-gypsies-and-travellers.

Brown, S. K., & Bean, F. D. (2005). Retrieved from http://www.migrationinformation. org/Feature/display.cfm?ID=442.

Bruce, D.R. (1984). "Cities: Gypsies venturing into American culture." *Chicago Tribune*.

Caillat, Colbie (2014). "Gypsy Heart." [CD]. Republic Records. USA.

Cameron County Press (1911, February 23). "Gypsies in America." *Cameron County Press*. Retrieved from: http://chroniclingamerica.loc.gov/lccn/sn83032040/1911–02–23/ed-1/seq-3/#date1=1836&sort=relevance&rows=20&words=gypsies+gypsy+Gypsy&search-Type=basic&sequence=0&index=19&state=&date2=1922&proxtext=Gypsies&y=0&x=0&dateFilterType=yearRange&page=2.

Carpenter, P. (2007). "Examining Borat and his influence on society." *Taboo, 11*(1), 15.

Ceneda, S. (2002). "Romani women from central and eastern Europe: A 'fourth world,' or experience of multiple discrimination." London: Refugee Women's Resource Project, Asylum Aid.

Ceyhan, S. (2003). *A case study of Gypsy/Roma identity construction in Edirne*. Yayınlanmamış Yüksek Lisans Tezi. Ankara: Ortadoğu Teknik Üniversitesi Sosyal Bilimler Enstitüsü.

Chohaney, M. L. (2012). "Secrets Beneath the Soil: A Mixed Methods Necrogeographic Investigation of Romany ('Gypsy') Memorial Sites." Doctoral dissertation, University of Toledo.

City of Alexandria. (2007, September 24). "Human Rights—What is discrimination." Retrieved from: http://alexandria.gov/humanrights/info/default.aspx?id=368.

Civil Rights Defenders (2016, May 23). "Roma register case against Sweden begins in Stockholm." *Liberties.Eu*. Retrieved from: http://www.liberties.eu/en/news/lawsuit-against-the-swedish-state.

Clark, C. (2004). "'Severity has often enraged but never subdued a gypsy': The History and Making of European Roma Stereotypes." In N. Saul and S. Tebbut (Eds.). *The role of the Romanies: images and counter-images of "Gypsies"/Romanies in European cultures* (226–246). Liverpool: Liverpool University Press.

Comanescu, L. (2015). "Representations of the Romaes in *My Big Fat American Gypsy Wedding*."

Council of Europe (2016, March 21). "Do Roma people need protection from themselves?" Retrieved from: http://Romastudies.eu/2016/.

Council of Europe (2018, January 1). "European Rome Rights Centre receives Raoul Wallenberg Prize for combating racism, rights abuse." Retrieved January 22, 2018 from: https://search.coe.int/directorate_of_communications/Pages/result_details.aspx?ObjectId=090000168077dd2b.

Covert, M. R. (2015). *The Impact of Assimilation on the Education of Roma Women in the United States*. Unpublished Manuscript. Georgia State University.

Crandall, C. C., & Stangor, C. (2005). "Conformity and prejudice." *On the nature of prejudice, 50*, 295–309.

Crocker, J., & Major, B. (1989). "Social stigma and self-esteem: The self-protective properties of stigma." *Psychological Review, 96*(4), 608.

Croucher, S. M. (2013). "Integrated threat theory and acceptance of immigrant assimilation: An qanalysis of Muslim immigration in Western Europe." *Communication Monographs, 80*(1), 46–62.

Cusack, C. M. (2011). "Placentophagy and Embryophagy: An Analysis of Social Deviance within Gender, Families, or the Home (Etude 1)." *Journal Law & Social Deviance, 1*, 112.

The Daily Pacific (1892). "All about the Gypsies, their origin, manners, customs and method of living." *The Daily Pacific*. Retrieved from: http://chroniclingamerica.loc.gov/.

Danova. S. (1998) (as cited in Erjavic, 2001). *Roma: Media*. http://www.rnw.nl/humanrights/html/mediaRomaa.html.

The Day Book (1913, May 01). "Kidnapped by Gypsies! A thrilling chase that led through three states." *The Day Book*. Retrieved from: http://chroniclingamerica.loc.gov/lccn/sn83045487/1913–05–01/ed-1/seq-18/.

Deaton, S. (2013). "Textual Analysis of the Portrayals of the Roma in a U.S. Newspaper." Master's Thesis, University of Central Florida. Retrieved from: http://stars.library.ucf.edu/etd/2527.

Decade of Roma Inclusion Secretariat Foundation (2012). Retrieved March 17, 2015, from: http://www.romadecade.org/about-the-decade-decade-in-brief.

Derrington, C. (2005). "Perceptions of behaviour and patterns of exclusion: Gypsy Traveller students in English secondary schools." *Journal of Research in Special Educational Needs, 5*(2), 55–61. doi:10.1111/J.1471–3802.2005.00042.x.

Derrington, C. (2007). "Fight, flight and playing white: An examination of coping strategies adopted by Gypsy Traveler Adolescents in English secondary schools." *International Journal of Educational Research, 46*(6), 357–367.

Derrington, C., & Kendall, S. (2004). *Gypsy Traveller students in secondary schools: Culture, identity and achievement*. Trentham Books.

Dobreva, N. I. (2009). "The curse of the traveling dancer: Roma representation from 19th-century European literature to Hollywood film and beyond."

Doherty, M. (2013, Aug 13). "Britain has a duty to help the most vulnerable Gypsies and Travellers." *The Guardian*. Retrieved from: https://www.theguardian.com/commentisfree / 2013/aug/13/gypsies-travellers-britain-duty.

Donald, B. B., & Brooks, B. T. (2008). "Immigrants and other cultural minorities as non-traditional plaintiffs: culture as a factor in determining tort damages." *Judicature*, 92, 220.

Du Bois, W. E. B. (1968). *The Souls of Black Folk: Essays and Sketches*. Chicago: AG McClurg, 1903. Johnson Reprint Corporation.

Erjavec, K. (2001). "Media representation of the discrimination against the Roma in Eastern Europe: The case of Slovenia." *Discourse & Society*, *12*(6), 699–727.

Esses, V. M., Medianu, S., & Lawson, A. S. (2013). "Uncertainty, threat, and the role of the media in promoting the dehumanization of immigrants and refugees." *Journal of Social Issues*, *69*, 518–536.

Euroactiv (2015). "France evicts 300 Roma per week." (2014, January 1). Retrieved March 17, 2015, from: http://www.euractiv.com/sections/social-europe-jobs/france-evicts-300-roma-week-311839.

European Youth Campaign for Soceity (2010). "August 2nd—Commemoration Day of the Roma Genocide." Retrieved March 17, 2015, from: http://ternype.eu/about-ternype.

Equality and Human Rights Commission. (2016, March). "England's most disadvantaged groups: Gypsies, Travellers and Roma." Retrieved January 9, 2018, from: https://www.equalityhumanrights.com/sites/default/files/ief_gypsies_travellers_and_roma.pdf.

Facebook (2016). "Quotes from online Roma discussion. No retrieval source given for the sake of anonymity."

Fangs for the Fantasy (2013, May 3). "Hemlock Grove—So Many Problems." Retrieved January 05, 2018, from: http://www.fangsforthefantasy.com/2013/05/hemlock-grove-so-many-problems.html.

Federal Writers' Project (1920). H. Schuler. *Tricked by Gypsies*. Retrieved from: https://www.loc.gov/resource/wpalh3.31100508/?sp=1&st=text.

Fernandez, V. R. (2016, August 1). "The Hidden Roma Heritage of Famous Comic Book Characters." Retrieved January 22, 2018, from: https://www.opensocietyfoundations.org/voices/how-pop-culture-can-help-roma-see-themselves-survivors.

Fonseca, I. (1995). *Bury me standing, the gypsies and their journey*. New York: Vintage Books

Foster, B & Norton, P. (2012). "Educational equality for Gypsy, Roman and Traveller children and young people in the UK." *The Equal Rights Review*, 8, 85–112.

Fryberg, S. A. (2002). *Really? You don't look like an American Indian: Social representations and social group identities*. Doctoral dissertation, Stanford University.

Fryberg, S. A., Markus, H. R., Oyserman, D., & Stone, J. M. (2008). "Of warrior chiefs and Indian princesses: The psychological consequences of American Indian mascots." *Basic and Applied Social Psychology*, *30*(3), 208–218.

Furumoto-Dawson, A., Gehlert, S., Sohmer, D., Olopade, O., & Sacks, T. (2007) (As cited in Heaslip, 2015). "Early-life conditions and mechanisms of population health vulnerabilities." *Health Affairs*, *26*(5), 1238–1248.

Gans, H. J. (1979). "Symbolic ethnicity: The future of ethnic groups and cultures in American Essays." *Ethnic and Racial Studies*, *2*(1), 1–20.

Gelbart, P. (2012). "Either sing or go get the beer: Contradictions of (Roma) female power in central Europe." *Journal of Women in Culture and Society*, 38, 22–29.

Gibson, M. A. (1988). *Accommodation without assimilation: Sikh immigrants in an American high school*. Cornell University Press.

Girlsaskguys (n.d.). "What are your opinions on Gypsy Travellers." [Online Forum]. *Girlsask-guys*. Retrieved from: http://www.girlsaskguys.com/social-relationships/q1860633-what-is-your-opinion-on-gypsy-travellers.

Gordon, M. M. (1964). *Assimilation in American life: The role of race, religion, and national origins*. Oxford University Press on Demand.

Green, C. (2016, Jan. 12). "Butlin's and Pontin's accused of keeping secret 'blacklists' of Traveller families." *Independent*. Retrieved from: http://www.independent.co.uk/news /uk/home-news/butlins-and-pontins-accused-of-keeping-secret-blacklists-of-traveller-families-a6808231.html.

Gropper, R. C. (1975). *Gypsies in the city: Culture patterns and survival*. Darwin Press, Incorporated.

Grover, S. (2007). "Mental health professionals as pawns in oppressive practices: A case example concerning psychologists' involvement in the denial of education rights to Roma/ Gypsy children." *Ethical Human Psychology And Psychiatry: An International Journal Of Critical Inquiry, 9*(1), 14–24. doi:10.1891/152315007780493825.

Hahn, D. (producer), Trousdale, G. & Wise, K. (directors) (1996). *The Hunchback of Notre Dame.* [Animated Film]. United States: Walt Disney Pictures.

Hall, E. G. (2001, June 01). "Gypsies: King of Con." *Police: The Law Enforcement Magazine.* Retrieved from: http://www.policemag.com/channel/gangs/articles/2001/06/gypsies-kings-of-con.aspx.

Hancock, I. F. (2002). *We are the Roma people* (3446). Hatfield: University of Hertfordshire Press.

Hancock, I. F. (2008). "The gypsy stereotype and the sexualization of Roma women." In *"Gypsies" in European Literature and Culture* (181–191). Palgrave Macmillan US.

Hancock, I. F. (2010). *Danger! Educated Gypsy: Selected Essays.* Univ. of Hertfordshire Press.

Hanson, H., K. Reichs, and P. Charles. "Bones." *The Turn in The Urn. Fox.* Los Angeles, California, 31 Mar. 2014. Television.

Harding, S. (2014). "Social exclusion: Cultural dissonance between Travellers and non-Travellers in British secondary schools." *Journal of Student Engagement: Education Matters, 4*(1), 25–34.

Harris, K. (2013, August 21). "Europe's Roma, racism gets worse in tough economic times." *Time Magazine.* Retrieved from: http://world.time.com/2013/08/21/roma-in-europe-age-old-discrimination-worsens-in-tough-economic-times/.

Heaslip, V. (2015). *Experience of vulnerability from a gypsy/travelling perspective: a phenomenological study.* Doctoral dissertation, Bournemouth University.

Herman, D (executive producer) (2012). "My Big Fat Gypsy Wedding." [Television Series]. The Learning Channel.

Heller, L. (2017). "Thirsting for Justice: Roma and the Human Rights to Water and Sanitation." *ERRC Blog.* Retrieved from: http://www.errc.org/blog/thirsting-for-justice-roma-and-the-human-rights-to-water-and-sanitation/164.

Higgins, A. (2013, May 9). "In an effort to integrate Roma, Slovakia recalls U.S. struggles." *New York Times.* Retrieved from: http://www.nytimes.com/2013/05/10/world/europe/in-slovakia-integration-of-roma-mirrors-early-struggles-in-us.html?_r=0.

Hirsch, M. L. (2012, Sept 4) "Women under siege." *Women's Media Center.* Retrieved from: http://www.womenundersiegeproject.org/blog/entry/forced-sterilization-big-media-stories-versus-the-big-picture.

Holland, K. (2016, Jan 22). "Dundalk Travellers told to put children into foster care." *The Irish Times.* Retrieved from: http://www.irishtimes.com/news/social-affairs/dundalk-travellers-told-to-put-children-into-foster-care-1.2506108.

Holland, T. (director). (1996). *Thinner* [Motion picture]. United States: Paramount.

Imre, A. (2003). "Screen Gypsies." *Framework: The Journal of Cinema and Media, 44*(2), 15–33.

Investment Watch (2016). "Roma gypsies treated like circus animals by Dutch football/soccer fans." *Investment Watch.* Retrieved from: http://investmentwatchblog.com/roma-gypsies-treated-like-circus-animals-by-dutch-footballsoccer-fans/.

Jasaroska, S. (2014). "Sign the petition to people harmed as a result of the negative and inaccurate stereotypes and hate caused by these shows." [Online petition]. *Causes.com.* Retrieved from: https://www.causes.com/actions/1669292-petition-to-bring-legal-action-against-the-national-geographic-tv-show-american-gypsies-tlcs-my-big-fat-american-gypsy-wedding-and-other.

Johnson, Andrew (March 27, 1866). "Veto Message." Online by Gerhard Peters and John T. Woolley, *The American Presidency Project.* http://www.presidency.ucsb.edu/ws/?pid=71978.

Jones, D. R., Harrell, J. P., Morris-Prather, C. E., Thomas, J., & Omowale, N. (1995). "Affective and physiological responses to racism: the roles of afrocentrism and mode of presentation." *Ethnicity & Disease, 6*(1–2), 109–122.

Jones, R. L. (Ed.) (2004). *Black Psychology* (4th edition). Hampton, VA: Cobb & Henry.

Jovanović, J. (2014). *Roma women's identities real and imagined Media discourse analysis of "I'm a European Roma Woman" campaign.* Doctoral dissertation, Central European University.

Kabachnik, P. (2009). "The culture of crime: Examining representations of Irish Travelers in *Traveller and The Riches.*" *Roma Studies, 19*(1), 49–63.

Kao, G., & Thompson, J. (2003). "Racial and ethnic stratification in educational achievement and attainment." *Annual Review of Sociology, 29*, 417–442.

King, C. R. (2015). *Consumerism on TV: Popular Media from the 1950s to the Present.* A. Hulme (Ed.). Ashgate Publishing, Ltd.

King, S. (1984). *Thinner: A Novel.* New York: Pocket Books.

Kriss, A. & Lipera, P. (Creators) (2012). "American Gypsies." [Television Series]. National Geographic Channel. USA.

Kushi, S. (2016, Jan 18). "Roma women of the Balkans: Battling intersectional oppression." *Open Democracy.* Retrieved from: https://www.opendemocracy.net/sidita-kushi/Roma-women-of-balkans-still-battling-intersectional-oppression.

La Ferla, R. (2012, March 1). "The Fortune Tellers Knew It." *New York Times*, E4.

Lacalle, C. (2009, Nov 10). "Racism and the Roma." *The Harvard Crimson.* Retrieved from: *http://www.thecrimson.com/article/2009/11/10/gypsies-gypsy-europe-against/.*

Lane, P., Spencer, S., & Jones, A. (2014). "Gypsy, Traveller and Roma: Experts by Experience."

Leavitt, P. A., Covarrubias, R., Perez, Y. A., & Fryberg, S. A. (2015). "'Frozen in Time': The Impact of Native American Media Representations on Identity and Self-Understanding." *Journal of Social Issues, 71*, 39–53.

Lee, E. J., Keyes, K., Bitfoi, A., Mihova, Z., Pez, O., Yoon, E., & Masfety, V. K. (2014). "Mental health disparities between Roma and non-Roma children in Romania and Bulgaria." *BMC Psychiatry, 14*(1), 1.

Levinson, M. P. (2007). "Literacy in English Gypsy communities: Cultural capital manifested as negative assets." *American Educational Research Journal, 44*(1), 5–39. doi:10.3102/0002831206298174.

Levinson, M. P., & Sparkes, A. C. (2005). "Gypsy children, space, and the school environment." *International Journal of Qualitative Studies in Education, 18*(6), 751–772. doi:10.1080/09518390500298212.

Levitz, S. (2012) (as cited in Beaudoin, 2014) "Federal immigration points system changed." *The Toronto Star*, December 19. Retrieved from: http://www.thestar.com/news/canada / 2012/12/19/federal_immigration_points_syste m_changed.html.

Liebkind, K., & Jasinskaja-Lahti, I. (2000). "The influence of experiences of discrimination on psychological stress: A comparison of seven immigrant groups." *Journal of Community & Applied Social Psychology, 10*(1), 1–16.

Lipkin, D. (creator) (2007). *The Riches.* [Television Show]. FX Network.

Little Falls Herald (1920, May 28) "Gypsies Visit City." *Little Falls Herald.* Retrieved from: http://chroniclingamerica.loc.gov/lccn/sn89064515/1920–05–28/ed-1/seq-3/#date1=1920&index=0&rows=20&words=CITY+gypsies+GYPSIES+VISIT&searchype=basic&sequence=0&state=&date2=1920&proxtext=Gypsies+visit+city&y=0&x=0&dateFilterType=yearRange&page=1.

Live Link (2016). "The fighting traveler women of Ireland." *Live Leak* [video]. Retrieved from: http://www.liveleak.com/view?i=4ef_1461940345&comments=1.

The Local (2016, Mar 03). "Third arson attack on Roma in Linz." *The Local.* Retrieved from: http://www.thelocal.at/20160303/third-arson-attack-on-roma-family-in-linz-austria.

Lonon, S. (2016, Jan 18). "Beware traveling scammers." *Tampa Patch.* Retrieved from: http://patch.com/florida/southtampa/beware-gypsies-travelers-sheriffs-office-warns.

Lyubansky, M., & Eidelson, R. J. (2005). "Revisiting du bois: The relationship between African American double consciousness and beliefs about racial and national group experiences." *Journal of Black Psychology, 31*(1), 3–26.

Maclane, R. & Rafkin, A. (1966). "The Gypsies." [Television series episode]. In Leonard, S. (executive producer), *The Andy Griffith Show.* Culver City, California of Desilu Studios.

Mago, S. (2016). Roma activists 2.0. *Rom Archive*. Retrieved from: https://blog.romarchive.eu/?p=5404.

Manzo, J. F., & Bailey, M. M. (2005). "On the assimilation of racial stereotypes among black Canadian young offenders." *The Canadian Review of Sociology*, *42*(3), 283.

Marafioti, O. (2012, May 15). "Why TLC's My big fat gypsy wedding doesn't represent the Roma." *Slate*. Retrieved from: http://www.slate.com/blogs/xx_factor /2012/05/15/ is_my_big_fat_gypsy_wedding_unfair_to_the_roma_community_.html.

Martindale-Hubbell. (2003). *Martindale Hubbell Law Directory 2003*. Martindale-Hubbell.

Mastro, D. E. (2009). *Racial/ethnic stereotyping and the media*. na.

Mastro, D. E. (2015). "Why the Media's Role in Issues of Race and Ethnicity Should be in the Spotlight." *Journal of Social Issues*, *71*(1), 1–16.

Mastro, D. E., & Atwell Seate, A. (2012). "Group membership in race-related media processes and effects." *The handbook of intergroup communication*, 357–369.

Mastro, D. E., & Greenberg, B. S. (2000). "The portrayal of racial minorities on prime time television." *Journal of Broadcasting & Electronic Media*, *44*, 690–703.

Matros, Y. (2004). "The Role of Language in Mystifying and Demystifying Gypsy Identity." In *The Role of the Romanies: Images and Counter images of Gypsys/Romanies in European Culture* (53–78). Liverpool: Liverpool University Press.

Meyers, S. L. (2006, Sept. 27). "Kazakhstan laughs as its officials try to ban Borat—Europe—International Herald Tribune." *New York Times*. Retrieved from: http://www.nytimes.com/ 2006/09/27/world/europe/27iht-borat.2952940.html.

Mickelson, R.A. (1989). "Why does Jane read and write so well? The anomaly of Women's achievement." *Sociology of Education, 62*, 47–63.

Miller, C. (2009). *The church of cheese: Gypsy ritual in the American heyday*. Gemma.

Minahan, J. B. (2013). *Ethnic Groups of the Americas: An Encyclopedia*. ABC-CLIO.

Morris, R. (2000). "Gypsies, Travellers and the Media: Press regulation and racism in the UK." *TOLLEYS COMMUNICATIONS LAW*, *5*(6), 213–219.

Murray, J. (Presenter) & Starkey, K. (Producer) (2016). "Romany Gypsy women." [Radio Program]. *BBC Women's Hour*. Retrieved from: http://www.bbc.co.uk /programmes/ b07b9r55#playt=0h10m52s.

National Association of Bunco Investigators (2015). "Conference training schedule: Elder exploitation and nomadic organized crime." Retrieved from: http://www.nabihq.org/en-us/ seminars,_training,_and_conferences/2015TrainingAgendaFinal.pdf.

Nazroo, J. Y., & Karlsen, S. (2001). *Ethnic inequalities in health: social class, racism and identity*. Health Variations Programme.

Nerds of Color (2017). "Erased and Ignored. Dick Grayson's RRoma Identity Comes to Light." *Nerds of Color Blog*. Retrieved from: https://thenerdsofcolor.org/2017/03/01/erased-and-ignored-dick-graysons-rRoma-identity-comes-to-light/.

New York Times. (1909, July 22). "Keeping out the Gypsies." *New York Times*, 6.

New York Times. (1909, July 23). "Flung their babies at the inspectors." *New York Times*, 14

New York Times. (1986, September 17). "Gypsy survivors of the Nazis hear pledge on aid." Retrieved from: http://www.nytimes.com/1986/09/17/us/gypsy-survivors-of-nazis-hear-pledge-on-aid.html.

New York Times. (2011, August 5). "Telling Fortunes, and, From Time to Time, Also Taking Them." Retrieved from: https://www.nytimes.com/2011/08/06/nyregion/in-new-york-fortunes-told-and-too-often-taken.html.

Nicoara, M. (2012, July 28). "American Gypsies needs to catch up with the reality of Roma people's lives." *The Guardian*. Retrieved from: https://www.theguardian.com/ commentis-free/2012/jul/28/american-gypsies-reality-roma-lives.

Nirenberg, J. (Ed.). (2011). *Gypsy Sexuality: Roma and Outsider Perspectives on Intimacy*. Clambake Press.

Nirenberg, J. (2014). *Gypsy Movements*. Tampa: Schlimmer Publishing.

Okely, J. (2014). "Recycled (mis)representations: Gypsies, Travellers or Roma treated as objects, rarely subjects." *People, Place and Policy Online*, *8*(1), 65–85.

Oleaque, J.M. (2014). "The representation of Gypsies in the media." *Vidas Gitanas Lugo Drom.* Retrieved from: https://www.accioncultural. es/virtuales/vidasgitanas/pdf_eng/vidas_git_art2_representacion_eng.pdf.

Open Society (2011). "Against her will: Forced and coerced sterilization of women worldwide." Retrieved from: https://www.opensocietyfoundations.org/sites/default/files/against-her-will-20111003.pdf.

Oprea, A. (2004). "Re-envisioning social justice from the ground up: Including the experiences of Roma women." *Essex human rights review, 1*(1), 29–39.

Parham, T. A., White, J. L., & Ajamu, A. (1999). *The psychology of Blacks: An African-centered perspective.* Pearson College Division.

Peralta, E. (2013, October 23). "Two Blonde Children Taken From Roma Families in Ireland are returned." Retrieved January 22, 2018, from: https://www.npr.org/sections/thetwo-way/2013/10/23/240288419/two-blond-children-taken-from-roma-families-in-ireland-are-returned.

Perea, J. F. (1993). "Ethnicity and Prejudice: Reevaluating National Origin Discrimination Under Title VII." *William and Mary Law Review, 35*(3), 805.

Perring, R. (2016, Feb 3). "French police storm shanty camp to evict 350 Roma Gypsies from Paris." *Express.* Retrieved from: http://www.express.co.uk/news/world/640795/Roma-gypsy-shanty-town-Paris-French-police-evict.

Persaud, T. (2010, October 26). "Christianity thrives among 'Gypsies' despite prejudice." *Christianity Today.*

Petrova, D. (2004). "The Roma: Between a myth and the future." *Social Research,* 111–161.

Pinterest (n.d.). "Gypsy Board" [pinterest board]. Retrieved from: https://www.pinterest.com / annieb5767/gypsy-board/.

Plaut, S. (2012). "Expelling the Victim by Demanding Voice: The Counterframing of Transnational Roma Activism." *Alternatives: Global, Local, Political, 37*(1), 52–65.

Plunkett, J. (2012). "Big Fat Gypsy Weddings has 'increased the bullying of Gypsies and Travellers.'" *The Guardian.* Retrieved from: http://www.theguardian.com/media/2012/oct/16/big-fat-gypsy-weddings-bullying-travellers.

Popplewell, J. (Director). (2012). *My Big Fat Gypsy Wedding.* United States: Firecracker Films.

Rechel, B., Blackburn, C. M., Spencer, N. J., & Rechel, B. (2009). "Access to health care for Roma children in Central and Eastern Europe: Findings from a qualitative study in Bulgaria." *International Journal for Equity in Health, 8*(1), 1.

Rivadeneyra, R., Ward, L. M., & Gordon, M. (2007). "Distorted reflections: Media exposure and Latino adolescents' conceptions of self." *Media Psychology, 9*(2), 261–290.

Roddenberry, G., and M. Snodgrass. "Star Trek: The Next Generation." *Up the Long Ladder.* Paramount Studios. Los Angeles, California, 20 May 1989. Television.

Rodriguez, V. [Roma Pop]. (2016, October 8). "NYCC '16 Racusm: Peter David Anti-Roma Statements at X-Men LGBTQ Panel" [Video File]. Retrieved from: https://www.youtube.com/watch?v=Z4QuxCNe89g.

Rojas, A. J., Navas, M., Savans-Jiménez, P., & Cuadrado, I. (2014). "Acculturation Preference Profiles of Spaniards and Romanian Immigrants: The Role of Prejudice and Public and Private Acculturation Areas." *The Journal of Social psychology, 154*(4), 339–351.

Roma Support Group (2012). "Roma mental health advocacy project." *Roma Support Group.* Retrieved from: http://romasupportgroup.org.uk/wp/wp-content/uploads/2011/08/Roma-Mental-Health-Advocacy-Project-Evaluation-Report.pdf.

ROMApop (2016). "Hate Speech Against Roma People at New York Comic Con 2016." Press Release. Retrieved from: ROMApop Twitter entry October 12, 2016.

Romea.cz. (2016, March 28). "Czech town offers Roma family accommodation in uninhabitable hotel." *Romea.* Retrieved from: http://www.romea.cz/en/news/czech/czech-town-offers-Roma-family-accommodation-in-uninhabitable-residential-hotel.

Rubin, L. (writer), & Giedroyc, C., Mahoney, V., Sakharov, A., Taylor-Johnson, S. Winant, S. (directors). (2017). *Gypsy* in L. Rubin (producer). Netflix.

Russel (2016). "Teenager claims school bully 'threatened to stab her' because of Gypsy heritage." *Brief Report*. Retrieved from: http://www.briefreport.co.uk/news/teenager-claims-school-bully-threatened-to-stab-her-because-of-gypsy-heritage-3823884.html.

Rutgers University (2016, Jan 11). "Obama appoints WGS Professor Ethel Brooks to U.S. Holocaust Council." [Online notice]. Retrieved from: http://womens-studies.rutgers.edu/events/808-obama-appoints-wgs-professor-ethel-brooks-to-u-s-holocaust-memorial-council.

RT News (2015). "'Good at rummaging through garbage': Italian official proposes Gypsies as waste sorters." Retrieved March 17, 2015, from: http://rt.com/news/229271-gypsies-roma-rome-garbage/.

Salo, M. T. (2002). "Gypsy and Traveler Culture in America." Retrieved January 09, 2018, from: http://www.gypsyloresociety.org/additional-resources/gypsy-and-traveler-culture-in-america.

Saul, N. & Tebbutt, S. (Eds). (2004). *Role of the Romaes: Images and Counter Images of Gypsies'/Romaes in European Cultures*. Oxford: Oxford University Press.

Schemer, C. (2012). "The influence of news media on stereotypic attitudes toward immigrants in a political campaign." *Journal of Communication, 62*, 739–757.

Schiappa, E., Gregg, P. B., & Hewes, D. E. (2005). "The parasocial contact hypothesis." *Communication Monographs, 72*(1), 92–115.

Schlueter, E., & Davidov, E. (2013). "Contextual sources of perceived group threat: Negative immigration-related news reports, immigrant group size and their interaction, Spain 1996–2007." *European Sociological Review, 29*, 179–191.

Schneeweis, A. (2017). 'The Imagined Backward and Downtrodden Other: Contemporary American news coverage of the Roma/Gypsy." *Journalism Studies*, 1–20.

Schneeweis, A., & Foss, K. A. (2016). "'Gypsies, Tramps & Thieves' Examining Representations of Roma Culture in 70 Years of American Television." *Journalism & Mass Communication Quarterly*, 1077699016682723.

Schultz, D. L. (2012). "Translating intersectionality theory into practice: A tale of Roma-Gadže feminist alliance." *Signs, 38*(1), 37–43. doi:10.1086/665802.

Serdult, V. (2016, Aug 4). "Hungary continues to segregate Roma school children." *The Budapest Beacon*. Retrieved from: http://budapestbeacon.com/featured-articles/hungary-continues-to-segregation-roma-school-children/37111.

Sigona, N. (2008). "The latest public enemy: Romaan Roma in Italy." *The case*.

Silver, Wigram, Downey & Lin (producers) & Ritchie (director) (2011). *Sherlock Game of Shadows* [Motion Picture]. United States: Village Roadshow Pictures, Silver Pictures.

Silverman, C. (2012). "Education, agency and power among Macedonian Muslim Roma Women in New York City." *Journal of Women in Culture and Society, 38*, 30–36.

Silverman, C. (2014). "Balkan Romani Culture, Human Rights, and the State: Whose Heritage? In Cultural Heritage in Transit: Intangible Rights as Human Rights (125–147)." Philadelphia: University of Pennsylvania Press.

Smolinska-Poffley, G. & Ingmire, S. (2012) *Roma mental health advocacy project: Evaluation Report*. Roma Support Group. Retrieved from: http://romasupportgroup.org.uk/wp/wp-content/uploads/2011/08/Roma-Mental-Health-Advocacy-Project-Evaluation-Report.pdf.

SPRC (2013). "Suicide among racial/ethnic populations in the U.S." [fact sheet]. Retrieved from: http://www.sprc.org/sites/default/files/migrate/library/Blacks%20Sheet%20August%2028%202013%20Final.pdf.

The St. Mary Banner (1915, November 27). "Making the way of the Gypsies harder." *The St. Mary Banner."* Retrieved from: http://chroniclingamerica.loc.gov/lccn/sn88064384/1915-11-27/ed-1/seq 6/#date1=1915&index=0&date2=1915&searchType=advanced &language=&sequence=0&lccn=sn88064384&words=Gypsies+gypsies+Gypsy+gypsy&proxdistance=5.

The St. Tammy Farmer (1916, Aprol 29). "Kidnapping of children by gypsies causes excitement I in Covington but examination of camp give no clew." *The St. Tammy Farmer*. Retrieved from: http://chroniclingamerica.loc.gov/lccn/sn82015387/1916-04-29/ed-1/seq-1/#date1=1916&index=0&date2=1916&searchType=advanced&language=&sequence=0&lccn=sn82015387&words=gypsies+Gypsies+gypsis&proxdistance=5&rows=20&ortext=Gypsies&proxtext=&phrasetext=&andtext=&dateFilterType=yearRange&page=1.

Stangor, C. (2009). "The study of stereotyping, prejudice, and discrimination within social psychology: A quick history of theory and research." *Handbook of prejudice, stereotyping, and discrimination*, 1–22.

Strauss, D. (2012) "Study on the Current Educational Situation of German Sinti and Roma." Retrieved from: http://sinti-roma.com/wp-content/uploads/2014/07/2011_Strauss_Study__ Sinti_Education.pdf.

The Sun (1913, April 06). "American women's experience with English gypsies-unattractive on close acquaintance." *The Sun (New York)*. Retrieved from: http://chroniclingamerica.loc. gov/lccn/sn83030272/1913–04–06/ed-1/seq38/#date1=1913&index=0&date2=1913& searchType=advanced&language=&sequence=0&lccn=sn83030272&lccn=sn83030431& lccn=sn86091025&lccn=sn91068129&lccn=sn95047216&words=gypsies+GYPSIES+ Gypsies+gypsy+GYPSY&proxdistance=5&state=&rows=20&ortext=Gypsies&proxtext=& phrasetext=&andtext=&dateFilterType=yearRange&page=1.

Sutherland, A. (1975). *Gypsies: The hidden Americans.* Long Grove, IL: Waveland Press.

Szlavi, A. (2014, January 1). "April 8th: International Roma Day." Retrieved March 17, 2015, from: http://one-europe.info/april-8th-international-roma-day.

Tasbeeh (2015). "Roma rants: The Hunchback of Notre Dame (Disney) critiques and concerns." *Rroma in the Arts.* [Tumblr Post] Retrieved from: http://rRoma-in-art.tumblr.com/ post/121214077396/Roma-rants-the-hunchback-of-notre-dame-disney.

Tereskinas, A. (2002). "Ethnic and Sexual Minorities in the Lithuanian Mass Media: Images and Issues." *CPS International Policy Fellowship Program*, 1–12.

Thomas, J. (2006, Aug 16). "Coercive sterilization of Roma women examined at hearing." *IIP DIGITAL.* Retrieved from: http://iipdigital.usembassy.gov/st/ english/article/2006/08/ 20060817104545 1cjsamoht0.678158.html#axzz4G8UJpWKE.

Thomas, S. & Tarantino, J. (Executive Producers) (2012). *Gypsy Sisters.* [Television Series]. The Learning Channel. USA.

Tobin, P. C., & Blackburn, L. M. (2007). "Slow the spread: a national program to manage the gypsy moth." *General Technical Report-Northern Research Station, USDA Forest Service*, (NRS-6).

Torres, L. (2010). "Predicting levels of Latino depression: Acculturation, acculturative stress, and coping." *Cultural Diversity and Ethnic Minority Psychology*, 16(2), 256.

Topeka State Journal (1921, April 05) "City Minus Gypsies." *Topeka State Journal.* Retrieved from: http://chroniclingamerica.loc.gov/lccn/sn82016014/1921–04–05/ed-1/seq-5/#date1= 1920&sort=relevance&rows=20&words=gypsies+GYPSIES+gypsy&searchType=basic& sequence=0&index=10&state=&date2=1922&proxtext=Gypsies&y=15&x=13& dateFilterType=yearRange&page=2.

Tóth, K. D. (2005). "Comparative study on the identity types of successful gypsies/travellers in Hungary and in England." *European Integration Studies*, 4(2), 121–131.

The Traveller Movement. (2015, October 15). "Cultural History." Retrieved January 09, 2018, from: http://travellermovement.org.uk/cultural-history/.

Tremlett, A. (2013). "'Here are the Gypsies!' The importance of self-representations and how to question prominent images of Gypsy minorities." *Ethnic and Racial Studies*, 36(11), 1706–1725.

Ureche, H. & Franks, M. (2007). "This is who we are: A study of the views and identities of Rroma, Gypsy and Traveller young people in England." *The Children's Society.* Retrieved from: https://www.childrenssociety.org.uk/sites/default/files/tcs/research_docs/ This%20is%20who%20we%20are%20%20A%20study%20of%20the%20experiences%20o f%20Rroma,%20gypsy%20and%20traveller%20children%20throughout%20England.pdf.

U.S. House of Representatives (n.d.). "The Civil Rights Bill of 1866." Retrieved January 22, 2018 from: http://history.house.gov/Historical-Highlights/1851–1900/The-Civil-Rights-Bill-of-1866/.

Van Cleemput, P., Parry, G., Thomas, K., Peters, J., & Cooper, C. (2007). "Health-related beliefs and experiences of Gypsies and Travellers: a qualitative study." *Journal of Epidemiology and Community Health*, 61(3), 205–210.

Van der Zee (2016, July 19). "Roma women share stories of forced sterilization." *Aljazeera.* Retrieved from: http://www.aljazeera.com/indepth/features/2016/07/roma-women-share-stories-forced-sterilisation-160701100731050.html.

Velez, A. M. (2012). "The Roma uncovered: Deconstructing the (mis)representations of a culture." Florida Atlantic University.

Walsh, C., Este, D., Brigette, K. & Giurgiu, B. (2011). "Needs of refugee children in Canada: What can Roman refugee families tell us?" *Journal of Comparative Family Studies,* 42, 599–613.

Whedon J. (producer) & Feige, K (Director) (2015). *Avengers: Age of Ultron.* [Motion Picture]. United States: Walt Disney Studios.

Whittington-Walsh, F. (2002). "From freaks to savants: Disability and hegemony from The Hunchback of Notre Dame (1939) to Sling Blade (1997)." *Disability & Society,* *17*(6), 695–707.

Williams, C. L., & Berry, J. W. (1991). "Primary prevention of acculturative stress among refugees: Application of psychological theory and practice." *American psychologist, 46*(6), 632.

Williams, D. R. (1999). "Race, socioeconomic status, and health the added effects of racism and discrimination." *Annals of the New York Academy of Sciences, 896*(1), 173–188.

Yabush, D. (1970, November 15). "Fiction Cloaks Gypsies' Lives." *Chicago Tribune,* 1.

Yin-Har Lau, A., & Ridge, M. (2011). "Addressing the impact of social exclusion on mental health in Gypsy, Roma, and Traveller communities." *Mental Health and Social Inclusion, 15*(3), 129–137.

Yuenger, J. (1987, September 20). "Gypsies the last outsiders: Whether it's society's fault or their own, most never 'fit in.'" *Chicago Tribune,* D1.

Zabara, N. (2014, Aug 8). "Roma people haunted by stigma." *The Trauma and Mental Health Report.* Retrieved from: http://trauma.blog.yorku.ca/2014/08/Roma-people-haunted-by-stigma/.

Index

accommodate, 72, 78, 79, 81, 84, 95, 149
acculturation, xxii, 32, 150, 163, 194;
    model, 71, 115
activism, 34, 48, 73, 104, 202–208
Al, xxii, 76–77, 127, 131, 162, 167, 184,
    193
Alana, 191
Albania, 140, 177
Allie, xxii, 138, 143–144, 173, 188, 206
America, xviii, xix, 2–3, 7, 11, 15, 16,
    25–26, 27, 29–30, 33, 34, 35–36, 37,
    55–58, 61–64, 97, 113–114, 127–128,
    137–139, 181–185, 189–190
American: Black, xv, xviii, 37, 38, 64, 70,
    114, 122, 175, 177; Council for Roma
    Equality, 204; *Gypsies* (Television
    Series), 29–30; Roma, x, xvi, xviii, xx,
    xxv, 35, 50, 118, 127, 166, 174, 199,
    210, 211
American Civil Liberties Union, 52
Andy Griffith, 20–22
Anne, xxii, 51, 137, 139, 152, 154
anti-Ziganism, xvii, xviii, 24, 203
anxiety, 112, 122, 123, 169
appropriation, 5, 33, 57, 175, 176
Ashland Tidings, 10
assimilate, xvii, 34, 39, 43, 46, 48, 54, 55,
    56, 76, 78, 79, 80, 85, 87, 90, 91, 92,
    148, 151, 152, 169, 192; assimilation, 1,
    10, 33, 35, 35–36, 36, 38, 44, 59, 67,
    73, 76, 79, 80, 94, 97–98, 99, 104, 156,

179; theory, 71–72
Atlanta, 33; *Atlanta Constitution*, 7–8, 33,
    39
Auschwitz, 207, 208
Austria, 55
Avengers, 17

BBC, 120
Benny, xxii, 105–106, 128, 131, 167, 175,
    179–180, 195, 198
Berry, John, 68, 71–72, 112, 133, 146, 155
blacklist, 55
Bones, 22
Borat, 16
Brooks, Ethel, 203
Buffy the Vampire Slayer, 23–24
Bulgaria, 13, 123; Bulgarian, 123
bullying, 5, 60, 112, 115, 117, 123, 137,
    139

California, 119
Canada, 3, 51–52, 206
career, 79, 86, 100, 147, 151
Chicago, 109; *Chicago Tribune*, 11
Christianity, 210
civil rights, 36–38, 63, 114, 122; Civil
    Rights Act, 69
college, 76, 78, 80, 83, 86, 88, 90, 91, 95,
    116, 138, 143, 147, 153–154, 156, 158,
    167
Comic Con, 17–18

Congress, 69, 114, 118, 201; Library of
Congress, 2, 201
court, 47, 62, 69, 86
crime, xvii, 8, 10, 11, 22, 24, 40, 59, 62
Criminal Minds, 24–25
Czech Republic, xv, 52, 66, 105, 193, 203

daughter, 72, 90, 99, 101, 120, 121, 137,
147, 148, 150, 152, 154, 155, 157, 160
David, Peter, 17–18
the *Day Book* , 8
DC Comics, 18
decade of Roma inclusion, 207
degree, 80, 92, 94, 97, 137, 174
depression, 112, 122, 123, 124, 136
discrimination, xvii, xviii, xix, 38, 39, 41,
42–43, 43–49, 58–61, 111
Disney, 14, 27, 185
Donald, xxii, 85–87, 118, 166–167,
182–183, 189–190, 193, 198–199, 199
drab, 77
duality, xviii, 146, 160, 190
Dutch, 193

economic, 80, 81, 84, 95, 107, 114, 124,
211
Eddie, xxii, 40–41, 87–89, 132–133, 142,
167, 185, 197, 199
education, 10, 11, 73, 76, 79, 80, 81, 83,
84, 85, 86, 88, 89, 93, 95, 96, 135–163;
higher, 143–146
Ellis Island, 110
England, xvii, xxiii, 59; London, 198
Esmerelda, 185
ethnicity, 4, 11, 17, 50, 51, 54, 60, 65, 79,
82, 89, 130, 135, 136, 137, 139, 143,
168, 169, 170, 171, 172, 180, 193, 194,
196
Europe, xvii, 5, 6, 7, 8, 11, 12, 16, 18–19,
25, 33, 44, 46, 50, 51, 54–55, 57,
58–61, 64–65, 96, 105, 119, 124,
129–130, 138, 169–171, 176, 177–179,
190–192, 196
European: Academic Network, 202; Roma,
xx, xxiii, 36, 66–67; Roma Grass Roots
Organization (ERGO), 206; Roma
Rights Centre, 33, 202, 206; Union, 135

Facebook, 52, 58, 118, 175, 205

Fangs for the Fantasy, 23–24
fear, 78, 79
feminism, xx, 14, 145, 189, 200
Fener, xxii, 41, 49, 89–90, 116–117,
149–150, 155, 183, 187, 189, 198
Fey, xxii, 35–36, 36, 51, 79–81, 113, 143,
205, 206
Florida, 11, 61–62, 64
fortune telling, 1, 11, 15, 21, 38–39, 52, 62,
63, 74, 75, 77, 80, 100, 107, 114, 116,
131, 165–166, 176
Foundation for Roma Education and
Equality, 204
France, xv, 110; French, 94, 110, 174, 187

gadje, xxiv, 36, 38, 39, 40, 43, 49, 50, 55,
75, 75–76, 80, 82, 83, 89, 93, 96, 131,
135, 136, 142, 160, 161, 197, 199, 209
Gayle, xxi, 99–102, 144, 159–160,
188–189, 193
gender, 81, 85, 99, 120–121, 136,
148–149, 151, 160, 196–197
Germany, xviii, 139; German, 51, 71, 106,
169
Gertie, xxii, 16, 40, 50, 63, 90–92, 147,
166, 167–168, 185–186, 193, 195–196,
208–209
Gilbert, xxii, 17, 46, 96–97, 119–120, 127,
130, 131, 162, 174, 184–185, 190, 193,
198, 205–206
girlsaskguys.com, 26–27, 56, 57–58, 59
Gracie, xxii, 28, 36–38, 81, 152, 153–154,
161–162, 205, 206, 207–208
Gropper, xvi, xvii, xviii, 75
GRT. *See* Gypsies, Roma and Travelers
(GRT)
gypo, 137, 142
gypped, 4
Gypsies, xv–xxiii, xvii, xxi, xxiv, 1, 2, 4, 6,
6–7, 8, 11, 14–15, 17, 20–22, 23, 26,
39, 40, 41, 42, 44, 48, 51, 52, 55,
56–60, 61, 62, 64, 69–76, 90, 91, 101,
109, 110, 114, 116, 117, 118, 120, 125,
127, 130, 131, 138, 140, 142, 144, 145,
147, 168, 170, 171, 173, 175, 177, 178,
179, 182, 183, 186, 191, 193; *Gypsies
in the City*, xvi; *Gypsy Movements*, 37,
204; *The Hidden Americans*, xvi–xvii;
Lore Society, 204; moth, 201

Gypsies, Roma and Travelers (GRT), xxiii–xxiv, 5, 12, 13, 59, 120, 122, 127, 139, 170

Hancock, Ian, xvi–xvii, xviii, xxiv, 29, 62, 136, 204
the *Harvard Crimson*, 52, 173
health, 110, 120, 122–125, 126, 210
Hemlock Grove, 23–24
Henry, xxii, 30, 42–43, 48, 50–51, 97–98, 127, 129–130, 130, 180, 182, 184, 197, 199, 206
hiding, 50, 51, 185–189
Hollywood, 17–18, 19, 119
Holocaust, 17, 35, 66, 124, 203–204, 207
homogenous, xxi, xxiii, xxiv, 5, 7, 11, 21, 59, 61, 120, 177, 178, 179, 192
housing, 126–128
Hunchback of Notre Dame, 14, 16
Hungary, 34, 66, 140; Hungarian, 106, 188–189

identity, 47, 64, 87, 92, 103, 107, 113, 122, 146, 163, 165–200
immigrant, 46, 51, 96, 97, 105, 105–106, 110, 115, 156
Initiative for Roma Music, 204
integration, 47, 80, 81, 92
International Roma day, 203, 207
International Roma Union, 204, 206
internalization, 171–172, 172
Irish, xxiv, 20, 22–23, 51, 65, 71, 94, 124, 126, 141, 177, 186, 187, 191; Ireland, xxiv, 34, 59, 139
Italy, 13; Italian, 15, 71, 109, 187, 189

Jewish, xviii–xix, 17, 44, 184, 193, 199
Jim Crow, xv
Jimmy, 191
Johnson, Andrew, 69–70
Josephine, xxii, 98–99, 152, 154, 168, 183
Journal of Roma Studies, 204

Kathleen, 141
King of Romania, 25
King, Stephan, 14

language, 86, 97, 113, 197, 198, 199

law, 52, 62, 64, 109, 149, 165, 169, 171, 201
Louisa, xxii, 45–46, 63–64, 82–85, 114, 132, 142, 150–152, 168, 206

Marafioti, Oskana, xvi, 116
marginalization, 42, 46, 67, 80
Marilla, xxii, 42, 77–79, 148–149
marriage, 74, 76, 77, 78, 86, 88, 89, 89–90, 90, 91, 92, 93, 94, 95, 96, 97, 100, 137, 147, 150, 151, 154, 157, 189
Martin Luther King, 37
Marvel, 17–18
Maryland, 52
media, xxv, 1–2, 3, 4, 5, 6, 53, 55, 56–58, 64, 115–120, 120–121, 138, 170, 171, 171–172, 174, 200, 205, 209
mental, 122–125, 126, 211
methodology, xix–xxi
Mexico, 119
Mike, 3
Miller, xvi
Minnesota, 63
misogynistic, 78
mistrust, 46, 48–51, 53, 64, 135, 146
movies, 2, 14–19, 119
My Big Fat : American Gypsy Wedding, xvi, 26–29, 61, 116; *Gypsy Wedding* (*MBFGW*) , 25–29, 34, 66, 115–118, 120, 121, 181

National Association of Bunco Investigators, 62, 63
National Public Radio, 34
Native American, 51, 103, 185–186
Nerds of Color, 18–19
New Jersey, 44, 55
New York, 18, 50, 67, 166
New York University (NYU), 204
newspaper, 2, 6–13, 52, 53, 55, 58, 60, 61, 61–62, 63, 64, 67, 109, 120, 170
nigger, 38
Nirenberg, Jud, 37, 204
nomadic, xxiv, 11, 77, 128
Norway, 141

Obama, Barak, 203
objectification, 14, 15

occupations, xxi, 7, 40, 45, 48, 61, 63, 73, 82, 85, 107, 129–133. *See also* career; work

Ohio, 175, 183, 205

online, 56–58

oppression, 108

passing, 36, 38, 42, 50, 194

patriarchal, 78, 145

Peaches, xxii, 38–40, 49, 74–76, 113, 157–158, 182–183

Phoebe, xxii, 94–95, 155–156, 168, 174, 187, 190

Pinterest, 138

police, 12, 33, 38, 40, 43, 45, 45–46, 47, 60, 61–65, 86, 110, 128, 132, 149; *Police: Law Enforcement Magazine*, 61–62

Portugal, 33

poverty, 52–53, 107, 120, 125, 141, 171

prejudice, xix, xxv, 6, 19, 20, 33–35, 41, 42, 44, 53–55, 55–58, 58–61, 110, 111, 112, 117, 127, 143, 153, 171–172

psychological, 112, 169, 170

race, 36, 37, 49, 62, 67, 79, 82, 89, 90, 95, 115, 116, 138, 153, 175, 176, 182, 187, 193, 196; racism, 4, 5, 8, 9, 14, 19, 25, 26, 43, 53, 55, 57, 59, 60, 68, 96, 111, 117, 122, 129, 137, 139; racist, 183, 187, 205, 209

The Riches, 22, 23

Rodriguez, Vincent, 18

Roma: discrimination, ix, x, xv–xvi, xxv, 5, 6, 28, 33, 34, 35, 36, 43, 47, 50, 59, 114, 122, 129, 144, 169, 194; Education Fund, 206; genocide remembrance day, 207; Romania, 54; Romanian, 124, 173, 193; ROMApop, 18; women, xx, 15–16, 20, 61, 62, 63, 64, 65, 65–67, 77, 78, 79, 80, 81, 89, 90, 93, 98, 99, 100, 101, 107, 120–121, 145, 155, 158, 159, 161–162, 177, 191, 196–197

Romanichal, ix, x, xxiv, 38, 39, 40, 48, 49, 75, 76, 83, 94, 103, 104, 107, 113, 131, 182, 186, 193, 197

Ruby, xxii, 40, 53, 63, 92–94, 114, 117, 160, 166, 168, 186

Rumnis, 85, 199

school, 40, 50, 58, 59, 60, 77, 78, 80, 83, 84, 85, 86, 87, 88, 91, 97, 98, 100, 103, 112, 141, 142, 153, 179. *See also* education

Scottish, xxiv, 62, 124

segregation, 140–141, 153

separation, 38, 39, 42, 48, 73, 77, 78, 80, 82, 91, 103, 146, 149, 156, 160

sexuality, 210

Sherlock Game of Shadows, 15–16

Sinti, xxiv, 35, 139, 169, 178, 191–192

slavery, xvii, 9

Slovakia, 66, 140, 179

Slovenia, 34

SNCC, 37

social services, 125–126

socioeconomic status, 93

South Florida Gypsy Crimes Task Force, 62, 63

St. Mary Banner, 8, 9

St. Tammy Farmer, 8

Star Trek: The Next Generation , 22

stereotypes, 7, 15, 17, 20, 23, 34, 41, 43, 44, 48, 61, 102, 116, 145, 171–172, 173, 174, 205, 209

sterilization, 66–67

stress, 124, 126, 169

suicide, 122

The Sun, 8

Sutherland, xvi, 75

Sweden, 122; Swedish, 187

Teddy, xxii, 47, 103–105, 106, 119, 194–195, 197, 198, 199, 206

television, 2, 3, 5, 19–31, 116, 117, 119, 174

Texas, 93, 165, 204

Thinner, 14–15

Time Magazine, 34

TLC, 25–26, 27, 28, 117, 205

Topeka State Journal, 1, 2

traditional, xxi, 43, 45, 48, 50, 61, 63, 64, 72, 73, 74, 77, 78, 79, 81, 82, 84, 86, 87, 88, 90, 94, 95, 97, 98, 99, 100, 101, 120, 130, 137, 147, 151, 158, 159–160, 162, 209

trauma, 123, 124, 125

traveling, 43, 45–46, 74–75, 77, 82, 83, 86, 89, 90, 95, 98, 107, 128, 131, 151,

165–171, 179; travelers/travellers, xxiv, 12, 13, 22, 55, 57, 58, 60, 62, 65, 122, 125, 126, 191, 202

United Kingdom, 5, 13, 36, 58, 117, 169–170, 171
United Nations, 204, 207
United States, xviii, xxiii, xxv, 4, 7, 25, 34, 35, 42, 44, 47, 51, 53, 56, 61, 73, 78, 79, 96, 97, 102, 107, 110, 118, 131, 172, 174, 175, 202, 208. *See also* America
university, 43, 46, 48, 53, 95, 100, 161, 174, 206. *See also* college

Vaidy, xxii, 40, 53, 95–96, 137, 142, 145, 157–158, 206

Welsh, 124
White, xvii, xxiv, 67, 74, 79, 80, 83, 90, 92, 95, 106, 113, 114, 135, 136, 137, 139, 140, 153, 177, 179, 191, 193, 194, 195
work, 75, 77, 83, 84, 86, 87, 93, 94, 95, 98–99, 100, 104, 112, 129, 154, 155. *See also* career; occupation

Yugoslavia, 140

About the Author

Melanie R. Covert is an assistant professor of psychology at Brenau University. She holds a PhD in sociology with a focus in race and urban studies. She holds an undergraduate and master's degree in psychology and practices as professional counselor. She comes from a Romanichal family and became passionate about Romani scholarship during her graduate studies. She lives in Georgia with her husband and German shepherd, Wilson.